W9-BLT-666

PRESCRIPTION FOR DISASTER

Books by Joseph J. Trento

The National Aeronautics and Space Administration
(with Richard Hirsch)

Prescription for Disaster

PRESCRIPTION FOR DISASTER

JOSEPH J. TRENTO

With *reporting and editing by*
SUSAN B. TRENTO

CROWN PUBLISHERS, INC.
New York

For Tate Baggett,
Meta and Niles Borop,
Nancy Trento,
and in memory of Tom Trento, Sr.

Copyright © 1987 by Joseph J. Trento

All rights reserved. No part of this book may be reproduced or transmitted in any form or by any means, electronic or mechanical, including photocopying, recording, or by any information storage and retrieval system, without permission in writing from the publisher. Published by Crown Publishers, Inc., 225 Park Avenue South, New York, New York 10003 and represented in Canada by the Canadian MANDA Group
CROWN is a trademark of Crown Publishers, Inc.

Manufactured in the United States of America

Library of Congress Cataloging-in-Publication Data
Trento, Joseph J. (Joseph John), 1947–
    Prescription for disaster.

    Bibliography: p.
    Includes index.
    1. United States. National Aeronautics and Space
Administration—History. 2. Astronautics—United States
—Accidents—1986. 3. Challenger (Spacecraft). I. Title.
TL789.8.U5T74   1987   363.1'24   86-24134
ISBN 0-517-56415-7

10 9 8 7 6 5 4 3 2 1

First Edition

Contents

Acknowledgments

"THERE WAS AN ORGANIZATION THAT WAS REGARDED AS being perfect, that suddenly doesn't do the simplest thing. My point of view was that you had to do all the simple things as well as the complicated things if you are going to succeed. That's the only way you can have an agency that can year after year deliver the goods." Those are the words of James Webb, who lead the National Aeronautics and Space Administration that took us to the moon and beyond.

The destruction of *Challenger* is not a story of technological failure—it is a story of political failure. To tell it, we relied on those who fanned the dream of manned spaceflight into a fire on the moon. We would like to thank Dr. T. Keith Glennan, James Webb, Dr. Thomas Paine, Dr. James Fletcher, Dr. Robert Frosch, James Beggs, and Dr. William Graham for sharing their stories. This book would not have been possible without the assistance of William Lilly, David

Williamson, and Dr. Robert Gilruth. We owe a special debt of gratitude to Dr. Hans Mark and the publisher of his upcoming memoirs, Duke University Press. We would also like to thank Willis Shapley, Dr. Robert Seamans, former Congressman Don Fuqua, former Congressman Harold "Cap" Hollenbeck, Dr. George Keyworth, Gen. Jacob Smart, Dr. John Naugle, Paul Dembling, Robert Aller, Robert Allnut, Tom Brownell, Richard Callaghan, former Senator Howard Cannon, Philip Culbertson, LeRoy Day, John Disher, Mary Lou Domreys, Charles Donlan, Milan Krasnican, Chet Lee, Charles Mathews, Gilbert Rye, John Yardly, Robert Freitag, Col. John Fabian, and Richard Smith. We would also like to thank those at NASA, the White House, CIA, and the Defense Department who asked that their identities not be revealed. Our gratitude also goes to Lee Saegesser at the NASA history office, Linda Durdall, and John Costello for their help. And a final word of thanks to James O'Shea Wade, our editor at Crown, and his assistant editor, Jane von Mehren. We have tried to get it right but any mistakes or omissions are our own.

Joseph J. and Susan B. Trento
Washington, D.C.

1

The Great Space Race

THERE IS NOT A HINT THAT SOMEONE OTHER THAN A rich lobbyist or lawyer lives in the beautiful Georgian-style house between the vice president's home and the National Cathedral in northwest Washington, D.C. It sits on a corner facing a small park near the embassies on Massachusetts Avenue. Everyday thousands drive by. Few if any know that the brilliant and sometimes enigmatic man who charted the nation's political and administrative course to the moon still lives here. Inside the big brick house there are no icons to indicate his achievements. Attractive Persian rugs, a beautiful Chinese bowl, and other antique furniture are more a tribute to his ability to make money before a young president called him back to Washington for another tour of duty. The home of James Webb is not that of an old man. It has no smell of medicine. It is comfortable and inviting. Inside there is the look of prosperity but not intimidating wealth.

Webb has a doctor's appointment; he had forgotten about it when he scheduled our first interview. I am directed up the stairs to where he is being tended to by his doctor so I can at least say I have met him. Outside a bedroom I hear his soft southern voice; he is telling a taller and younger man to get ready. Webb, looking very different than he did in 1962, is trying to use a walker to travel the five feet to a massage table. Each step is a victory. I stand in the hallway watching the old man struggle as the younger man looks on. Webb realizes I am there but ignores me as he fights to inch forward. The spring sun catches the dust in the air and glints off the metal of the walker. The old man is methodical; he defies the illness. Two minutes pass as he carefully makes his way to rest on the massage table. Watching him move from chair to table reminds me of the giant mobile launchers he had built to accommodate the thirty-six-story-tall Saturn V moon rockets. They traveled the three and a half miles from their assembly building to the launchpad at the same deliberate and painful pace. And like the Saturns, Webb reaches his destination. Just getting to the table is victory enough for him. At eighty-two, his goal is to hold off Parkinson's disease. In 1962 he marshalled the same cunning and grit to push the nation's science and technology ahead several generations.[1]

Webb was the keeper of John Kennedy's promise. He shepherded a government bureau that was largely based on intangibles like pride, the desire to explore, and the dreams of the future, past economic, technological, and political obstacles. Webb does not grant interviews. He lectures and he hands out literature he has written. He acknowledges questions, but his answers are tinged with caution.

"I'm Jim Webb." A strong hand is offered. The hair is gray and short. The face is still strong and full. He apologizes for the conflicting appointments and asks me who I have interviewed. I go through part of my list. He tells me to call him in a couple of days. He has had a very bad night. He treats Parkinson's disease as just another difficulty to be managed, like an annoying journalist.

Webb is not a gentle old man. He tries to be a political sphinx who will not speak ill of his political enemies or argue that space is America's future. Eighteen years after leaving NASA he believes that if there is a civilian space program after *Challenger*, it should be one entered into with conviction and passion. He says he believes the country must make the decision and it must look to the president to offer the options—either explore space or do something else. "That comes from the leader," he says. "I was lucky enough to have worked for that kind of leader."

John Fabian, a pilot of considerable skill, managed to make the leap from the corps of "blue suiters" in the Air Force to the ranks of the astronauts. No small achievement since Navy flyers have been favored overwhelmingly for astronaut slots throughout the history of manned spaceflight. Now Fabian has the exterior of an ordinary middle-aged American. But most middle-aged Americans have not been thrust into orbit on a Space Shuttle. Most have not spent years and years training for a few days in space. In fact, most Americans have no idea how difficult, how complicated, and how frustrating life in the astronaut corps can be for a flyer. And Fabian was not even a shuttle pilot. He was a mission specialist. He chafed at not being able to push the buttons that implement the software that make the shuttle fly. But Fabian took what he could get and that was his piece of history. On his wall is a mission emblem for a flight that never flew. It hangs in place of his second mission emblem. To save money on the now routine program, Fabian said, "NASA had decided not to give any more of them out to the crews." He got his two missions. One of them was to fly with Sally Ride when she became the first American woman in space.

But for Fabian the burning desire to be in space had to be weighed against his family's desire for a normal life. He decided to take a new job running an operation so secret that the office he works in is a vault in the basement of the Pentagon. Colonel Fabian is in charge of all Air Force assets in space. Though Fabian will not talk about it, he oversees a fleet of satellites that scan and poke and use their sensors to tell us what is happening around the world as it happens. His world is far bigger than the one he left at NASA. The Air Force program spends three times more than the civilian agency. Yet he can say very little about what he does now.

On January 28, 1986, Fabian was running on a treadmill in the flight nurses office at Houston. As a former shuttle astronaut he continues to get his annual flight physical from NASA. He was filling out paperwork for the exam when a doctor called him in. The doctor pointed to the loudspeaker on the wall. All both men heard was a hiss. Fabian's stomach churned. Just over a minute into the flight of Mission 51L all communications, all telemetry from *Challenger* were lost. A nurse came bursting in saying, "It was beautiful, just beautiful." She looked quizzically at the stricken faces in front of her. She had watched the lift-off. She had seen the big slow rollover of *Challenger* and watched the climb. And satisfied another good mission was off she turned her back and walked away. Nine miles up, the 4.5 million pounds that was *Challenger*, most of it fuel, exploded.

Grief should be private. But it wasn't for John Fabian or his friend Sally Ride. Donald J. Kutyna, an Air Force general who is Fabian's superior, was appointed to the Rogers Commission to investigate the accident. So was Sally Ride. Fabian was assigned to assist Ride. He watched her sit with the other panel members trying to control her considerable emotion in this public setting. "It just unraveled like Watergate," Fabian said. "We felt betrayed. It was one thing to understand the technical reasons for the solid rocket explosion. But NASA had always put its people above everything. To hear how they put off and covered up the needed repairs and to know it killed your friends is a little hard to take."

One night after a particularly tough day for the commission, Fabian decided to rummage through his notes when he was first selected as an astronaut in 1978. He and his thirty-four other classmates were to get their first introduction to the shuttle from the legendary NASA engineer Dr. Max Faget. Faget had played a major role in every manned NASA vehicle. He had figured how to get astronauts back from the moon through the searing 25,000-mile-an-hour reentry. His impish personality threw cold water on the stereotyping of NASA scientists as nerds. He lectured the new astronauts for an hour and a half on the new reusable spaceship. Yet when Fabian looked at his notes, all he had committed to paper was the date, the room number, and one line from Faget: "The biggest mistake we have ever made was putting solid rocket boosters on the shuttle."[2]

Fabian loved NASA. At least he loved the NASA that he had known and had grown up with. So did Francis R. "Dick" Scobee, Michael John Smith, Ellison S. Onizuka, Judith Arlene Resnick, Ronald Edwin McNair, Gregory Bruce Jarvis, and Christa McAuliffe. But the NASA for whom those seven died and for whom Fabian and his colleagues repeatedly risked their lives was an organization that had badly degenerated. Gone were the essential qualities—the energy, the hope, the unity, and the honesty—that NASA had relied upon to bring its astronauts back safely from the moon.

Born out of crisis, NASA had been the most unique political experiment in the country's history. The politicians who nurtured it, the administrators, scientists, engineers, astronauts, and technicians who made it live, led us from fear of the Soviets to a sense of pride and accomplishment we have not been able to duplicate.

Had it not been for national humiliation there would have

been no American space program. When scientific bureaucrats decided that an eighteen-month period between 1957 and 1958 should be declared an International Geophysical Year (IGY) they had no idea they were unleashing the most intense period of scientific and engineering activity in world history. Only a world bureaucracy could come up with an eighteen-month year.

On July 29, 1955, the United States had rushed out an announcement saying that the Naval Research Laboratory (NRL) would develop and launch the world's first satellite—Vanguard—for the IGY. The United States beat a similar Soviet announcement by twenty-four hours. It would be a long time before the United States would beat the Soviets again. On August 3, 1957, the Soviet Union launched the world's first Intercontinental Ballistic Missile (ICBM). Two months later, on October 4 at 7:30 A.M. on a clear Friday morning, another Soviet ICBM lifted off from a launchpad at the Tyuratam Test Range in Kazakhstan, and carried *Sputnik I* ("Traveling Companion") into orbit. It weighed 184 pounds, traveled at 18,000 miles an hour at 560 miles in altitude and it passed over the United States. Its radio voice was a strange beeping sound. Ostensibly Sputnik was a result of projects the Soviets began in 1955 for the IGY.

Interest in space had been building for years. At the end of World War II both the United States and the Soviet Union captured many of the scientists and engineers who had created Hitler's remarkable rocket program. The U.S. captured 130 of the Nazi regime's most brilliant rocket scientists, including Dr. Wernher von Braun. The Soviets captured 6,000 scientists and mechanical engineers who had constructed and launched the rockets von Braun and his U.S.-captured colleagues had conceived and designed.

The Soviets went to work immediately launching captured V-2 rockets and refining the technology. But von Braun and his group got far less encouragement and support. Rescued under a project called "Paperclip," the Nazi party affiliation and SS membership of many of the scientists were erased from their biographies to avoid future immigration and public relations difficulties. Also hidden were the thousands of dead who labored as slaves for the Nazi rocket program. Von Braun and his colleagues ended up at Fort Bliss near El Paso, Texas, where they, too, shot off captured V-2 rockets. By the summer of 1950, they had joined the contractor employees at the Army Ballistic Missile Agency (ABMA) in Huntsville, Alabama, and began development of what was to become a battlefield IRBM called Redstone.

Beginning in the late 1940s the U.S. Air Force began the serious examination of space activity. The three military services all had separate research programs, but in order to not stop work on a U.S. ICBM, the Pentagon had prevented Wernher von Braun's U.S. Army rocket team from building and launching a rocket that could orbit a satellite. Instead the NRL got the assignment. The payload they were trying to put in orbit when *Sputnik I* went up weighed but a fraction of the Soviet satellite.

The morning after the launch of *Sputnik I*, with the country "near hysteria," Eisenhower called a meeting. The president was furious about press reports quoting two Army officers saying that the von Braun team could have put its satellite up a year earlier. Eisenhower asked Donald A. Quarles, a Department of Defense official, if the reports were correct. "There is no doubt, that the Army Redstone, had it been used, could have orbited a satellite a year or more earlier," Quarles told the president. He tried to mitigate it by saying that using secret military technology would force secret U.S. ICBM research into the open. It was clear, however, that such fears had not bothered the Russians. That afternoon the president met with Dr. Deltev Bronk of the National Science Foundation and asked him about Sputnik. Bronk told the president that we could not always "go chang-

ing our program in reaction to everything the Russians do."
Eisenhower was not so sure.[3]

On November 3, 1957, the Soviets launched *Sputnik II*
into orbit, a 1,121-pound payload with a dog named Laika ("Little Lemon"). The military and political implications of what had
happened were ominous and clear. Editorials proclaimed the
Soviet successes a technological Pearl Harbor. Lyndon Johnson,
then the Senate Majority Leader, grabbed onto the issue of
the Soviet achievement and used his Defense Preparedness Subcommittee to warn the country of the dire consequences of
Sputnik. Johnson and Senators Henry Jackson and Stuart Sym-
ington blamed Eisenhower. Hydrogen bomb inventor Edward
Teller made continuing headlines with his testimony about the
Soviet threat before Johnson's committee. Ironically Teller,
who had predicted the Soviets would make war in space in those
hearings, would a generation later be advising Ronald Reagan
on how to do what the Soviets had never been able to achieve.[4]
The new reality in 1957 was the knowledge that the Soviet
Union could use the same missiles that had launched benign
payloads to deliver nuclear warheads. What was going on behind closed doors at the Pentagon and in Congress was even
more alarming than Teller's testimony. A report from the National Security Council leaked out; it became known as the
Gaither Report. The report concluded that the Soviet Gross
National Product, while less than a third of the United States,
was increasing at a much faster rate. It warned that the Soviets
were equal to the U.S. in military spending and that they were
prepared to build 1,500 warheads and massively expand their
conventional forces. But the most fearsome item in the report
was the prediction that by late 1959 the Soviets would have one
hundred operational nuclear-tipped ICBMs ready to launch
against the United States. News of the report fueled the politicians' apprehension and the media hysteria.

Lyndon Johnson asked for a copy of the report with the

classified portions deleted. Eisenhower refused Johnson's request. Eisenhower felt that the report did not take into account numerous American advantages including its far-flung military bases, its international economy, and its much more efficient industrial base. But the president recognized that the report could compound the hysteria Sputnik had caused.[5]

President Eisenhower had not neglected the national defense as Lyndon Johnson and others charged. But his Pentagon subordinates, including Secretary of Defense Charles Wilson, had made an enormous tactical and political error by refusing to authorize some of von Braun's experimental Army rockets for a satellite program. Wilson listened to his military advisers and decided that U.S. development of an ICBM by the Air Force and the Army's work on intermediate range ballistic missiles (IRBM) had to take priority over civilian scientific research projects for the IGY.

And Eisenhower had his own secrets. The Navy was developing the Polaris submarine program under Adm. "Red" Rayborn. Polaris would carry sixteen new solid-fueled, nuclear-tipped rockets that could destroy targets as its launcher submarine hid on the ocean bottom. It was a revolutionary military development that was done under budget and completed ahead of schedule.[6] Polaris, and later Poseidon and Trident, would give the United States a remarkable undersea edge for almost three decades.

What the Pentagon was counting on was an Air Force program for an ICBM called the Atlas. By 1954 hydrogen bombs weighing 60,000 pounds were being tested. It became obvious to defense planning officials that a mating of warhead and missile would result in a formidable weapon. A committee of experts concluded that warheads small enough to sit on an ICBM could be fabricated. Brig. Gen. Bernard Schriever, who would later mean a great deal to the civilian program, was put in charge of the crash program. His job was to deliver an Atlas with the capability to deliver an H-Bomb from the heart of the United States to a target in the Soviet Union.

Von Braun's Redstone group was left in the dust. It was kept busy working on a vehicle called Jupiter, a derivative of Redstone. All of these projects were actually underway when the shockwave of Sputnik hit Washington. Eisenhower expressed frustration over the heavier lift capability of the Soviet boosters. "Why," he asked, "did we not have a bigger lift capacity?" The answer was in our ability to produce small warheads. The U.S. boosters simply did not need to be as large. Twenty years later we would learn that the Soviet vehicles were big and relatively crude, because Soviet nuclear weapons were enormous and only a large rocket could deliver them.[7]

The R-7 Soviet booster was not the imagined giant that U.S. scientists and defense planners feared.[8] No taller than a puny Redstone, R-7 did not use a few large engines, but twenty small ones to produce an incredible one million pounds of thrust. By comparison von Braun's Redstone could deliver only 75,000 pounds. But of course the Soviets had to have the bigger lifting power in their rockets because they did not know how to make nuclear weapons small enough.

On December 6, 1957, as Lyndon Johnson was berating the military on its lack of space preparedness, the United States' first effort to orbit its own satellite was about to be attempted. For the first time a national television audience was able to watch a launch. The black and silver Vanguard rocket stood seven stories tall like a giant pencil over its launching pad. At zero fire and smoke covered the bottom of the rocket. After lifting four feet off the pad, the Vanguard exploded.

The credibility of Eisenhower's Department of Defense in keeping von Braun's team out of the satellite project immediately came into question. Eisenhower realized what a horrible choice the NRL project had been. Now it was up to von Braun's group to get "something up" right after Sputnik. Eisenhower asked his new Secretary of Defense Neil McElroy how long it would take for von Braun to launch a satellite. Von Braun told McElroy sixty days. Gen. John Medaris, von Braun's boss, corrected his civilian employee and told McElroy ninety days. Using a Jupiter C, which was really a souped-up Redstone, von Braun's team worked around the clock to get off a launch. On the night of January 31, 1958, von Braun's rocket, dubbed *Juno I*, capped with a six-foot-tall striped satellite called *Explorer I*, was launched at 10:48 P.M. The United States was in the space business.

Von Braun believed he was a victim of Pentagon politics, but he also believed in destiny. He had once spent two weeks in prison because the Nazi command suspected (correctly) that the only reason von Braun was building rockets was because he wanted to explore space. He envisioned the first manned space station in 1935 as well as a reusable space shuttle that would travel from earth to the station. He was already the public voice for manned exploration of space. He made speeches and wrote books about it. In his mind he designed giant rockets capable of going to the moon a hundred times.

But there were other visionaries. Richard Bissell of the CIA was already working on designs with the Air Force on photographic observation satellites in polar orbit. These satellites could drop film canisters to earth for recovery. The age of remote sensing intelligence was being ushered in.

The Russians kept launching heavier and heavier payloads. On May 15, 1958, reality hit home again. In honor of the accession of May Day, the Soviets successfully orbited a 3,000-pound payload called *Sputnik III*. The CIA informed Eisenhower that the Soviets were developing a manned orbital program. The president was incredulous. He could not understand why the Soviets thought the propaganda war was worth such expense and effort.

Eisenhower knew that Johnson and the rest of Congress

would never allow such a Soviet feat to go unanswered. Eisenhower was adamant that the military not be given additional programs and power. And that meant that he was not going to put a manned space program in the Pentagon even though military research had yielded interesting information on what man might find in space. Eisenhower became convinced that only a civilian agency could keep interservice rivalry from hampering manned space research. Since the National Advisory Committee on Aeronautics (NACA) was already in existence and the civilian agency enjoyed a good relationship with the Pentagon, it would be a logical place for such research. NACA had developed advanced aircraft and rocket planes beginning with the X-1 that Chuck Yeager flew to break the sound barrier, and all the planes up to the X-15.

Eisenhower had seen for himself how the Soviets made space an international issue by orbiting Sputnik over country after country. The reality of civil space had to be dealt with. Eisenhower was in no position to complain about the Soviets orbiting over the United States, since he had advocated an open skies policy for both sides. Eisenhower feared the arms race spreading to space. In his mind the only approach was to have civilian run space programs for civilian purposes.[9] Lyndon Johnson was demanding a space program in an entirely new government agency. Eisenhower went along on the condition it be civilian controlled.[10]

Johnson went to work. In creating a consensus on a civilian agency, Johnson reached out to the NACA for suggestions on the legislation. Paul Dembling, who was general counsel for NACA, met all over Washington with people who had an interest in the new agency. But when it came time to see the military's supporters, Dembling found himself in an interesting situation. "Senator Styles Bridges, who was chairman of the Armed Services Committee, would not meet with us in his office on the Hill. And the reason for that was that he would take too much flack from the military if he met with us civilians who were going to push for a civilian agency," Dembling remembers.[11]

To keep the military from scuttling the bill, Johnson arranged to give the Pentagon only twenty-four hours to comment on the legislation. The Department of Defense read it so quickly that it was convinced the bill simply extended the status quo and changed the name of NACA to the National Aeronautics and Space Administration. When Johnson received the bill in the Senate on April 2, he told his colleagues that the legislation must "have been whizzed through the Pentagon on a motorcycle."[12] Johnson fended off attack after attack on the bill. By now the Pentagon realized that a civilian rival of huge proportions was being created. The Pentagon argued that it had already put up the first satellite and, with the new Advanced Research Projects Agency (ARPA), it should handle all space activity.

Eisenhower was having trouble with his own appointees. Roy Johnson, who came from General Electric to run ARPA, said publicly he didn't understand why there was any need for a civilian agency. But fellow Texan Sam Rayburn, Speaker of the House of Representatives, joined Johnson in strongly urging a civilian agency. The bipartisan team of Johnson, Rayburn, and Eisenhower prevailed and on July 29, 1958, the legislation was signed to change old NACA and its centers into the National Aeronautics and Space Administration (NASA). In August 1958, Eisenhower appointed T. Keith Glennan, president of Case Institute of Technology, as NASA's first administrator.

Glennan, a lifelong Republican, was not new to the ways of Washington. He was a member of the National Science Board when it funded the Vanguard program. It was Glennan who urged the board to send a telegram to the Soviets congratulating them on Sputnik on the grounds that they had always come in second before and it was now time to "give them the kudos while they deserved them." Years before he had served on the Atomic Energy Commission and so presumably he knew his way around town. [13]

Neither the legislation nor Glennan's appointment did anything to assuage the Pentagon. In effect, what the Air Force, Army, and Navy viewed as their rightful territory was being handed over to a civilian interloper. That resentment would haunt the agency for its entire history. From birth, NASA was hurled into the brutal world of military interservice rivalry. Although most of the military space programs were immediately turned over to NASA, to placate the Air Force, a project called Dynasoar was announced. Dyna-Soar, or the X-20, was the obvious next step after the X-15. It would allow a piloted spaceship to be launched on a rocket and glide back from space to a conventional landing.

On August 18, 1958, Eisenhower ordered the new civilian agency to undertake manned spaceflight. Relying on the so far very unreliable Atlas D ICBM, a 2,000-pound capsule would be designed, tested, and eventually launched with a man aboard. On October 5, 1958, only a little more than a month after taking over, Glennan approved the first manned American space effort—Project Mercury.

One of the first orders of business was taking over control of centers that had previously been under other government agencies. By far the most sensitive incorporation involved merging the von Braun group at ABMA in Huntsville. The Army postponed and fought the takeover for a year before it was officially removed from the space business. Even the realm of the new ARPA was invaded and several projects it started were turned over to NASA, including their "Man-In-Space-Soonest" project.

David Williamson, who came to NASA from NACA, remembers being sent by Glennan to help take "control" of the ABMA. "The boss sent a group of us down there. I was honored to be a member. We were supposed to do a personal inventory of the people, the work that is going on, the dreams and aspirations and come back with a plan for sorting. And this is what I set out to do. We walked into a conference room and saw all the Germans sitting all over the place. I sat down. And then von Braun comes in and everybody stands up and clicks their heels."

Another center was the Jet Propulsion Laboratory (JPL) run by Dr. William Pickering. One of JPL's first projects was to crash a probe into the surface of the moon. This project was supposed to be the answer to the Soviet's already successful Luna series. Williamson remembers Abe Silverstein, who at that time ran all spaceflight, bumping into full-scale models of the project and finding them so badly engineered he wanted to cancel the entire program. "But that was only part of it. JPL, Pickering, named the project Ranger without authority from NASA. Silverstein once had a dog named Ranger, and it was a bad dog."[14]

Project Vanguard and two hundred of its top employees were also transferred to NASA into what was to become the Goddard Space Flight Center in Greenbelt, Maryland. This center was established to be mission control for the unmanned program and much more. Glennan was beginning to realize that all this activity was costing more money than he had ever imagined. Eisenhower told Glennan, "I don't care what you do as long as it is good, civil, and stays under a billion dollars." But now Glennan was looking at more than a billion. In a year the United States had actively decided to explore the moon and the planets and send a man into space and none of it came cheap. "Ike was not a space cadet," Glennan recalls. "Nor was I. I am by nature conservative. Ike never told me what to do. In the thirty months I held the job he became increasingly aware of the activity. He supported it, but on the several occasions I was with him he made the statement that the moon is there and would be there for a long time. And it didn't make much difference whether we did it in five or fifteen or fifty years from now."[15]

The military tried to share the limelight with NASA. Publicly, Gen. Bernard Schriever, the brilliant head of the Air Force ICBM program, claimed his group was helping in the civilian effort. Privately, however, Schriever was leaking stories to the press about Discovery, a surveillance satellite that could be recovered in midair near Hawaii with pictures taken of earth from space. These stories annoyed Glennan and he called the general and said to him, "I really would like to understand what the Discovery is all about so I can understand these statements. He said, 'Fine. I'll set it up' and he did." Glennan and his budget people flew to Edwards Air Force base on a new 707 and received briefings all day. By the time they arrived back in Washington at 2:00 A.M., Glennan realized he had learned very little about Discovery except that the Air Force was about to embark upon a satellite program that was a radical divergence from NASA's. What the Air Force was really developing was an orbiting spy platform with remote sensing devices for use by the military services, the CIA and the National Security Agency.

But that experience was only among the first of NASA's brushes with spying. On May 1, 1960, President Eisenhower received word from his aide, Gen. Andrew Goodpastor, that the Soviets had shot down a U-2 high-altitude spyplane. The United States claimed that the plane was a weather aircraft belonging to the old NACA flying out of Turkey.[16] When Glennan saw samples of U-2 photography, he found them "amazing" and immediately realized the possibilities for satellite spying. In fact, on "Meet the Press" a reporter questioned him about the U.S. ability to take high-resolution pictures of foreign territory with the TIROS weather satellite and whether it would be used for reconnaissance. Glennan replied, "If the optics are that good, we will degrade them. Our business is getting on with the understanding of the atmosphere."[17] Glennan felt that detailed earth observation was something best left to the military. That concession by Glennan is today the heart of the entire military space program. Years later NASA would have to struggle with the defense community over what pictures it could take from space.

As the first administrator, Glennan was more concerned with the day-to-day operation of the agency. The law that Bureau of the Budget analyst Willis Shapley helped draft to create the new space agency was a unique one that featured unprecedented flexibility for a government agency. The agency had only two politically appointed jobs, the administrator and his deputy. It had exemptions from the Civil Service Act built into it. The administrator could fire incompetents and hire new employees relatively quickly. It allowed employees to be commandeered from other government agencies and retirees to be brought back to government for the new effort. It could also develop its own procurement policy.[18]

Shapley attributes much of NASA's early success to the fact that it was designed to be an elite agency, which was the way Congress wanted it. But what really made NASA different was that it was also a flat organization. A mid-level employee at NASA could get an answer from the deputy administrator faster than a three-star general at the Pentagon could from one of his clerks. A middle manager at NASA could speak for the administrator of the agency when the Pentagon could not get the head of one of the armed services to speak with authority.[19]

To the conservative Glennan, Wernher von Braun was "the space cadet above all space cadets, this fellow who was going to the moon. He was a blue sky thinker but he was the most conservative engineer I have ever dealt with. He never had a failure." Von Braun had the ability to give Eisenhower the only request the president made of NASA, a heavy lift capacity. Glennan says, "The only time Mr. Eisenhower really exhibited a concern was, I guess, when we were into the Saturn in early 1960. I was talking to him one day about budgetary matters and as I left the office he said, 'Keith, I want you to know that anything we can do to increase the thrust of the launch vehicles I will support.'" Glennan talked to von Braun and found that it would cost an extra $100 million a year to increase the lift capacity for the Saturn program. Eisenhower provided the extra funds.

Despite Eisenhower's support for the big Saturn F-1 engine program, Glennan and others at NASA remained convinced that there was not enough public support for a massive manned space effort. In mid-1960, however, a NASA engineer named George Low walked into Glennan's office and laid out a detailed plan for a circumlunar voyage called Apollo. Low did not dare suggest doing what he and his colleagues felt they could do—land a man on the moon and bring him back safely. Low was a quiet man who pushed his big dreams as hard as he thought he could. Eventually he would be in a position to make fateful decisions about the Space Shuttle. Decisions that reflected his own view of manned flight more than the needs of NASA.

Although NASA enjoyed substantial public and congressional support, there was one person on Capitol Hill who could bring the program to a dead stop. He was a man capable of putting fear into even the most confident NASA officials when they were called before him. Congressman Albert Thomas (D-Texas) controlled the House Appropriations Subcommittee for NASA and he loved terrorizing bureaucrats. David Williamson remembered NASA witnesses being badgered to the point of tears by Thomas. His hearing room was in the basement of a House of Representatives building. What Thomas wanted was a major NASA installation located in his congressional district. When Glennan first came to NASA, one of the first calls he remembers getting was from Thomas. "'Well doctor, my it is good to see you back here.' There were pleasantries back and forth and then he [Thomas] said, 'now . . . you are going to need some more research and development laboratories and one of them I think could be in Houston . . . at Rice Institute,'" Glennan recalls. For several years Thomas and Glennan went back and forth on the Houston lab with Glennan refusing to give in. Finally during NASA's second year Thomas had grown impatient with Glennan's refusals and he told the NASA administrator. "He said, 'Doctor, stop the bullshit. You've got $14 million in there for Goddard and you will get not one penny unless you build another laboratory.'" Glennan refused but Thomas never gave up.

Managing the spending of huge amounts of money became a big problem for NASA. Eisenhower was still reluctant, as he put it, "to hock the family jewels to beat the Russians." Therefore, when Glennan submitted a ten-year plan for NASA to Congress, it was roundly attacked for doing too little at too slow a pace. The plan was delivered just as the Soviets began successfully to explore the moon and planets using unmanned probes. The plan included Apollo as a second-generation spacecraft after Mercury, one that could carry three men into orbit and, in the 1970s, even around the moon. But Eisenhower had no interest in a second manned program and neither did Glennan.

For Glennan, a self-labeled conservative, many of the missions and dreams of his NASA team seemed beyond reach. "I am just not a visionary and wasn't then," Glennan says. He was an engineer by training and a forceful manager. He would willingly manage visionaries, and Project Mercury was a vision. Of all the trauma Glennan encountered at NASA, Project Mercury was by far the most severe. Its size and scope would be unprecedented. The cost would run over $100 million.

For Mercury, the military would be playing several critical roles. The Air Force was needed to provide the unproven Atlas

ICBM booster for the orbital missions that would be launched from their facilities in Florida. The Atlas was still a highly unsuccessful rocket. Since the small Mercury capsule would be landing at sea, the Navy was needed to help recover the capsule and astronaut after the flight. Finally, and perhaps most important, men needed to be found to fly in the capsules.

To coordinate Project Mercury in 1959 Glennan created a Space Task Group. The group had to virtually fabricate the reality of manned spaceflight. To do the job Glennan picked Robert R. Gilruth, a man who was almost Glennan's opposite in temperament and personality. Gilruth was a shy man who looked ten years older than he was. He had spent his life designing airplanes. He loved pilots and if he had an obsession it was to find a way to keep them alive. Gilruth could fashion a vision into a reality and still keep the affection of those who did the job for him.

As chief of the Space Task Group, Gilruth, who ran the Pilotless Aircraft Research Division at NASA's Langley Research Center, became the de facto chief of Project Mercury. Prior to Mercury, his team was launching sounding rockets with models of airplanes on their noses to determine the aerodynamic effects on aircraft design. Also working at Langley was Max Faget who worked in the Flight Research Division. Abe Silverstein and George Low, propulsion experts who ran the Lewis Research Center, would join with Gilruth and Faget in forming the nucleus for Project Mercury. The four had secretly lobbied the old NACA for manned spaceflight for years. Their dreams of space exploration had been partially realized with the X-1 through X-15 rocket planes. But now the actuality of spaceflight had to be formed from educated guesswork.

At the beginning Project Mercury was all over the place. B. Porter Brown was the first NASA employee at Cape Canaveral. He found that he was not welcome. Donald Yates, the Air Force general who ran the Cape, refused to assign a single launch site for Mercury-Atlas and Mercury-Redstone qualification tests. When NASA appealed to the Pentagon, it lost the battle. The five Atlas launchpads were reserved for launching the world's first spy satellites.

Contracts for the manned version of the Atlas were given to General Dynamic's Convair Division in San Diego. The McDonnell Aircraft Company in St. Louis was selected to build America's first spacecraft. At Huntsville, von Braun's team was working on plans for a Mercury-Redstone booster. To keep track of the man in orbit, a radio tracking network had to be developed so the satellite could communicate almost continuously with earth.

Astronaut selection was a relatively simple matter. President Eisenhower ordered the military services to provide the first "pilots." More than five hundred service records were screened. NASA wanted men under 5′11″, college educated, with families, and the best possible test pilot records. It was not until the list was cut to 110 that the men were brought to Washington in groups and told why they were being prodded, poked, and tested. On April 9, 1959, Glennan, skeptical about it all, introduced the seven Mercury astronauts at a press conference in Washington. This was the first time he met them. Neither Glennan nor NASA understood what they were about to unleash. The press attention was unending and total.[20]

Unlike Glennan, Gilruth befriended the astronauts and suffered over the fact that their lives were in his hands. Gilruth would not go on with Mercury unless he was absolutely certain his astronauts could get off an exploding Atlas. He had little faith in the Atlas rocket and dreaded the idea that one of "his boys" might be blown to bits on his command. On April 12, 1959, his mind was somewhat eased. The first successful test of an escape system that could lift the astronaut and capsule off an exploding Atlas took place. With Mercury, a tradition started at NASA in manned flight. A tradition that precluded any budget savings in areas of mission safety. No part of Mercury, Gemini, and later Apollo got more attention than escape systems and astronaut safety.[21] Only in 1972, with the approval of the Space Shuttle design, did NASA abandon that tradition.

The pressure on the hundreds who worked under Gilruth was immense. His assistant on staff matters, Paul Taylor, dropped dead of a heart attack at age forty-six. And the nearly four hundred who worked on Project Mercury in 1959 had no clear future. Glennan was not pushing Eisenhower for any further manned programs, despite his ten-year plan for NASA. Mercury was scheduled to end in 1961 when Glennan hoped this "ridiculous competition with the Russians would be over."[22]

Quality control was everything in Glennan's operations. One of his first actions was to establish an office of quality assurance, a move that upset Gilruth and others. They said it would be taken as a sign of distrust and add another layer of unnecessary bureaucracy. Glennan says that Gilruth told him "'that it was just another layer of control over us. Our whole life has been built on quality control and assurance.' I said, 'I am sorry, Bob, but that's what it is going to be because I've got to know independently that these things are reasonably safe and reasonably operable.'"

Williamson says the atmosphere at NASA was charged with excitement and hope. "The whole business of fun at NASA was that nobody had done any of the technical stuff before. It was a clean slate. That's always a challenge. The second challenge was that you learned by failure, that was very important. Failure was not penalized because it was inevitable. . . . When you had a major failure and something did not work, there was no sense of guilt."

One reason that there was no punishment for failure was Hugh Dryden. He and Jimmy Doolittle had run the old NACA. Dryden was the picture of old-fashioned propriety and kindness. He was an explorer out of the old school. Glennan, the no-nonsense manager, selected Dryden to be the man who represented the spirit of science in the new agency. Dryden understood politics and politicians, but his honesty was so acute that it cost him the job of being NASA administrator. Before Mercury, Dryden publicly described a von Braun proposal to shoot a manned capsule on a suborbital trajectory as having all the value of shooting a "woman out of a cannon in a circus." Congress was outraged and Dryden was destined to earn the unofficial title of NASA's technical conscience. Glennan thinks "that Hugh was just too honest. He didn't dissemble a bit. You know he was a lay preacher and he was just the epitome of the goodness of man."

Despite the perception that Eisenhower remained aloof, he would be angry when roadblocks were thrown in the way of the program. Glennan, after a particularly trying period and as a good manager should, asked for an appointment with the president to see if Eisenhower approved of what he was doing with NASA. For the first time, he requested to see the president alone. "Within fifteen minutes he was stomping around the room and banging the table saying, 'Goddamn it, Keith, we can't let them do that to us.' And I remember saying, 'Goddamn it, Mr. President, I agree with you.'"

2

The Kennedy Years

T. KEITH GLENNAN HAD ALWAYS EXPECTED DEATH TO strike the American space program in flight. But in January 1986, as Glennan was driving from downtown Washington to his home deep in the western Virginia suburbs, no event could have been further from his still agile mind. He had lived more professional lives after he left NASA, and had put space behind him. Glennan is an old-fashioned man who betrays little emotion about what he pioneered. In the living room of his highrise condominium there are no model spacecraft or pictures. There is a pretty and well-used wooden dining table at which Glennan sits and reads by a big expanse of glass overlooking Lake Anne in Reston, Virginia.

Often history is hidden away in Washington. People look for it along the Mall at the Smithsonian. It seems almost unfair to the children who play around the lake that they are unaware that this reluctant midwife to the space age is in their midst. For all the gargantuan tasks Glennan was told to begin during his career, none was more mystifying to him than manned spaceflight.

At eighty-two, Glennan still looks and sounds like the boss. He had instilled in NASA's "marching army" the pride of quality control. He never punished his managers for failure. He encouraged the technical arrogance in NASA that was derived from the "by the book" management that says every nut, every bolt, every replacement part, every piece of wiring has a traceable chain of responsibility. Glennan did not love manned spaceflight, and perhaps he did not even understand why the Congress and the country shared such a vision. But if we were going to do it, we would do it right. That was what he promised Ike.

In the twenty-six years after Glennan left NASA he took pride in the legacy he had left. He viewed himself as the designer of the foundation. He was the manager who brought the field centers together, wrestled with the military and gave what he called "the blue sky thinkers" a chance to try to make history. But on the morning of January 28, 1986, T. Keith Glennan was only thinking about getting back to his home. It was a beautiful January morning in Washington with a bright blue sky and the kind of crispness you can only get on a cold winter day. When he heard the awful news of *Challenger*'s fate, it did not take long for him to react as the boss. "Sure I felt some emotion," and then quickly the always present manager says, "I was glad it did not happen on my watch. I think one had to expect this.

"You know they simply didn't have quality assurance that went right up to top management independent of everything else. . . ."[1] Glennan says that the idea that NASA would have those responsible for reliability reporting back only to the center they worked for was an invitation to trouble. When Glennan ran NASA and established the independent Office of Quality Assurance, its purpose was to provide an outside auditor who could bypass those responsible for a mission and go directly to the administrator's office to correct a problem. Quality assurance had been so downgraded by 1985 that a NASA field center like Marshall could keep the lid on a problem. If something did happen, and Washington heard about it, headquarters could deny it because technically the field center did not have to pass on bad news. So headquarters had "deniability." In 1958 deniability was not something NASA management worried about.

Time was the enemy then. While Glennan insisted there was no race underway with the Russians, the public and Congress did not view it that way. And neither did the team Gilruth headed for Project Mercury.[2] They understood they had to forge a practical approach to beat the Russians. Instead of the spaceships envisioned in Buck Rogers and by von Braun, the crew at Langley ended up with a "man in a can." Max Faget's blunt-ended, bell-shaped design would be the precursor of all American spacecraft.

The engineers at NASA had wanted to build a bigger and more sophisticated vehicle. In fact, designs passed around in 1958 included some craft that look remarkably like the Space Shuttle. But the materials and knowledge simply were not available yet. Since the boosters were not yet powerful enough for more ambitious capsules, Faget's bell shape won out because it weighed half as much as other proposals. At the Marshall Space Flight Center in Huntsville, von Braun's team was preparing a new more powerful Redstone for a suborbital flight. At the Cape, testing was beginning on the Atlas ICBM to man-rate it for the later Mercury orbital flights. The NASA engineers were convinced they could get it all to work, but they had no idea if they could beat the Russians.[3]

Not since the Manhattan Project had technology faced so many unknowns. Gilruth and his team were looking beyond the edge of everything known about flight. Could a man survive a flight on an ICBM? How rough a ride would he encounter? Early tests showed that the bigger the rocket the more pronounced was an effect called "pogo," a shaking of the entire stack of stages in flight in a vertical motion. Pogo could virtually shake a spacecraft to destruction. Would the capsule work? Could it protect the astronaut from reentry? How hot would it get inside that Mercury capsule as the ablatives of the heat shield burned away. If the astronaut got into trouble on reentry the plasma formed by the capsule traveling 17,500 miles an hour would block out all radio communications for the most critical time of reentry.

To find out if the concept of a blunt-ended capsule worked, NASA put an early Mercury test model on an Atlas. They called the mission Big Joe and fired it on September 9, 1959. It was the middle of the night when the Atlas engines lit the palmetto of the Cape. For 120 seconds the Atlas climbed as she was supposed to, lifted in part by the hopes of those who understood that she would have to be safe enough to carry a man. Then it all went wrong. The big outboard engines did not drop away so the lone sustainer engine in the middle had to bear the load of the two dead and heavy rocket motors. No one knew the capsule was never put in the correct reentry position. Instead it broke loose from the Atlas at 350,000 feet and free-fell back through the friction of the atmosphere at 15,000 miles an hour.

Charles "Chuck" Mathews, who lead the team launching the Atlas that day, remembers what happened. "For a long while we didn't know what was going on. The communications with the down-range elements were very poor. . . . General Yates, who was in charge of the Atlantic Missile Range, because there had been so many failures, always made a point of having a press conference immediately after any launch whether it was a success or a failure. . . . He kept calling us and saying, 'I gotta hold this press conference,' and we kept saying, 'Wait awhile.' . . . I hung around another half hour very forlornly."[4] Mathews drove from the launch site south through Cocoa Beach and the towns that led to Patrick Air Force Base where Yates' press conference was just breaking up. Mathews was immediately called to the phone and told that the Navy had sighted the Mercury capsule. By the time Mathews got back to Yates, most of the press had gone and many of the next day's headlines heralded, incorrectly, the saga of the lost capsule. Although no one knew it for seven hours, the capsule had worked perfectly and was recovered by the Navy.

Although Big Joe proved the success of the capsule design, NASA had more than enough failures with the Atlas. And for every major failure they would test again. NASA insisted on man-rating Atlas by putting it through enough stress to understand all the reasons the booster might blow up with a man on it. Because of the fear of the Soviet program, the pressure to get a man in space was immense. But the pressure did not affect Glennan or his subordinates. The Atlas would go through test after test. A generation later, a budget-poor NASA would declare the entire reusable shuttle system fully operational *after only four flights, none of them unmanned.* Things had changed.

Atlas had power, but not brute power. It stood as tall as a nine-story building. Its steel gleamed in the sunlight. It looked tough and invulnerable. In fact, its skin was paper thin. It had to be kept under constant pressure or it would collapse like a crushed beer can. "It was at the edge of technology," Glennan recalls, and "that can be frightening. Those things were like a balloon, very thin skinned. And the strength in those depended on how well the launch went. If they got into a shear situation they would find that the damn thing would collapse." Atlas was not meant to carry man. Its purpose was to carry a nuclear warhead to destroy a city. In flight Atlas worked like a big inflated tire that could take the bumps and vibration and still reach its target. It would turn out that NASA's insistence on man-rating

Atlas would make it a more reliable ICBM, but not without a considerable price.

As the first NASA administrator, Glennan was the first to have to live with the prospect of sending men to fly on the nose of rockets that routinely blew up. Glennan believed death would come during Project Mercury. Up until 1959 Mercury was nothing more than theories. In 1959 Mercury would move from a design program to a test program. It would also introduce the idea of manned spaceflight to the public.

All of these tests led up to the flight of Mercury-Atlas I in the summer of 1960. For the first time the rocket and capsule were subjected together to the worst conditions it could face in flight. One minute into the flight, when that combination of speed and atmosphere met the Atlas at what engineers call Max Q, the Atlas blew up. The metal collar, the adapter that joined Atlas to Mercury, collapsed. For Gilruth it meant massive reassessment. Months of redesign and testing would slow down the program. The failure hardly reassured the American public as the Soviets continued to use their 10,000-pound lift capacity to humiliate the United States.

As the election year of 1960 heated up, Glennan continued to make speech after speech claiming that the United States was not in a "space race with the Soviets." [5] But that summer Vice President Richard Nixon was campaigning against a charismatic young senator who publicly challenged Eisenhower, Nixon, and Glennan. "We are in a strategic space race with the Russians and we have been losing . . . ," John Kennedy argued. He berated Nixon for what he called "the missile gap," which would prove to be a myth. But it was a myth even Eisenhower believed, given the intelligence he was getting and the Soviets' public demonstrations. Comments by Lyndon Johnson, Kennedy's running mate, about the "slow-motion Republican space

program" cut deep. Nixon countered that Kennedy was irre-
sponsible in his use of space as an issue.

What Kennedy represented was a boldness to try things
that might fail, a "quit playing it safe" attitude. He symbolized
those who fought in World War II—men who had a less cau-
tious and more optimistic approach than those of the preceding
generation.

Because it was an election year, Eisenhower's space policy
and Project Mercury attracted media and congressional critics
who were harsher on the Republican than the Democratic presidential ticket. In the middle of the campaign the Russians
launched two dogs, Strelka and Belka, along with assorted
smaller animals, on a suborbital journey and successfully recovered them. A month later Nikita Khrushchev attended the
United Nations session and said matter of factly that the Soviet
Union was now prepared to put a man in orbit.

Some members of Congress tried to urge Glennan to take
more money to catch up with the Soviets. Glennan would politely tell them that if he felt that NASA needed more, he would
be back. He also heard from Congress about other matters—
contracts. One contract was for modifications to the man-rated
Redstone for Mercury. When NASA awarded the contract to
someone other than Chrysler, Glennan received a visit from
members of the Michigan delegation. "I answered their questions for an hour and a half and finally I said, 'I wonder if you
realize that had this award gone to Chrysler that they would
have built ninety-five percent of it in Florida,' and the whole
thing [meeting] collapsed," Glennan laughed. He never heard
another word from the congressmen.

The Soviet spectaculars continued and intelligence brought
to Glennan warned that the Soviets were coming close to a
manned launch. After the Mercury-Atlas I failure, the situation
did not improve. On election day, 1960, the first qualification
flight of a production Mercury capsule exploded aboard a "Little

Joe" booster 165 seconds after lift-off from NASA's Wallops Island, Virginia, facility.

Two weeks after Kennedy won the presidential election, the Mercury-Redstone combination was ready to be tested. The Rocketdyne engine roared, and at a height of one inch, it shut down. The escape tower carried itself away to 4,000 feet as the rocket settled back down on the platform. As a bizarre postscript, the drogue and main parachute popped out of the top of the earthbound rocket like a child's party favor. It was the height of public humiliation for Gilruth and his team. The media fried NASA and blamed the administration for spending too little too late. But the Soviets were having their own problems getting a man into space. On December 2, 1960, two Soviet dogs were cremated on reentry. Less than a month later, the same Mercury-Redstone combination was launched again, and this time it worked. Gilruth and his team hoped that the United States might be first in space with a manned suborbital mission on the Redstone.

Almost immediately after the election, Glennan was routinely asked for his resignation by the newly elected administration. Glennan was out of town so Hugh Dryden had David Williamson, Glennan's deputy, find something Glennan had signed, put it up against an office window, and trace the signature for the resignation.[6] Space no longer mattered much to Eisenhower and Glennan. Plans for the three-man Apollo orbital flights were cancelled. Talk of circumlunar trips were now openly scoffed at by the lame-duck Eisenhower White House.

Gilruth's team did not know what to expect from the new administration and neither did Glennan. But the one thing he clearly did not expect was to be ignored. Through November, December, and January there was no sign that Kennedy was going to pick a successor to Glennan at NASA. Growing concerned and angry, Glennan could not understand why they did not at least name Hugh Dryden acting administrator. Glennan remembers, "I called Jerry Parsons at the White House and I said, 'Goddamn it, Jerry, this is the seventh-largest department in the government. Why can't somebody press them to get an administrator appointed?'"

A few days before the inauguration Glennan decided to make an appointment with Lyndon Johnson to express his worry. "Lyndon never called me Keith; he called me doctor. And that office of his. In it were the most beautiful gals and they were all over that office by God. He was harder for me to see than Ike," Glennan recalls. Glennan finally got Johnson on the phone. "I said, 'Lyndon, I am concerned about leaving this office with nobody in charge. I don't understand why you don't ask Hugh to serve as your acting administrator and I want to offer you any help I can.' He said to me, 'Well, Doctor, when I need your help, I'll call you.'"[7]

Glennan was further alienated by the man who would become Kennedy's Science Adviser, Dr. Jerome Wiesner of MIT. Wiesner issued a hurried report to the president on space policy that was critical of Glennan. "It was the kind of report that looked like it had been put together in three weeks," Glennan said. The message it sent to the Mercury team was not comforting. "By having placed highest national priority on the Mercury Program, we have strengthened the popular belief that man in space is the most important aim of our non-military space effort. The manner in which this program has been publicized in our press has further crystallized such belief. It exaggerates the value of that aspect of space activity where we are less likely to achieve success, and discounts those aspects in which we have already achieved great success and will probably reap further successes in the future," Wiesner wrote.[8] Wiesner also chastised NASA (and indirectly Glennan) for not giving up on the Atlas, which had failed five times in a row with various NASA payloads. Wiesner suggested that the more powerful Titan ICBM, being developed for the Air Force, could give the

United States near booster parity with the Soviets. NASA did not know that the report and Wiesner's other comments, which so angered Glennan, were not being taken seriously by the president-elect.

NASA anxiously waited for Kennedy to name his new administrator. Agency officials expected someone with a scientific background from Wiesner's committee would be selected. But while Kennedy had little in common with his new Vice President, Kennedy agreed with Johnson about the passions that the Soviet efforts seemed to stir in the American public. Both men had been traveling for months and faced a restless electorate. Johnson told Kennedy that Congress would not be satisfied with playing second fiddle to the Soviets.

As Lyndon Johnson gave up the power he had so carefully cultivated in the Senate, he passed the chairmanship of the Senate Committee on Aeronautical and Space Science to Robert S. Kerr of Oklahoma. Although Kerr and Johnson were friends, they were very different men. Kerr exuded wealth. Oil had made the Kerr-McGee Company successful and the nuclear age made it enormous. It was at Kerr-McGee that James Edwin Webb, a transplanted Carolina boy, learned how to operate on a grand scale. In his youth, Webb was a Marine pilot. Later he ran Harry Truman's Budget Bureau and served in the State Department. Webb also knew the space business. He was on the board of directors of McDonnell Aircraft, the contractor for the Mercury capsule. Handpicked by Senator Kerr, Webb did not want to be NASA's second administrator. He asked such luminaries as Clark Clifford to appeal to President Kennedy to get him out of it. At the age of fifty-four, he had led a complete life. But Kennedy told Webb that he saw NASA as a cornerstone for his administration and that he intended to make the most out of the agency. Although Webb would tell people he was the "nineteenth choice" for the NASA job, there was little evidence to support that contention. Kennedy wanted NASA to provide the hard evidence that the country was moving forward again. Webb understood that this would be no ordinary presidential appointment.

With his mentor, Senator Kerr, chairing his confirmation hearing, Webb had little fear of scientists who complained he did not have the technical background to run NASA. Kennedy and Johnson and now Kerr understood what Wiesner and his fellow scientists did not understand—NASA was as much a spirit as a science. It would serve as a popular framework on which to improve our educational and technical capabilities. It would bring a kind of populism to technology.

In 1961 Webb was bursting with energy. He was a stocky 5′ 9″ and had a reputation for impeccable manners. Webb knew little about the technical side of NASA. His tough, full face belied the fact that behind it was an extraordinarily complex man who would either become a scapegoat for the failure of America to succeed in the new space age or the man who administrated America into the future. When Webb took over NASA he sent a very meaningful message to what Hugh Dryden dubbed his "marching army." Dryden, the technical and scientific conscience of the agency, was reappointed as deputy and Robert Seamans, who stood a head taller than Webb, remained the perfectionist general manager.

Just before Webb assumed leadership of NASA, the unsuccessful Mercury program began to turn around. On January 31, 1961, von Braun's Redstone gave a chimp named Ham the ride of his life. Ham endured glitch after glitch on the flight, and almost drowned when the Mercury took on seven hundred pounds of seawater through the hatch after landing. Once the hatch was fixed, Gilruth and his team believed that a man could be launched and safely returned.

For Webb the Mercury-Atlas II (MA II) test could succeed and push the Mercury program forward, or it could fail and cause a frustrated public to pressure Congress into calling a halt to it all. Robert Seamans and Abe Silverstein were finally persuaded by Gilruth that a "quick fix" collar to strengthen the connection between the Atlas rocket and the Mercury capsule would solve the problem. At 9:12 A.M. on February 21, 1961, MA II ignited. At one minute after lift-off the forces of Max Q attacked the bellyband connecting Atlas to Mercury. This time there was no failure. At a press conference Gilruth told the reporters that a man could have survived the flight.

But the first manned flight would be on von Braun's rocket. Ham's flight indicated that the Redstone rocket overaccelerated. Von Braun, despite his visionary tendencies, was a very conservative engineer.[9] Based on the recommendations of his Marshall team, he wanted the first manned Mercury-Redstone mission delayed for one more test flight. With the Soviets so close to their first launch, Webb was under tremendous political pressure to get a man up. But he, like Glennan, understood that NASA could survive the humiliation of being second to the Russians with a man in space. To launch carelessly because of emotion would be like signing a death warrant not only to an astronaut but perhaps to NASA. On March 9, *Sputnik IV*, weighing five tons, was recovered with a dog called Chernushka. Von Braun's extra test went off without a hitch on March 24. A day later the Soviets recovered yet another dog from orbit. The dogs rode in ships weighing five times more than the Mercury capsule.

On March 22, 1961, a frustrated Kennedy called in Webb, Dryden, and Seamans to find out how NASA could close the gap with the Soviets faster. Kennedy's budget adviser, David Bell, and NASA budget specialist, Willis Shapley, had already met with Webb.[10] While they had approved the first massive doses of money for Mercury and the Saturn program, no decision on further programs had been made. And in fact, Kennedy had first rejected a massive program. Webb says, ". . . You've got to remember that Ted Sorenson became convinced that we were going to have to do something in space. Dryden told Kennedy, when he first turned us down on our request, and told him [Dryden] he was not ready to address space. Dryden told him you were going to have to address it whether you wanted to or not after the Russian program. This was the thing Kennedy finally realized, that he could not escape important and big decisions on the space program by putting them off." [11] But it was clear by March 22 that Kennedy wanted to go much further. He said he wanted the Saturn booster program, which Eisenhower encouraged for its lift capabilities, pushed harder and faster and he wanted it done immediately. Kennedy was frank in the meeting. He wanted to know where and when the United States could surpass the Soviets. A month later Kennedy ordered Johnson to figure out how the United States could beat the Russians in space. On April 28 Johnson gave his report to the president and it said in part: "To reach the moon is a risk, but it is a risk we must take. Failure to go into space is even riskier. . . . One can predict with confidence that failure to master space means being second best in every aspect. In the crucial areas of our Cold War world, in the eyes of the world, first in space is first, period. Second in space is second in everything."

Although various scientific advisers including Wiesner opposed a lunar adventure, Kennedy began to believe that the energy he saw at NASA could be generated nationwide. With Webb he had the manager to do the job. But there was still opposition in Kennedy's own house. Secretary of Defense Robert McNamara was pushing for a manned mission to Mars. Webb, forever the political operator, appeared to be conservative on the idea of going to the moon. He told Johnson that without McNamara's wholehearted support for the lunar transportation system, there was little chance of success. David Williamson says there was a method to McNamara's position: "McNamara had said that the Russians are sufficiently far ahead of the United States in rocketry that we are probably going to get beaten if we try to pick the moon. It's too easy a target for them to beat us. So let's pick Mars. McNamara was being very clever about that because if you pick Mars you obviously break the decade [1970] and you go out in never-never land so that the work that gets done is pure research and never competes for resources, either money or industrial or academic or political resources, with the Defense Department. So he may have been honest, but he also was clever." [12]

But Kennedy had no interest in far-off adventures. He wanted a test for the country. He wanted a deadline. He was willing to risk humiliation to see success during his tenure. McNamara and Webb were ordered to look at the logistics for a trip to the moon. In one of their few cooperative efforts, the two men worked together on the report. Kennedy had made it clear to McNamara that his reasons for going to the moon were to revitalize American science and technology. McNamara embraced the inevitable. The secretary of defense had other problems including the refusal by contractors and the armed services to accept modern cost-accounting methods in the Pentagon. By April 1961, he began to believe that if there were a huge civilian program to compete with the military, it could well put the aerospace lobby back under control. McNamara told the president that unless something like a lunar program were undertaken, unemployment in the aerospace industry would rise alarmingly.

In early April 1961, three astronauts of the original seven, John Glenn, Virgil "Gus" Grissom, and Alan Shepard, were in final flight training for the first suborbital mission. As the ground crew prepared the Mercury-Redstone for its first manned launch, crushing news came from Moscow. Maj. Yuri Alekseyevich Gagarin, using the radio call sign *Swallow*, lifted off from the Baikonur launch site on April 12. His flight lasted eighty-nine minutes. Although he was nothing more than a passenger since the control system on the *Vostok I* was totally automatic, he was the first man in space. The consequences of Webb's decision to let von Braun test the Redstone booster again became apparent. After sending his congratulations to the Soviet Union, President Kennedy said, "The news will be worse before it gets better."

As if to prove him right, on April 25, 1961, during the next Mercury-Atlas test, the Atlas rocket had to be destroyed. However, ten days later came what the country and Congress had so longed for. Alan Shepard climbed aboard the Mercury-Redstone and flew in space for fifteen minutes and twenty-two seconds. Although compared to the Soviet achievement the American effort was technologically puny, the American public reacted ecstatically.

The flight was broadcast live on television and the holds in the countdown and the minor technical problems were there for all to see. Kennedy watched the launch and the reality of the Shepard flight hardened his resolve. At a press conference the day of Shepard's flight a reporter asked Kennedy about the open coverage of the launch. Kennedy was adamant: " . . . I think everybody ought to understand that we are not going to do what the Russians did, of being secret and just hailing our successes. If they like that system they have to take it all, which means that you don't get anything in the paper except what the government wants. But if you don't like that system, which I don't, then you have to take these risks. And for people to suggest that it is a publicity circus, when at the same time they are very insistent their reporters go down there, does seem to me to be unfair. What is fair is that we recognize that our failures are going to be publicized and so [are] our successes and there isn't anything that we can do or should about it."

Kennedy decided to set himself up for what could be heartbreaking failure. Confidential polls ordered by the White House showed that only about a third of the general public supported the idea of going to the moon.[13] Kennedy decided to educate the public and turn his back on the advice of many scholars, economists, and his own science adviser. Just before he announced the lunar decision, Kennedy had botched the Bay of Pigs invasion based on advice he took from experts. He took the blame and went on. Now he would make a decision based on his own intuition and political sense. In May, Kennedy told Congress: "This nation should commit itself to achieving the goal, before the decade is out, of landing a man on the moon and returning him safely to earth. No single space project will be more impressive to mankind or more important for the long-range exploration of space; and none will be so difficult or expensive to accomplish."

Deep within NASA, an engineer named John Disher had been brought from the Lewis Research Center in Cleveland to be part of a very special group. Working for George Low, Disher was one of three NASA employees charged with figuring out if Lyndon Johnson's and now Kennedy's dream of sending a man to the moon could be accomplished. But Disher and his colleagues did not know if it was even really possible to get to the moon. [14] NASA General Manager Robert Seamans remembers looking up at the moon from a Washington park the week of Kennedy's decision and thinking: "How can we do it? It is so far. We must be mad." [15] David Williamson says Webb made NASA understand Kennedy's motivation. "Kennedy wanted, and he was articulate about it and he didn't stick to the same set of words each time, but he wanted to energize America—pull America together. He wanted to wake up the moribund industries, the high-tech industries, although they weren't called that. He wanted some way to crack the academic aloofness from the national affairs world. He wanted to confront the Russians with a success of a democracy and he did not want to confront them with something that had a direct military application. He very much did not want to do that." [16]

For Webb problems were multiplying. He had just had the

largest civilian project in human history thrust upon him. The president wanted him to lead an agency to the moon when his technical team could not even get a one-ton capsule in earth orbit. And for Gilruth, still struggling to get men in orbit, the thought of such a challenge was astounding. Kennedy had "told us to make our dreams come true," Gilruth remembers, "and now we had to figure out how to do it." [17]

As the team and the money began to grow, Webb got a message from Bernard A. Schriever, who was responsible for all Air Force ICBMs including the troubled Atlas. Then Seamans' aide David Williamson recalls what happened. "There is a famous secret telegram dealing with all of it and it was sent to James Webb saying don't make it [NASA's Atlas tests] public, because if you fly a big public mission on my Atlas and my Atlas breaks, I won't be able to lie to Congress and to the people of America about how far ahead of the Russians we are. That's not what he said but that's what he meant. What he said was that it will hurt national security because it will give the Soviets a feeling that our deterrent isn't credible. Okay, well that's a legitimate argument. In fact it [the Atlas] wasn't credible and wasn't going to be credible for about three years. What he was saying in a premature way, we [NASA] will tell everybody in the world that we're not as good as we think. And that is one of the big differences between the old NASA and DOD [Department of Defense] throughout. We never thought to use secrecy for embarrassment reasons of that kind."

Relations between Webb and McNamara were never cordial or warm. [18] But the two had mutual bureaucratic enemies who often forced them into an odd alliance. For all of Lyndon Johnson's interest in space, his role after the Apollo decision grew smaller. The Kennedy White House made certain there were channels to the president for both McNamara and Webb other than the National Aeronautics Space Council (NASC) that Johnson chaired. The main conduit was the Bureau of the

Budget (BOB). Budget analyst Willis Shapley helped conduct the rigorous budget reviews that McNamara and Webb were willing to endure in exchange for clear access to Kennedy. Webb, who once headed the BOB, even bypassed its director, David Bell, who was his former deputy. "He knew the rules and I knew the protocol and I just sort of thumbed my nose at him. And I dealt directly with the president. . . . You see I had this relationship with Kennedy that meant I could talk to him about anything like that," Webb recalls.

Although it was deep and personal, the antagonism between McNamara and Webb never went so far as to prevent a job from getting done. Shapley recalls them as "two completely different kinds of people, both brilliant in their own way. And they could not stand each other."

But Webb and McNamara agreed on basic policy matters more than they disagreed. That was not the case with Webb and Kennedy's science adviser, Jerome Wiesner. Williamson says that Wiesner feared that Webb's NASA was going to eat up the entire United States research and development budget. "And that means Jerry's friends and the biological people and the high energy people and the little group that wrote for the science community were not going to be all that loyal to Jerry because he wasn't going to have the patronage. The patronage was going to be through the big bucks," Williamson says. Webb was not a scientist but he understood self-interest. He knew that the way to win the support of science, industry, politicians, and bureaucrats for Project Apollo was to give them a personal stake in the action. In the end Webb beat Wiesner. Williamson says he did it because he never took him on directly. "Webb had a knack, which I sat there as a kid and just admired, which is to let you and someone fight, and he would vector things. Here comes an absolutely irresistible force directly at Jim and what Jim does is he looks at the time, blows it over his shoulder, whistles up a friend, says, 'I really think we ought to do that,' steps aside and lets the two collide. The effect of the vector is just along the line he picked."

The decision to go to the moon caused NASA to grow beyond anyone's wildest expectations. Webb instinctively understood that to ensure the survival of the agency, it needed broad support from the technical, university, and scientific communities. Webb became a political broker on a grand scale. The contracts for the big Saturn V moon rocket were spread from New York to California. When a cranky Robert Gilruth was told that his Langley Memorial Center would no longer be home for manned spaceflight and that he would be expected to move to Houston, Texas, he was more than a little upset.

Gilruth loved Virginia's eastern shore where he could sail his boat and be close enough to Washington to keep track of the politics that increasingly controlled his life. He was a brilliant aeronautical engineer who thrived on flying with his test pilots and spending hours with them over drinks discussing and debating how he could make his planes better. Now he was running a program that was bigger than anything he had imagined. Although Gilruth was the senior statesman of the space program, he could be startlingly naive when it came to the money and politics that determined if his dreams became reality. But nothing stung him like the idea of moving to Houston. So in late 1961 he found himself alone with Webb, the only two passengers on the old NACA DC-3 that NASA was using. Gilruth remembers gathering his courage and attacking the issue with Webb head on. "We were bouncing around the back and I said, 'Mr. Webb, why in the world would you want to make us leave Virginia? Here we have got that beautiful big place at Langley Field, and there is a lot of land and all that good saltwater around there. I've got my boat. Why do we have to go to Houston of all places?' And he said to me, 'Bob, what the hell has Senator Harry Byrd (D-Virginia) ever done for you or for NASA?' I said, 'Well nothing that I know of.' And then he reminded me that Congressman Albert Thomas came from Houston. That's how Webb worked."

Webb says Kennedy played his space politics close to his vest. "He did not tell the people on his staff. It was a very personal relationship where he knew about what I was doing but not specifically. He knew that Johnson was very anxious to get something in Texas and we talked about that. I told him that Johnson was not trying to influence the contracts. Well as I began to settle with Houston I told him that. And he was talking to Albert [Thomas] one day on the phone about two or three things he wanted Albert to do and Albert says, 'I don't know if I can do that, these are difficult things,' and Kennedy says 'Now Albert, you know, Jim Webb is going to put that space installation in your district,' and Albert says, 'Well now Mr. President in that case.' And Kennedy gave him many things beyond the space program. But I didn't tell Albert. Kennedy told him."[19] It was the closeness of the Webb and Kennedy partnership that gave NASA such power within the government. NASA would survive on its momentum through one disinterested president after another until the destruction of *Challenger*.

Gilruth emerged from the Soviet triumphs and the frustrating setbacks and failures of Mercury as a man who paid so much attention to detail and to the lives of his astronauts that he would literally be worried sick. NASA aides remember Gilruth getting so upset that he would vomit into a wastebasket.[20] If Webb, Dryden, and Seamans had to carry out the task of administratively going to the moon, Gilruth and his teams had to turn it into a reality. "When the president decided to do it we had no idea. I mean we had looked at it in an abstract way but to think about doing that when we could not even get a Mercury capsule in orbit seemed so impossible," Gilruth says.

According to Seamans, Kennedy's feelings for the space program were genuine and delays and failures did not deter him. "There is no question that it was personal interest. He understood the effect it was having on the public. And after the Shepard flight and he saw the way Shepard handled himself, Kennedy understood we would succeed." Also Seamans knew of Kennedy's fascination with the scale of the program. From the projected sizes of the rockets (one was supposed to be as big as the Washington monument) to the worldwide Mercury Tracking Network, the manned spaceflight program was enormous. Arnold W. Frutkin traveled the world setting up the tracking network. He made agreements with countries that allowed Project Mercury to be in constant communication with the new Houston center. Connecting the $41 million network together was 102,000 miles of teletype, 60,000 miles of telephone, and 15,000 miles of high-speed data circuits. After adding to that the new telemetry links and connecting them all to seventeen ships and sites around the world, the Mercury communications network was waiting and ready.

On July 21, 1961, Gus Grissom flew the second and last suborbital flight. Either a failure by Grissom or the explosive bolts that attached the hatch to the capsule resulted in the sinking of *Liberty Bell 7*. But the capsule again proved manworthy, and Gilruth decided to cancel further suborbital flights. It was time to fly the Atlas. But two weeks after Grissom's flight, the Soviet Union launched Maj. Gherman S. Titov on a seventeen-orbit journey. United States intelligence learned that the same launcher and craft that was used on the Gagarin flight was used again.

The first test of a new thick-skinned Atlas with a robot playing the role of astronaut went well. Although it did not yet have an astronaut on board, a Mercury capsule and Atlas booster finally orbited. In spite of criticism, Gilruth insisted on one more orbital test flight of the Atlas and the capsule, this time with a monkey aboard. In the meantime, on October 27, 1961, Kennedy got a phone call from Webb that gave the president reason for great hope. Von Braun's team had not only been busy with the little Redstone for Mercury, but they and the contractors had also fabricated and built a behemoth rocket called Saturn I. While the press busied itself with Mercury, that morning NASA fired off its own civilian designed, built, and operated launch vehicle. Saturn I, all seventeen stories of it, produced 1.3 million pounds of thrust and flew 215 miles into space. The gap was closing.

On November 28, Enos the chimp became the first American primate in orbit. Speculation rose in the press that the 168-hour work weeks at the Cape would mean that John Glenn would fly into orbit in the same year as the Soviets. NASA, under intense pressure from the media and members of Congress to get Glenn into orbit, had Dryden answer: "You like to have a man go up with everything as near perfect as possible. This business is risky." After the eighth time Glenn's flight was postponed, a reporter asked Kennedy about the delays. His response was heartening to Gilruth: ". . . I think we ought to stick with the present group who are making the judgment." Early in the morning on February 20, 1962, Bob Gilruth and John Glenn rode to the top of the Atlas gantry together. Gilruth remembers looking down at Glenn lying on his back in the Mercury capsule. "I put John Glenn into that spacecraft by myself . . . and we shook hands . . . and he said, 'Well Bob, I'll see you in a few hours.'"

Gilruth rode back down the big rust-red gantry to live through the delays of the launch. He remembers the fear: "You know, you did everything you could. You went over each one of those things with a fine-tooth comb and you checked all the clearances in the pumps, because a lot of times those pumps could catch and cause a fire." At 9:47 A.M. Mercury launch control lit the bird and Glenn was on his way. Outside of minor problems everything went well until the telemetry showed that *Friendship 7*'s heat shield was loose and was being held only by the straps of the retro-rocket motors. When Gilruth got word of the trouble, the awful knotting fear that he had felt for three years was there again. Engineers decided that all they could do was keep the retro-package on the heat shield instead of discarding it as planned. If one of the three retro-rockets failed to fire, this plan would have to be abandoned because the solid fuel would explode and destroy the capsule during the heat of reentry. Although Glenn was never told about the trouble, by the halfway point of his last orbit he had guessed what the problem was. During reentry the ablative shield did its job. After a long day Gilruth greeted Glenn on Grand Turk Island and received a message from the White House: "I also want to say a word for all those who participated with Colonel Glenn at Canaveral. They faced many disappointments and delays. The burdens on them were great. But they kept their heads and made a judgment, and I think their judgment has been vindicated." That evening Gilruth began to believe that the dream Kennedy had made his own was now possible. At Houston the Army Corps of Engineers was turning one thousand acres into the Manned Spacecraft Center. From this new center three manned projects would be simultaneously orchestrated—the remainder of Mercury, a new two-man project called Gemini, and the Apollo lunar landing project.

Throughout the early Mercury program up to the Glenn flight, a huge technical battle was brewing within NASA. How would NASA get to the moon? A decision had to be made on which way to go and how much money would need to be spent. The success or failure of the entire Apollo mission rested on this decision. Wernher von Braun and his Marshall team, along with many other leading experts, argued that the best way to go was to build a super rocket and go directly from the earth, land on the moon, and come back. To make such a trip would take a rocket nearly six hundred feet high with ten million pounds of thrust. Tentatively dubbed NOVA, the cost and management of such a launch vehicle would be astronomical. Gilruth's people had another way to go. But first he had to convince von Braun. Gilruth argued, "A set rendezvous was something people thought, my God, you know that's a tough thing to do way off on the moon. And I used to say, 'Well, if you can't rendezvous with another spacecraft, how the heck do you think you're going to go down on the moon and do all that kind of stuff.'" One by one the supporters of von Braun's direct descent approach gave way to Gilruth's lunar orbit and rendezvous until eventually von Braun was convinced. Gilruth's concept of having a manned lunar module leave a lunar orbiting "mothership" ended up saving billions.

On January 25, 1962, NASA told Wernher von Braun to fulfill his life's ambition—design and build the rocket to take men to the moon. Dubbed the Saturn C-V, it would be capable of sending forty-five tons to the moon. The new Saturn would be as tall as a thirty-story building and could put the weight of 120 Mercury capsules in earth orbit. Gilruth, who was still sweating over the Atlas, was now to develop a manned spacecraft that would ride a rocket that would put out the cumulative horsepower of six hundred Boeing 707s taking off at the same time.

3

Shooting
the Moon

ON A HOT SEPTEMBER MORNING IN 1962, THE YOUNG
president of the United States spoke at Rice University in
Houston as Webb looked on: "We set sail on this new sea
because there is new knowledge to be gained and new rights
to be won, and they must be won and used for the progress of
all people. For space science, like nuclear science and all technology, has no conscience of its own. Whether it will become
a force for good or ill depends on man."

Although they came from different worlds, Kennedy understood James Webb's ability to manage and manipulate his
programs into reality. Kennedy in turn provided Webb unwavering support even through periods that were technologically tough. Webb had an uncanny knack for not
boxing himself in a corner.

Shortly after Kennedy told Congress that the United
States was going to the moon, Webb marshalled his program

heads and asked them how much it would cost for them to develop a program to go to the moon. Paul Dembling, NASA's general counsel, was in Webb's office when the first figures came in: "He got a figure of $10 billion. He says, 'Come on guys, you're doing it on the basis that everything is going to work every time, every place, no matter what you do.' So they came back with a figure of $13 billion. And he goes up to the Hill with that $13 billion figure. And Albert Thomas, chairman of the Appropriations Committee for NASA, said to him, 'What are the run out costs?' He said, 'Well, Mr. Chairman, $20 billion.' And later on going back in the car, Brainerd Holmes said, 'Where the hell did you get that figure from?' He said, 'I put an administrator's discount on it.' That's the words he used, an administrator's discount. He said, 'I've read enough about it,' and then he mentioned a book, *Weapon Acquisitions Process* . . . that was pretty popular in those days. He said, 'I looked at all those and I figured I had to put on a discount so I put on my own evaluation of it and that's how I came up with the $20 billion.'"[1]

Kennedy also insulated Webb and the astronaut corps from Lyndon Johnson's political demands. And Webb was lucky. The Kennedys took a great personal liking to the astronauts. The polished public performances by Shepard and Glenn helped the program immeasurably with the White House according to Robert Seamans who was NASA's general manager at the time. "I think that the Kennedys realized that they had a real asset in Alan Shepard. . . . When John Glenn came along they realized they had another great asset and invited them to their pool parties and so on."[2]

Robert Gilruth had gotten the message from Webb that his future and the future of the new Manned Spacecraft Center would be in Houston, Texas. Gilruth's first visit to the tract of land Humble Oil donated for what Congressman Albert Thomas referred to as "my laboratory" was about as awful as he had feared. Gilruth was sent to Houston and arrived to tour the site just after Hurricane Carla roughed up the city. Gilruth recalls "being worried about what would happen if a hurricane hit while we were controlling a flight." [3] Charles "Chuck" Mathews, one of Gilruth's deputies, is a big man with a reputation for getting things done. Mathews was transferred from Langley to Houston to work on the Apollo program. He remembers his first few months in Houston: "When we [NASA] moved down to Houston we were actually in twenty-six different locations all over the city. . . . We still had John Glenn to launch in that time period and we had committed to two other programs [Gemini and Apollo]. . . . We were in an old fan factory. I had a very nice office myself, but the rest of the guys, it was pretty crummy. . . . When I was assigned to Gemini, I couldn't even find the place. It was in an old GAO building. It was only two floors occupied, one by Gemini and one by some other government agency. The rest was full of rats," Mathews recalls. [4] Gilruth hated everything about the move, but accepted it as a political trade to get the manned space program what it needed.

Webb thrust Gilruth into a very public role as he led his 750 employees west. "Bob was very astute . . . a very shy and somewhat introverted person. You'd be surprised how strong a person he was in terms of getting his way if he really wanted to. And not by head-on collisions," Mathews remembers. As Gilruth would admit later, the welcome NASA got in Houston was nothing short of amazing. The Texas generosity at first overwhelmed the new residents. And for Gilruth that meant a great deal. His astronauts did not make very much money and the $25,000 each received from *Life* magazine and the free homes built for them by the local community eased their financial burdens. "All of a sudden," Gilruth remembers, "they went from rags to riches. They had to be seen with all the high muckedy mucks and their wives didn't have much to put on their backs. They made something like $8,000 or $9,000 a year."

But Gilruth had bigger problems than adjusting to Texas. Project Mercury was child's play compared to the lunar landing. Computers and electronics needed to operate the Apollo spacecraft had yet to be invented. Three astronauts instead of one would be needed to maneuver the giant spacecraft. The Apollo astronauts would need to learn how to use the new radars and computers to chase, find, and dock with another spaceship for the lunar mission to be successful.

The Lunar Excursion Module (LEM) would be far different from its mothership. Apollo would be built to withstand a 25,000-mile-an-hour reentry from the moon to the earth. LEM would fly only in space, and would never bear more than one-sixth of the weight of earth. But LEM, which was really two spacecraft, had the toughest job of all. It would land on the moon. It would carry experiments and, when a mission was complete, it would carry two astronauts and lunar samples back to the waiting Apollo mothership. To do that, LEM's crew compartment and upper stage would have a second rocket engine and fuel supply that would use its squat first stage as a launching pad. Two men would have to handle a launch that normally took thousands. "It was light years beyond Mercury," according to Gilruth. "We had to have a way for all of us to know how to maneuver these spacecraft. We had to be able to work outside the capsule in case something went wrong and to be of any use on the moon. I mean there isn't much point in landing if you can't go outside."

For Gilruth it meant that NASA could not wait the projected four years between the end of Mercury and the first manned tests of the Apollo system. A program had to be devised to give the astronauts experience in all aspects of the lunar flight. A program called Gemini, using a two-man capsule, was the solution. NASA and its crews had to learn how to launch and rendezvous spacecraft while in flight. The Atlas did not have the lift capacity to put anything bigger than Mercury up, and Mercury was not sophisticated enough to rehearse the lunar flight. The Air Force's new Titan ICBM, however, was another matter. It was powerful enough to launch two men aboard a more sophisticated spacecraft. By the time the Gemini decision was made in December 1961, NASA officially proclaimed it the training program for Apollo.

Webb says he undertook Gemini as insurance against a possible Apollo failure. "Mercury would not have lead us very far. With Gemini we would have learned a great deal about spaceflight and its capability. If we had an insuperable obstacle and had to stop Apollo, if our equipment wouldn't work or it is too difficult a job, if we really didn't see how to overcome some difficulty in getting to the moon, we would have still done the next most important thing," Webb says. [5]

McDonnell, which built Mercury, was selected to build Gemini, a true spacecraft with twice the interior volume of Mercury. What Gemini represented was the capsule the original Space Task Group wanted to build had NASA not faced the pressures of Congress brought on by the Soviet successes. Gemini would have an advanced on-board computer and radar system. It would have a docking collar to mate with other spacecraft. A service module would be attached during spaceflight to its aft end containing some startlingly new devices, including fuel cells that would produce both electrical power and water so the spaceship could remain aloft up to two weeks at a time. And unlike any of the Soviet capsules, Gemini could raise and lower and change the plane of its orbit. [6]

From Webb's viewpoint it was a system that would keep manned flight visible during the tough and drawn out Apollo development program. From the NASA engineers' viewpoint it was a dream come true. A true seat-of-the-pants research and development program that would pour information into the developing Apollo program. "We actually ended up with average two-month launch rates which only recently has the shuttle exceeded. No other program ever launched that fast. . . . We got program information very timely to support the Apollo program," Mathews observes. The lunar program could well have ended in failure without the data and experience of Gemini. Apollo evolved from Mercury and Gemini. Ten years later, when NASA made the decision to build the Space Shuttle, little attention was paid to evolutionary programs. There was not enough money. And NASA had developed the arrogance of success. After all, the Space Shuttle was their fourth-generation vehicle.

Almost from the start Gemini was dogged by many of the same problems that plagued Mercury, including booster problems. NASA was getting little cooperation from the Air Force in preparing Titan for manned flight. In Gilruth's view Titan simply had to be "man-rated." And if that meant a rift in the unsettled peace between NASA and the Pentagon, so be it. Gilruth had men to put on the moon and his orders came from the commander in chief. The Titan would remain a symbol of the strife between the Air Force and NASA all the way into the 1980s.

For much of the NASA team Mercury was becoming a memory. Von Braun's group at Huntsville was concentrating on Saturn. North American Rockwell in Downy, California, was building engineering copies of the Apollo. Across the Los Angeles Basin in Canoga Park, the mountains that outline the San Fernando Valley would light up nightly as engine after engine was tested at Rocketdyne. Through it all, the Jet Propulsion Laboratory was developing a series of probes to orbit the moon and to crash-land and soft-land on its surface so the Apollo scientists could pick the best landing spots for the manned moon missions.

As each succeeding Mercury flight was launched, it became obvious that the management challenge in coordinating Apollo was growing more and more difficult. Webb answered the challenge by setting two criteria. One was that NASA would always have enough engineering and quality-control staff to make certain that the contractor's work was continually checked and verified. The other decision was "all up testing." The crash nature of Apollo into unknown technology made much of the program a crapshoot. Instead of testing each component and testing it again, fully assembled launch vehicles would be fired off. This approach was the only chance of meeting the lunar landing deadline. But it meant that NASA was risking a great deal on every test. It was a method approved by President Kennedy who understood that we still faced a superior Soviet program.[7]

While Kennedy was satisfied that the openness of the U.S. program was catching on around the world, the launch of Maj. Andrian G. Nikolayev aboard *Vostok III* reminded everyone which nation was still ahead. Just as American officials breathed a sigh of relief that this was only a repeat of the earlier Titov flight, the CIA told Webb that another five-ton Vostok was orbited with a man in it. The Soviets had launched two spaceships with two cosmonauts at the same time. Cosmonaut Pavel R. Popovich was supposedly sighted by Nikolayev. The Soviets made much of the flight of *Golden Eagle* and the *Falcon*. But what struck Gilruth and his colleagues was that no attempt was made to rendezvous. As big as the Soviet crafts were, their pilots had no control over them. Gilruth wondered if no rendezvous was attempted in the Soviet flights because they were going to build a booster even bigger than the Saturn V and try to go directly to the moon.[8]

No matter what the Soviets were doing, Gilruth decided that the lessons of Mercury had been learned. Carpenter and Schirra flew successful flights. Webb agreed with Gilruth and decided to cancel Mercury after Gordon Cooper's flight. On May 16, 1963, Mercury ended with a relaxed Cooper, the calmest of the astronauts, drifting off to sleep just before lift-off.

Mercury cost $384 million, nearly four times its original esti-
mate. But the United States put men in space and nobody died.

Meanwhile the Soviets pressed on. Nikita Khrushchev ordered his civilian space program managers to come up with
more flights to surpass the promise of Gemini and Apollo. But
the Russian scientists and engineers had gone as far and as fast as
they could. The big boosters were impressive, but the Soviet
capsules were no more than huge, crude life-support systems.
According to CIA sources the constant interference of the
Soviet party chairman set back the Russian program.[9]

Khrushchev demanded that a giant Saturn I–class booster
be built and launched before the United States'. The Soviets
suffered failure after failure in engine development tests. The
chairman also demanded that Segregi P. Korolev, the brilliant
architect of the Soviet program, eclipse Gemini and Apollo with
the first three-man capsule. Korolev had only the *Vostok I* capsule that was designed for one cosmonaut. According to a
September 1962 CIA memo, he ordered the capsule stripped
of all but the required equipment for survival, and three seats
installed. Because Soviet cosmonauts never landed with their
craft, but parachuted in full spacesuits at 24,000 feet, the
cramped quarters in *Voskhod I* required that the capsule parachute to the ground with the crew. In the summer of 1963,
President Kennedy was briefed on troubles in the Soviet program and the death of several top Soviet scientists and technicians in a series of suicides and "accidents." On June 16, 1963,
the Soviets again launched a cosmonaut. This time it was a
woman, Valentina V. Tereshkova, who joined Valery F. Bykovsky in orbit. Although Bykovsky's flight lasted more than
119 hours, again the two craft did not change their orbit. The
bits and pieces of information coming out of the Soviet Union
were revealing a very slowly evolving program that had only an
outward appearance of major progress.

While the Soviets were experiencing serious trouble with

their landing and life-support systems, Gemini was also having technical and financial difficulties. But despite the bad news, Webb had little trouble working his will on Capitol Hill. Congressional leaders knew of Webb's immediate access to Kennedy. The relationship between Webb and Congress has to be put in the context of the times, according to Willis Shapley. Shapley, a scholarly looking man who worked intimately with Webb, says that until Vietnam began undermining the credibility of the executive branch, Congress generally took the word of the administration. Shapley and others felt that Webb's intuitive understanding that this trust could not be abused was a major reason for his success. Webb hated to go back to Congress during the year for programs needing additional funds. He preferred to make his pitch once a year. Going back for more he felt weakened his credibility. A dispute over that very practice with Brainerd Holmes, his first Apollo manager, caused Webb's first major crisis. Webb, angry that Holmes had leaked word of this dispute to the press and White House, fired Holmes.[10] Another reason for Webb's success was that he would not allow NASA to fall behind its contractors technically. He demanded that NASA employees always know more about their programs than the contractors working for them. When the electronics of Apollo seemed to be beyond the agency's knowledge, Webb pushed through a NASA electronics center at MIT.

Webb also understood that Kennedy had broader mandates than going to the moon. The president also wanted educational improvements such as better staffing for graduate schools and better equipment for university laboratories. Critics in the military and scientific community were silenced when Webb promised the scientific community that Apollo would not soak up all the country's scientific expertise. According to Shapley, Webb promised "for every person we take out of the pool, we will put two back. He said, 'We are going to start a sustaining university program.'"[11]

While Kennedy's legislation for increased funds for education sat languishing on Capitol Hill, Webb quietly went to the Bureau of the Budget and requested money for his new Universities Space Research Association and other similar programs. Shapley remembers Webb's low-keyed request for the programs. "I am not asking you to agree to it, I am just asking you to agree not to stop me." Many accused Webb of merely trying to "buy support" for NASA, but his new education programs would change the technological face of present-day America by pouring tens of thousands of advanced degree holders into the technical community.

But Webb had other problems, including the irrepressible Wernher von Braun. Webb noted on trips to Huntsville that his own brand of interagency rivalry was developing between the Marshall and Houston centers over Apollo. Von Braun used his German technicians not only to design and develop, but also to fabricate the Saturn test vehicles. Now von Braun was even pushing to construct the giant Saturn V at Marshall. Concerned about too much power being located in one center, Webb ordered the booster construction phased out of Marshall, other than for test vehicles. Webb also told von Braun to stop accepting hundreds of paid speaking engagements that were in direct violation of NASA employment regulations.

Although NASA worked out its differences with the Air Force over the Atlas booster during the Mercury program, similar problems on a bigger scale were repeating during Gemini. This time NASA was buying both the Titan boosters and the Agena rockets stages from the Air Force. NASA was totally dependent on the Air Force to keep to schedule. Unfortunately that was something the Air Force did not do. "They kept changing prices on us because of their procurement," David Williamson remembers.

Webb also faced quality-control problems. Products made for the military and then given to NASA were too often unacceptable. The military became frustrated with NASA's quality-control inspectors, who were considered by contractors to be the toughest to deal with. Webb faced charges from the DOD that such "nitpicking" was holding up Pentagon projects. For Webb the Gemini program proved trying. His managers projected the cost at $350 million including all development and hardware. These costs were soaring into the billion-dollar range largely because of troubles with the Air Force. Just as NASA settled on an advanced version of the Titan ICBM, a Titan II, for Gemini, Webb's deputies told him that the Air Force announced a vehicle called Titan III, capable of lofting 30,000 pounds into low earth orbit. The Air Force wanted NASA to fly Gemini on the new vehicle. John H. Rubel, an assistant secretary to McNamara, informed Seamans that NASA would have to wait for the new advanced Titan. By December 1961 Webb persuaded the Air Force to sell NASA the Titan II in exchange for NASA's support for the Pentagon's Titan III as long as NASA did not have to use it for Gemini. The proposed Titan III had about the same lift capacity as the first generation Saturn IB, a duplication of effort not lost on NASA management.

Officially the DOD wanted the big Titan to launch Dyna-Soar, the X-20 space glider. This military "space fighter" was in effect a crude and small Space Shuttle and a pet project of Gen. Curtis LeMay, the U.S. Air Force Chief of Staff. LeMay wanted nothing to do with a civilian agency and felt the Air Force should have its own space program. McNamara had no intention of allowing Pentagon contractors to open yet another procurement floodgate. So under the name "Blue Gemini" a new project was born. The project would provide manned observation posts from a small space station for fourteen-day periods. The Air Force astronauts would use Gemini capsules to shuttle back and forth to earth. But because of weight limitations, the "space stations" would only be a ten-by-six-foot cylinder, crammed full of equipment. Since the Gemini capsule opened up like a gull-winged sports car, a standard docking port was impossible. An elaborate inflatable system was proposed that would fit over the two vehicles like a pressurized tent. NASA engineers considered the Rube Goldberg contraption a dangerous joke. Their ridicule reflected the growing conflict between the military and civilian programs.

Politically Webb believed that a separate Air Force program using the same equipment would help get the Titan II man-rated for NASA.[12] McNamara, who was attempting to negotiate control of space between the earth and the moon away from Webb, proposed that Gemini become a joint NASA-Pentagon program that the Department of Defense would run. Webb was furious. Some saw McNamara's ploy as merely another attempt to sabotage the lunar landing. NASA assigned a retired admiral, W. Fred Boone, to prepare a report to keep NASA out of the partnership. But Webb understood what McNamara was really trying to do. The secretary of defense wanted Dyna-Soar killed and the "Blue Gemini" program was a good excuse to get rid of it. Webb was not about to endanger Apollo to help solve Pentagon problems. (This policy would be totally reversed by the time the first Space Shuttle flew.)

Through intermediaries like Shapley, Webb gave McNamara some room to maneuver. Gemini would be paid for and managed by NASA with the Pentagon contributing some military astronauts. This agreement was hardly a concession because Gilruth was only recruiting from the military anyway. On paper the Pentagon would buy the remaining hardware from Gemini for its "Blue Gemini" program. A board of NASA and DOD officials with strictly advisory authority would recommend possible military experiments. Webb conceded just enough to allow McNamara to say that Gemini was superior to Dyna-Soar and he was cancelling LeMay's pet project.

McNamara had studies in hand showing that automated

spy satellites, largely designed by Richard Bissell's CIA team, were the Air Force's real future. More than a billion dollars would be spent on the Dyna-Soar and a proposed Manned Orbiting Laboratory (MOL) that would never be orbited. According to CIA and NASA sources, those programs served as the perfect cover for a vastly increased CIA–Air Force spy satellite program. McNamara's decision to build Titan IIIs had nothing to do with manned flight. In the world of 1962, surveillance satellites required huge amounts of fuel to maneuver into position to take pictures and send them back in film canisters. Further, the bigger the satellite, the better the stability. Lightweight manned capsules did not have the stability of the heavy new generation of reconnaissance satellites McNamara and his technology experts were intent on putting up. Intelligence experts who look back on McNamara's decision to build Titan III for the big spy satellites praise the decision.

Today in the Air Force they call the technology "look down." In the "black" or secret world of space—the world that spends more than half of this country's funds for space—"look down" is the key. What began with the Discovery program taking relatively crude pictures showing Soviet tank factories, would evolve into a program where live television pictures could be obtained showing the rivets on a Soviet ICBM. The Air Force had a space race of its own and, with the help of the CIA in the late 1960s, it was able to win it.

With Gemini still bogged down and Apollo development progressing slowly, the money seemed to hemorrhage out of NASA. In the midst of these NASA troubles, President Kennedy decided to visit NASA facilities in Florida, Alabama, and Texas. Webb recalls seeing Kennedy just before they went on the trip. "I told him, 'We have several real problems and you are going into a campaign and how do you want to handle the space program? Do you want Lyndon to carry the ball? Do you want it to appear the Space Council made the decisions? Do you want it to appear it is your doing? What do you want?' He says, 'Well Lyndon is all right, but I have to carry this. Nobody short of me can carry this.'"

On November 21, 1963, in San Antonio, Kennedy spoke at the dedication of the Aerospace Health Center. His message was another of support during a bad time for NASA:

> There will be setbacks and frustrations and disappointments. There will be, as there always are, pressures in this country to do less in this area as in so many others, and temptations to do something else that is perhaps easier . . . but this space effort must go on. The conquest of space must and will go ahead. That much we know. That much we can say with confidence and conviction.
>
> Frank O'Conner, the Irish writer, tells in one of his books how, as a boy, he and his friends would make their way across the countryside, and when they came to an orchard wall that seemed too high and too doubtful to permit their voyage to continue, they took off their hats and tossed them over the wall and they had no choice but to follow them.
>
> This nation has tossed its cap over the wall of space, and we have no choice but to follow it. Whatever the difficulties, they will be overcome. Whatever the hazards, they must be guarded against.

That night in Houston at a tribute to Albert Thomas, Kennedy talked about how he and Thomas would be regarded in 1990 and hoped that they had made wise decisions. Then looking at this old man Kennedy said, "Your old men shall dream dreams, your young men shall see visions, the Bible tells us, and where there is no vision, the people perish."

At half past noon the next day Kennedy was shot dead. Conservative Republican Bob Seamans remembers. "You know, Kennedy was down at the Cape six days before he was shot . . . and I was down there with Webb and we showed him around. . . . And so we finally got off the Saturn I that he looked at when he was down there. . . . And the night before we got the launch off, we had to have extra guards around to keep people from going out and putting Kennedy's name on it." [13]

After the Saturn I was launched the blockhouse and pad crews all urged Seamans to call Jacqueline Kennedy and tell her of the first big success of the lunar program. Seamans went over to the mansion in Georgetown where she moved after the assassination and brought a model of the Saturn to show her. She called in the children. Seamans says he will never forget seeing the president's son reach for the Saturn. "There really was a tremendous tie" between the program and its murdered champion. The astronauts had become JFK's personal friends. No government agency carried Kennedy's mark more clearly than NASA and no government agency would miss his support more.

That awful Thanksgiving week after the murder, President Johnson announced that the place from which Americans would embark for the moon would be called the John F. Kennedy Space Center. Less than a year later, Chairman Khrushchev was removed from power. The two world leaders who began the race to the moon were gone.

Now that he was no longer kept away from the day-to-day operations of NASA by Kennedy's staff, Johnson became a serious irritant for both Webb and Gilruth. Like Khrushchev, Johnson pushed for action in the program. On March 18, 1965, Alexi Leonov opened the hatch on his *Voshbod II* and stepped into space. The flight came just a few days before Virgil Grissom and John Young made the first orbital flight in Gemini on March 23, 1965. The publicity edge garnered by the Soviet spacewalk did not sit well with Johnson. But Gemini maneuvered in orbit and that's what NASA needed to go to the moon.

Gilruth replaced the first manager of the troubled Gemini program with Chuck Mathews. After celebrating one of the successful Gemini flights, Mathews spent the day with the crew being honored in Washington. He learned that evening what it was like to get the Johnson treatment. "So we were standing in this reception line at the State Department . . . and people began snapping some pictures. And it didn't seem like it was the normal kind of thing. . . . The photographer was getting very close, obviously taking full face photos. Turned out these were passport photos. . . . The president decided we'd go over to Paris. That night . . . he made that decision and nobody had known about it," Mathews remembers. When Mathews told Johnson he had to debrief the crew and get ready for another flight, he remembers Johnson's response. "You know, Mr. Mathews, if I can't use these people to make a better image than we have in the world, you may not have another flight." [14]

On December 4, 1965, Frank Borman and James Lovell were launched on what would be the longest flight in manned space history up to that time. A week later, in NASA's most daring maneuver yet attempted, a second Gemini was poised to meet the first in space. Astronauts Walter Schirra and Thomas Stafford sat atop the Titan on the morning of December 12 when the booster was lit. Although the mission clock started, Schirra did not feel the vehicle move. He was sitting on a live booster that had shut down. Instead of ejecting as procedure dictated, Schirra's coolness saved the mission. Three days later the two capsules were within inches of each other orbiting the earth.

To meet its goals, Gemini still needed to dock two spacecraft successfully and then redock again before the system planned for the lunar flight could be certified as safe. On March 16, 1966, in late morning, two rookie astronauts began their chase of the Agena. After rendezvous, Gemini docked with Agena. As the docked spacecraft passed out of the range of downlinks, trouble started. The combined spacecraft began rolling. Unknown to the astronauts, a thruster on the Gemini was stuck in the "on" position. Believing that the problem was caused by the Agena, the astronauts undocked only to find that the spacecraft began spinning uncontrollably. Only by firing the reentry control system could the spinning be stopped before the astronauts blacked out. The poise demonstrated by Neil Armstrong "left a very great impression" on Gilruth.

In November 1966, the last Gemini mission was flown with Edwin "Buzz" Aldrin outside the capsule for five and a half hours. Like Mercury, Gemini was a lame duck to a much bigger program. Virgil Grissom, who kicked off Gemini, was in full training to fly the first manned Apollo mission and begin the trek to the moon. In Washington, Webb was getting intelligence reports that showed the United States forging ahead in the art of spaceflight. The reports said the Soviet booster program was in shambles.

For Webb the handwriting was on the wall. Political support for the program was waning as the war in Vietnam seemed to occupy more and more of the president's attention. To reduce chances of NASA becoming a target for budget cuts, Webb abolished NASA's long-range planning office. Webb did not want a high profile program for an increasingly critical Congress or White House to chop away at.[15] The Air Force's protectors were already making an end run on NASA's post-Apollo budget. Hopes for a major era of space workshops and Apollo applications flights appeared to have no real chance in Congress. According to his associates, Webb was convinced these attitudes could be turned around if the lunar landing was a success. But he knew he stood little chance while Apollo was still unproven.

The first big cuts in Webb's proposed budget came in fiscal 1967. He had submitted a budget for fiscal 1967 of $5.58 billion which was cut to $5.02 billion by Johnson and the Congress. Webb was prepared to go to the political mat if the lunar landing program itself were threatened. But the eloquent support of Kennedy was not there to stir the population and the Congress.

To compound Webb's troubles, Air Force Gen. Samuel Phillips, who was on loan to NASA, was running into second-rate work in all phases of the Apollo production line. Phillips warned Webb that the Saturn V–Apollo system would not be ready for a lunar launch if the quality did not improve. The complex Lunar Excursion Model (LEM) especially was falling behind.

At the Cape, the mosquito-infested Merritt Island was transformed. Dominating the scene was the Vehicle Assembly Building (VAB), a huge building where the Saturn Vs for Apollo would be stacked on giant mobile launchers inside the building. The United Nations Secretariat Tower could fit through the 48-story-high VAB doors. Together the mobile launcher and first Saturn V totaled 20 million pounds. But while the moon complex was taking shape, the first launch of Apollo would take place a few miles away on Pad 34.

On October 25, there was an explosion during a pressure test of the Apollo service module tanks at North American Rockwell in California. Apollo managers feared that the Grissom capsule, which was already delivered to the Cape, might have similar problems. After satisfying themselves that the 204 Mission was safe, flight rehearsals began. On January 27, 1967, there were 1,100 people readying the first Apollo mission.

It was a clear beautiful winter day. After lunch the astronauts ascended to the white room that was part of the service tower surrounding the spacecraft. Chaffee, Grissom, and White slid into the couches. First the inner hatch was closed, then the outer hatch, and finally the launch shroud sealed them into

Apollo. Grissom complained to the blockhouse that the environmental control system caused the breathing mixture in the capsule to smell like "sour milk." The unit had been fixed several times to no avail. As the sea level atmosphere was pumped out of the cabin and replaced with pure pressurized oxygen, test conductors tried to straighten out an open microphone that was throwing communications out of kilter. With fits and starts the launch procedures went on for five hours, necessitating a shift change. The astronauts remained sealed in the capsule.

Inside the capsule the crew was relatively comfortable. The Apollo couches were roomy and adjustable and the instrumentation was accessible. At 6:30 P.M. Astronaut Deke Slayton, who wished he were witnessing the activity inside the Apollo with the crew, settled for a seat in the blockhouse next to capsule communicator Stuart Roosa. At 6:31 the radio circuit came alive with Grissom's voice: "There is a fire in here." On the access arm leading to the white room, pad team leader Don Babbitt shouted to his crew to "get them out—now." As he reached for an intercom to notify the blockhouse, flames breached the capsule and the pressure wave threw Babbitt to the deck.

An RCA employee had one job—to watch a monitor trained on the window of the command module. He watched in helpless horror as a bright glow came from his screen. He could see the silver spacesuited arms of one of the astronauts fumble for the hatch. For three minutes the flames increased until smoke obscured the camera lens. The men in the blockhouse heard the crew screaming for help and moaning in pain. The pad crew fought the flames in the white room which was soon scorched by them. Five minutes and twenty seconds after Grissom's scream, the outer shroud was removed and the two hatches opened. Inside Apollo, Grissom and White were on top of each other. They had obviously struggled to get out. The rookie Chaffee was dead in his couch. The astronauts died not of burns but of asphyxiation. To make matters worse, NASA lied about details of the fire. The agency announced that the astronauts died instantly. In fact, hundreds of people heard the screams of agony over an open voice circuit that was preserved on tape.

Webb called the president and told him the news. The president told him to investigate what caused the fire and fix it. Webb agreed but let Johnson know that if someone had to go over the tragedy it would be the administrator. Johnson, who was personally heartbroken by the deaths, told Webb that it had to be cleared up by NASA. Langley Director Floyd Thompson was appointed by Webb to head the NASA accident investigation board. Webb asked members of Congress to hold off on their own inquiries until NASA completed its investigation. Coincidently, the head of North American Rockwell was in Washington for a review of the manned program and for the signing of a new space treaty. NASA General Counsel Paul Dembling was in the meeting. "When the Apollo fire occurred, Rockwell North American was due some incentive bonuses because they got the capsule there on time and everything else. But Webb—I was sitting there when he told Lee Atwood [the head of North American Rockwell]—said, 'I'm not going to pay you any bonuses. I can't face the American people and tell them we're going to pay the contractor bonuses after three people got burned up.' So he said, 'You can sue me. You can do whatever the hell you want. I am not going to pay you. We're going to enter into a new contract.' And they started discussing a new contract," Dembling said.[16]

Webb has his own recollection of those events: "I thought that they had not dealt with the government in good faith in [the] preparing of the contract. They had a lot of people out there who didn't want to do it our way . . . but our way had to prevail if we were really going forward with Apollo. . . . I told them they had to do certain things. . . . They said we are not going to do them and I stood up at the table and I said, 'All right, Lee, these are not negotiable, if you are not going to do them I am going to take away every goddamn contract work that you have with us if I can and give it to somebody else.' . . . And I called in five contractors and asked them to submit bids to finish the Apollo program and put them in the mail. There was nothing behind the scenes. Their executives [North American] flew from California . . . and said, 'We will do what you ask.'"[17]

But one senator, Walter Mondale, decided to go after NASA. If Mondale had gotten his way there would have been no massive Space Shuttle program—and no *Challenger* disaster. He believed that the massive spending by NASA for a manned space program was not necessarily the best use of our resources. But the genesis of Mondale's suspicions about NASA's veracity went back to the Apollo 204 fire. Mondale was leaked a series of reports covering 1965 and 1966 that General Phillips' staff put together. Known in NASA as the Tiger Team Reports, these documents were frank assessments of how the program was progressing. Mondale also had the notes of a North American Rockwell inspector who was so frightened with what he saw at the Cape that he went public. The inspector, Thomas R. Baron, had been fired twenty days before the tragedy.

That winter was long and awful for Webb. At hearings Mondale demanded that Webb testify under oath and grilled him about the fire. David Williamson, who was an aide to Seamans, happened to sit behind Mondale in the hearing room that day. "He had a four-inch-thick document on his lap behind the desk that only I could see and he was reading from it," Williamson remembers. As Mondale asked Webb under oath about the "Phillips Report," Webb politely told Mondale he had never heard of such a report. Mondale kept asking him about the report, which he was hiding on his lap, and charged that Webb was covering up. Paul Dembling remembers Webb and Apollo head George Mueller returning from the confrontation. "And I asked Webb, 'How did it go?' And he said, 'Mondale kept asking me about this damn report called the Phillips Report and I don't know what he's talking about and I asked George Mueller and he said No he doesn't know what he's talking about either.'" But Dembling had gotten a copy of the report that afternoon and told Webb about it. Webb was incredulous and Dembling remembers him saying, "They kept asking me and I told them we didn't have anything. I'd never seen anything. And there was no such report."

Webb was furious. To those at the hearing it appeared that Webb was lying to Mondale. Webb debated whether to send over the report to Mondale officially, which he knew Mondale already had. Webb knew Mondale could not publicly reveal he had a copy because portions of the report were confidential. Since Mondale was a member of Congress, Webb decided to send the report to the head of the General Accounting Office (the investigative arm of Congress), who would be custodian of the report and Mondale could go and inspect it. Mondale was furious and felt Webb had hoodwinked him. According to aides, Webb then did something that was uncharacteristic. Webb went to see Mondale, and a Webb aide remembers him asking Mondale, "In all due humility, Senator, what have we done wrong? Why are you so down on us?" Webb wanted to know why Mondale was upset and what he could do to rectify the situation. He and other visitors from NASA were standing in front of Mondale's desk. The senator sat back in his chair and instructed Webb, "I intend to ride this for every nickel's worth of political power I can get out of it. I don't give a hoot in hell about the space program or about your future," a NASA official with Webb recalls Mondale saying.[18]

Three weeks before the 204 fire a NASA medical director named Charles Berry warned about just such a ground event. In the end, NASA's investigation concluded that the Apollo fire was an accident waiting to happen. The capsule was poorly designed and poorly wired. The report said NASA failed in its management responsibility to make certain even the most ordinary circumstance had not been overlooked.

For Gilruth, who had lost three other astronauts in plane crashes, the 204 fire was his ultimate nightmare. He broke into tears when he learned that the doctors could not get the bodies out of the capsule because their spacesuits fused with the molten nylon inside. NASA did not then know that a Soviet cosmonaut was killed in a similar accident four years earlier.

As the recriminations over the 204 fire continued to boil, the Soviet program was flying. *Soyuz I*, a genuine three-man craft that featured a separate reentry capsule, flew its maiden voyage on April 23, 1967. Cosmonaut Vladimir M. Komarov had altitude control problems during his entire flight. On the seventeenth orbit Moscow Mission Control told him to end the mission. He climbed into the reentry capsule and separated from the mothership after twenty-six hours of flight. But the Soyuz parachute system failed and another space traveler died. Within NASA and the Soviet program, the losses of these four men had the survivors in both countries sharing a profound and real grief. Webb wondered aloud if both accidents could have been avoided if the two programs were combined. Thousands of new materials were tested for Apollo. Webb hired Boeing to help integrate all the contractors. North American was checked and checked again. The race had slowed but not stopped.

At precisely 7:00 A.M., on November 9, 1967, ten months after the fire, NASA was about to find out if Wernher von Braun was all he was supposed to be. As the sun touched the ground and the horizon came to life, Saturn V breathed her fire for the first time. The clamps held down the skyscraper of a rocket until all 7.5 million pounds of thrust broke her free. She leaned away from the launch tower and began to climb. It was only then that the roar and the vibration reached the VAB and the press center. Nothing like it had ever been seen or heard before. The moon rocket with its Apollo command and service modules on board flew. Apollo reentered at 40,000 kilometers an hour. Webb took NASA from an agency flying the Redstone rocket with 75,000 pounds of thrust to the Saturn rocket with 7.5 million pounds of thrust in six years. He used up much of his credit in Congress to pull the agency through the 204 ordeal. He could afford no more fires or lost astronauts. The Russians could still get to the moon first.

4

Flight of
the Sun God

THE FIRST THING YOU NOTICE IS THE SAILBOAT. YES, there are plenty of sailboats in Kilmarnock, Virginia, but none like this one. There is no design like it in Tidewater. She was handmade in Houston, and her master sailed her back from there through the intercoastal waterway. Then you notice the house, plain and low, with the big boat bobbing next to it. Inside, it is airy and elegant, and you tend to look out to the water. Bob Gilruth had to send men to the moon before they let him come home to Tidewater. They say at NASA that Gilruth was the heart, the inspiration. He looks old, but he was old-looking in 1961. He remembers the good times. And if you press him, he remembers the bad times too. For him, James Webb is still "Mr. Webb." Gilruth has the gift of civility. He is the living embodiment of what NASA was supposed to be—effective, curious, and humane. To meet Gilruth is to understand a definition of the kind of public servant who could not be intimidated, but who cared about and was responsive to his subordinates.

In the aftermath of *Challenger*, Gilruth understands the pain. But the agency he gave so much to bears little resemblance to the one that allowed the Space Shuttle to blow up. Gilruth more than most people understands the risk of manned flight. He cannot understand why NASA had no escape system. He cannot figure out why NASA did not fix the solid rockets. He does not understand how the agency acquired the attitude that propelling people millions of miles into space using chemical explosives could either be routine or safe.[1]

Before NASA there was another Gilruth, the Gilruth who is the engineering genius who holds most of the major patents for the hydrofoil. The Gilruth who had the idea to take scale models of future jet aircraft and fly them on sounding rockets because wind tunnels were not good enough for him. It was these credentials he brought to Houston. He led the "marching army" in Houston after the 204 fire. No one was more determined to turn Apollo into the flight of the Phoenix than Gilruth. After all, Chaffee, White, and especially Gus Grissom had been his boys.

Webb put everything on the line to come back from the fire. Using all his influence he succeeded in getting a half a billion dollars more from Johnson and the Congress to complete the redesign of Apollo. These numbers were huge in the late 1960s. Webb used guilt to win his case. He argued that without the money the program would fail and those who refused to vote for these funds would bear the responsibility.[2]

The LEM, which was to drop two astronauts on the Sea of Tranquility, cost fifteen times its weight in gold. All these expenses came at a time when there was a growing revolt against all technology. It came at a time when many Americans saw military, civilian, and industrial technology as some sort of monolithic evil. It was hard for men like Webb, so totally achievement oriented, to understand how a program devoted to a non-military goal could come under such heavy fire. But the big target was the cost. The support facilities for the lunar landing ran more than $2.2 billion. The communications facilities alone for Apollo cost the $380 million that was spent for Mercury. Add another billion to operate the system and that was just a small part of Apollo's total price tag.

Webb was hired to manage a national dream, a political statement, and a technological drama on the grandest of scales. When the 204 fire turned it into a nightmare, he steered it back on track. He used all his markers in Congress to garner support. He made his people kick the contractors in line. Man would fly Apollo in 1968. For the public the lunar adventure was beginning to unfold. But Webb understood that for NASA and the 400,000 who labored on Kennedy's goal, it was almost over. Layoffs were already starting. Johnson, mired in Vietnam, wanted NASA to succeed but made it clear to Webb there were other priorities. NASA seemed almost irrelevant as the country took to the streets to protest the war. In January 1968, President Johnson appointed Dr. Thomas O. Paine to replace Robert Seamans as deputy administrator of NASA. Webb says that President Johnson told him he was not going to run again and they agreed on Paine, a technician, because he was capable of guiding Apollo through its flight program. In early 1968, Senator Eugene McCarthy announced for the presidency and nearly defeated Johnson in New Hampshire. Bobby Kennedy joined the race. Johnson made public his decision not to seek reelection. Webb's only job was to make certain NASA had the resources to complete the lunar landing. To pay for the lunar project the White House and the Congress had all but wiped out any future manned programs. And then there was the matter of how

Paine was selected by the White House to be Webb's deputy administrator.

Paine was called in by Johnson and became uncomfortable. He remembers the president telling him "that I was only subject to confirmation by the Senate, and that the administrator of NASA had nothing to do with my selection and would have nothing to do with my appointment." Paine refused the job under those circumstances fearing that he would become nothing more than a White House spy. "Well, I wasn't going to be one," Paine said. "There are plenty of people who would volunteer for that job. I was not one of them. I didn't need the job anyway. So in the discussion that followed I said, 'Look, it's a fascinating job but I've never met Mr. Webb.' I said, 'If Mr. Webb asks me to take the job, then yeah, I'd be interested.'"[3]

Ten minutes later Johnson called Webb and set up a meeting between the two men. What Paine found was a very busy man. "He was about to rush up to the Hill. I think he had about twenty-five minutes to decide whether or not we were going to get married, a girl he'd never met. Pretty tough decision. . . . He said, 'Look, we don't have very much time. I have got to run up to the Hill and I've never met you, you've never met me.' He said, 'I'll tell you what we'll do . . . I'll give you the names of a number of people I know and I think you might know who are here in Washington and in the community in general. There are a lot of them who are people you should know, so one of the things that will interest me is if you know them. But the main thing that is going to interest me is what you think of them. So let me give you the names and you give me your unvarnished assessment of those people.'" Webb asked Paine one other question. Since Paine was in line to become head of General Electric, Webb asked him why did he want to come work in the government at such a critical time in his career? Paine's answer, that he wanted to broaden his experience to include five years of government service, sold Webb on him.

At the end of the twenty-five minutes Webb politely told Paine how much he enjoyed meeting him and said, "I hope very much you will accept the job and I am going to call the White House and tell them I am going to do everything I can to attract you to the job," recalls Paine. Although Webb understood and appreciated Paine's loyalty, it was obvious to Webb that he was in his own race to complete the lunar program before the consensus he labored so long to create fell apart.

Webb says Paine's version is not accurate. Webb says that President Johnson told him in January 1968 that he would not seek reelection. It was then that Webb says he decided to leave with Johnson. Webb said, ". . . So what I did was to arrange with Johnson that I would retire when I reached sixty-two. That he had appointed Tom Paine as my deputy at my request and that he could appoint Tom as acting administrator. I would not take any commitment that wouldn't permit me from coming back if Tom Paine got killed. . . . So Tom then agreed that he would stay a year without pressing to be administrator. . . . Now Tom immediately did push."[4]

During the horrors of 1968, anticipation of a lunar landing receded in the public's attention. Hundreds of Americans were dying every week in Vietnam. The Tet offensive that opened 1968 demonstrated that Americans controlled nothing in Vietnam for very long. In April 1968, the riots that followed the assassination of Dr. Martin Luther King consumed Washington. Inside NASA headquarters men conspired to go to the stars while five blocks away rioters looted a department store. Webb found himself politically playing for time. He hoped that the elements he brought together as he faced the pressures of a lame-duck presidency would stay together.

Technologically, the program continued to progress until the second flight of the Saturn V took off on April 4, 1968. Pogo, the violent up and down motion that had been a problem on other rockets, was worse because of Saturn's enormous height. The shaking exceeded the design limits of the Apollo and the LEM. There were more complications. A panel in the lunar adaption section of Saturn actually blew out during the flight. Two of the five second-stage engines shut down prematurely. Although the NASA public relations machine treated the flight like a success, it was considered a failure by Low and Mueller. Webb told Paine to find out what went wrong and fix it. Paine found real trouble. What Paine learned from his investigation was not exactly a confidence builder. He found rocket engines wired in reverse, as well as vibration problems and engine problems. For Richard Smith, who would be center director at the Kennedy Space Center during the *Challenger* accident, Apollo VI's troubles revealed a different and more aggressive NASA: "We would find out what was the matter and fix it and go fly."[5]

It took a thousand engineers to solve the pogo problem. Confident that the Saturn V's problems could be corrected, George Low and Christopher Kraft pushed for a manned circumlunar mission. It was decided that such an audacious mission could be conducted in early 1969. Gen. Samuel Phillips, Apollo Program Director, urged his colleagues to keep the mission a secret until approval was obtained from Webb. Paine was brought into the process since Webb and Mueller were in Vienna at a United Nations conference on space. On August 14, 1968, the heart of the Apollo management team met with Deputy Administrator Paine in Washington to make their pitch. Paine asked all twelve at the meeting where they stood. All voted for a manned flight into lunar orbit. But before Apollo would fly men, it would lose its leader.

In his brief time under Webb, Paine concluded that

Webb "felt that NASA would have the finest management structure and the best administration and that NASA would serve as a model . . . to other agencies in the federal government, state government, local government, and, indeed, around the world as a model on how to run a program." But Paine is convinced that Webb was not so comfortable with facing the failure of day-to-day operations. "I think Jim [Webb] saw, that my goodness, if we have any failures it would really reflect on the whole system. I don't think he was really looking forward with tremendous enthusiasm to the actual launching with men aboard. He had been as badly burned as the astronauts had in the Apollo I fire. And he was very conscious of the fact, though everything had been rebuilt the way it should have been, he had been surprised before and he could be surprised again," Paine recalls.

Webb understood that summer that his efforts to keep NASA running by delaying long-range planning may have backfired. Paine believes that Webb's reluctance to engage in long-range planning had more to do with Apollo: "I am not sure Jim ever thought we would do Apollo. Maybe he had his doubts and felt that, well, we probably wouldn't make it in '69, probably '70 or '71, and gee, let's not get a bunch of long-range plans which people will laugh at if we're not successful." While Webb was a brilliant manager, there was no real purpose for NASA after Apollo. For the future, any serious new program, like a manned mission to Mars, a space station or a Space Shuttle, would require at least five to fifteen years to develop and cost many billion more dollars. And Webb firmly believed that it wasn't NASA's role to sell new programs, it was NASA's roll to carry them out.

It was an October day in Washington. Webb was feeling buoyant. The night before Ladybird and the president had dropped by his house to help him celebrate his sixty-second birthday. That morning the seventh floor at NASA was busy. Webb decided he would go to see the president to make a push for the Apollo program based on what the Soviets were doing. Intelligence clearly showed that the Soviets had no Saturn V class boosters, nor even the power to send men on a successful circumlunar flight. But they did have a huge orbital program ahead with grave military implications. David Williamson remembers working over some highly classified estimates of what the Russians were doing on a yellow legal pad in his office. "Webb swooped in, grabbed up my papers and left the office." Webb was on his way to the White House to see President Johnson. All Williamson could think of was the fact that Webb had notes that were top secret in his hand and that Williamson was responsible for them.

Paine was sitting in his office when he got a strange call from Webb's wife Patsy saying a neighbor just heard on the radio that Webb had resigned. Paine said he told Mrs. Webb, "'Jim was here half an hour ago. He just went over to the White House. He was going to see the president. Just a friendly visit. Nothing to do with resignation.' 'Well thank goodness,' she said. 'I can't imagine how something like that could happen.' 'Well neither can I,' I said."

That afternoon, Jim Webb, who was nicknamed the "fastest mouth in the south," returned to headquarters in a condition that Paine described as "not exactly coherent." Paine reconstructed what he thought happened during the meeting between Johnson and Webb. "He went over there for this very friendly purpose of saying, well, thank you for coming to my house, and, gee, it's nice to see another birthday roll around. And somehow he got on the subject of, well, you reach my age and I guess you have to start thinking about retirement. And that was not the sort of thing you said to Lyndon Johnson. That was like saying, 'Well, Mr. President, I don't know whether I ought to stick around in your administration or not.' At least I think that is the way LBJ took it at that particular moment. Now LBJ was a very complex man and he may have had a lot of other things on his agenda. After all, Jim Webb had been part of the Kennedy administration. . . . LBJ said, 'Well, Jim, you have really done a magnificent job for your country and we are going to be sorry to see you go. Let's go tell the press.' And while Jim was still sputtering he was standing in front of the press corps in the Fish Room and President Johnson was saying that 'Mr. Webb has just told me it's his intention to retire. Today's his birthday, and I've accepted with great reluctance.' At least that's the public perception of what happened," Paine says. "My own guess is there is more to it. Since I think the right thing probably happened. I am a little reluctant to believe it was quite as chancy as Jim indicated that it was or LBJ acted quite as erratically as the surface appearance would lead you to believe."[6] Webb says Paine "knows better than that."[7]

Paine inherited NASA and the lunar landing program. Now the pressure of success or failure fell on his shoulders. Apollo had yet to fly in space with a man on it. The first manned mission after the fire was dubbed Apollo VII. There would be an exhaustive two-week check of the Apollo service and command modules. The flight would combine everything that Grissom, White, and Chaffee were going to do with the endurance test flights that were delayed due to the disaster. The first manned Apollo flight worried Paine. "The last time we had put astronauts in that capsule we killed them. And though we thought we had rebuilt the thing, you never knew." Commander Schirra and his crew proved just how good the new Apollo was.

For Paine the job of acting administrator was not easy. Money was harder and harder to come by. Johnson conducted many of the budget meetings himself. "At the time of the annual budget crisis he [Johnson] would call me over. I would sit in the Oval Office on the couch and he would sit on the couch opposite; next to him would be the budget director with a big black book. And he'd say, 'You know we're terribly sorry, Dr. Paine, but you know, times are tough.' . . . I remember once going over there and as I left the Oval Office after getting $75 million that I thought was terribly important, the budget director protested vigorously saying, 'But Mr. President, you committed that we were going to make this strict all across [the board]. If you are going to let people do this, all our numbers are out.' . . . 'Give him the money; he needs it.' And having been taught at General Electric when you get the order, get the hell out the door. . . . President Johnson said, 'Just a minute, Dr. Paine.' I said, 'Yes?' 'I just wanted you to know that I am aware you have extracted $75 million from me.'"

Apollo VII's success had met NASA managers' criteria for approving the lunar orbit flight. NASA's charter was to go to the moon, and seven years after Kennedy made the commitment, the hardware and the crew were ready. On November 21, 1968, Paine wired the news to his subordinates. The United States was going to the moon for Christmas.[8]

He recalls the reaction to his decision. "'How can you make such a decision?' they were asking. 'The last time you flew this thing unmanned you had seventy anomalies, as you like to call them. How could you possibly put a man on it? And if you were going to put a man on it, how could you possibly send a man to the moon?'" But Paine felt differently. "And as far as I was concerned, it was just the opposite. I had the feeling that these things that happened, every one of which had shown us a weak spot and shown us precisely how to fix it, had given us a hell of a lot better bird than if nothing had happened."

Mission Commander Frank Borman was not comfortable with the insertion of a lunar orbit. It meant that the Apollo main engine had to work flawlessly or the crew would be trapped in orbit. Borman did not trust the engine because when the de-orbit fire was needed to return to earth, Apollo would be on the dark side of the moon where there was no communication. Borman made his feelings known to Gilruth. "Borman didn't mind flying around the moon," Gilruth recalls, "but he didn't want to retro fire into lunar orbit." So Gilruth and Borman struck a deal. "I said if it worked perfectly you will fire into lunar orbit. If it isn't, you will just let it drift around the moon and come home. That was the deal and it worked perfectly and they fired into lunar orbit," Gilruth remembers.[9] To him Apollo VIII was good for NASA for more than technical reasons. "I think the Russians would have gone all out to orbit the moon if we hadn't done it when we did. . . . We preempted that. If they had orbited the moon, our press would have said they had won. Our press would have said, 'My God, skunked again,'" Gilruth remarked.

One month after Paine's decision to approve Apollo VIII, at precisely 7:51 in the morning on December 21, 1968, the firing room's command was verified and ignition of the five F-1 engines began. At Kennedy and Houston the eight million parts that had sent 2.5 million bits of data that indicated Apollo VIII was ready, now received the ultimate test. During launch sequence, 2,700 points on the vehicle and payload were being monitored and were returning 150,000 signals a minute. The crew reached a maximum of four times their weight on earth during lift-off. At 10:17 A.M. the crew refired the Saturn third stage and left earth orbit for the moon. To a tortured country that had lost leaders to assassination and its young to war, the flight of Apollo VIII offered hope. A billion people across the world watched its flight. And Borman read a prayer to the people of the earth:

Give Us, O God, The Vision
Which Can See Thy Love In The World
In Spite Of Human Failure.
Give Us The Faith, The Trust,
The Goodness In Spite Of
Our Ignorance And Weakness.
Give Us The Knowledge
That We May Continue To Pray
With Understanding Hearts,
And Show Us What Each One Of Us
Can Do To Set Forth
The Coming Of The Day
Of Universal Peace.

As Borman, James Lovell, and William Anders orbited the moon that Christmas Eve they read from Genesis. The Apollo engine fired them out of orbit. When Houston heard the news, Gilruth understood that despite the frustrations, the setbacks, and the fire, Kennedy was right, the deadline could be met.

Lyndon Johnson had tears in his eyes the night the crew read Genesis. On January 9, 1969, Johnson performed his last official act concerning the United States space program in which he had played such a huge role. He presented medals to the Apollo VIII crew. When he left for Johnson City, the president had seen much of his world crumble. His brother, Sam Houston Johnson, said that "there was nothing Lyndon wanted more than to be in office when the lunar landing came, nothing." Paine was amazed by Johnson's fascination with space. "He liked to tell stories about when Sputnik first went up and he was out at the ranch on the banks of the Pedernales looking up at the sky and seeing Sputnik going across and thinking that, my God, he was privileged to be observing a whole new era to the human race. He really believed that."

For the men who created and nurtured Apollo—Kennedy, Webb, and Johnson—there would be no opportunity to taste the glory. America elected Richard Nixon to the presidency, a man who had little use for either space or any other program that reminded the country of John Kennedy. The Nixon administration kept Paine as administrator. Paine concluded the reason he, a Democrat, kept his job was that Nixon did not want to sacrifice a good solid Republican if there were a failure. "The feeling was that if he put a good political appointee and there was a tragedy, the White House would wind up as the villain of the case. . . . There was a feeling that look, these guys have spent $20 billion, and it's either going to work or not going to work. Let's leave the ones who have spent the $20 billion in charge," said Paine.

The Apollo IX mission with James McDivitt, David Scott, and Russell Schweickart was a full dress rehearsal of all the lunar systems in earth orbit. Early that spring word came to NASA that President Nixon, anxious to reap political capital from the space program, would appoint a panel to define his space goals. Paine wanted to be ready. So as most of NASA was buried in Apollo, Associate Administrator for Manned Flight George Mueller took on a new assignment. Mueller, a tough visionary, reached into the office planning Apollo X and recruited an engineer named LeRoy Day. The two men had worked together on Gemini. Day, a tall man who came to NASA from the Navy where he worked as a civilian, was known as one of the brilliant young engineers of Apollo. He was working with Sam Phillips on the Apollo Test Program when Mueller summoned him from the Apollo office a few blocks from NASA headquarters in Washington.

Day was consumed with Apollo as the deadline neared and he had little idea of what was going on in the rest of the agency.

Mueller, not one to dwell on social niceties, simply said, "I want you to head up the Space Shuttle effort," Day recalls. Day had no idea what Mueller was talking about. He looked at Mueller's blackboard, which had a list of things to be done on it. He was a little uncomfortable. Mueller went on as if Day really understood what he was saying. "He went to the blackboard and started talking about these things that had to be done and we needed to start meeting with the Air Force, and we had to make decisions about what we were going to do with this rocket technology and so forth, and I said, 'George, stop. I don't understand what you are talking about. I don't even know what the Space Shuttle is.' . . . 'Right,' he says. 'I want you to head up the Space Shuttle effort.' We're just two weeks from Apollo X. I asked him if he talked to my boss Sam Phillips about this and he says, 'No, I haven't, but I will.'"Mueller then told Day that he was being transferred immediately to the Space Shuttle program. Day thought "immediately" meant just after he finished his work with Apollo. The next morning he started the new job. Day was issued what he described as a standard GS-14 desk and a yellow pad and told to think about a reusable spaceship for easy access to space.[10]

On May 18, 1969, Apollo X left for the moon without the expertise of LeRoy Day. For the astronauts aboard, the Saturn V at first proved to be an easy-riding vehicle. Then the ride turned into a mass of vibrations. Communication became difficult. The command module gauges could not be read. Finally the ride smoothed and thoughts of aborting the flight ended. For Comdr. Thomas Stafford and Eugene Cernan the mission was bittersweet. They came within a few miles of the lunar surface but never landed.

Publicly the Nixon administration seemed very supportive of the space program. Vice President Agnew sat in the firing room for the launch of Apollo X. In reality there was no support and, even worse, little interest. For Paine, access to the president was nonexistent. For the first time in the history of NASA, the administrator found himself dealing with low-level aides rather than the chief executive. While Agnew was publicly effusive about the program, NASA officials felt that his attention span and his ability to understand even the simplest concepts of the program were very limited.[11]

On July 16, 1969, Apollo XI left for the moon. Neil Armstrong, a civilian, struggled with dust and a shortage of fuel in his LEM called *Eagle*, but on Sunday, July 20, 1969, at 4:17 P.M. EDT the lunar race was over. Kennedy's pledge was kept; his timetable of within the decade met. That same day in a last-ditch attempt to upstage Apollo, an unmanned Soviet craft failed and crashed into the moon.

Suggestions that USS *John F. Kennedy* make the Apollo XI recovery were immediately squelched by Nixon appointees within NASA. Instead, Richard Nixon, standing on the deck of the USS *Hornet*, waved to the astronauts through the glass window of an isolation trailer. Bob Seamans remembers. "One of the most remarkable things that happened . . . was Nixon going out on a carrier when the astronauts came back from the moon. He greeted them out there and he made a statement that this is the greatest human event since the creation . . . and every other time that anything happened that was initiated by the Kennedys, he'd turn his back on it or try to destroy it."[12]

The flights continued. But with each flight, public interest and political leadership waned. Paine was unable to keep the Nixon budgets from getting smaller and smaller. Apollo XII took off on November 14, 1969, with Paine holding an umbrella over President Nixon's head as they watched the lift-off. Paine remembered Webb's theory that administrators and presidents were bad luck at launches. The Saturn V was struck by lightning twice during ascent. Fortunately the Saturn and its millions of pounds of volatile fuel escaped destruction, and Apollo XII landed on the moon in the Ocean of Storms. For Paine, seeing Nixon at the launch was a revelation. "Each time we had another launch and the entire world converged and the networks and everything else, his interest went up farther. He and everyone else in the administration suddenly became aware of the fact that this crazy President Kennedy stunt, my God, suddenly, hey, this is real and this is really something the American people are terribly excited about."

On April 11, 1970, Apollo XIII blasted off. During the mission a movie called *Marooned* was playing around the country. It was about astronauts stranded in space aboard an Apollo. On the way to the moon the public and political complacency was shattered. An explosion ripped through the Service Module draining it of oxygen. The lives of the astronauts were in the hands of Gilruth's team in Houston. He and his people could not help Grissom, Chaffee, and White, but this time there was a chance to save Lovell, Fred Haise, and John Swigert.

The crew activated the LEM and used it as a lifeboat. Since they were in translunar injection when the explosion came, they had to stay with the crippled ship around the moon. Lithium hydroxide canisters from the LEM were used to cleanse the precious oxygen. Houston transmitted a contingency plan on the private communications channel. The astronauts drew straws on who would be sacrificed should there not be enough air to breathe. In fact, due to the care of the crew and the round-the-clock monitoring and creativity of Houston, all three men survived. On reentry, the LEM that saved their lives could do them no good, but the powerless Apollo carried them home.

Gilruth and Paine knew the Apollo team was losing its edge. The big mission was accomplished, and a new budget era was ushered in. The old Bureau of the Budget soon became Nixon's Office of Management and Budget (OMB). George Shultz was in charge and Donald Rice became NASA's budget examiner. He was not friendly to the program. The first cut the Nixon administration targeted was the remaining Saturn V boosters. Four planned lunar flights were cancelled. In many ways the Saturn V was the heart of NASA. While technologically imperfect, the big booster gave NASA the power to put the weight of a pair of locomotives in low earth orbit. A combination of launches using Saturn could orbit a full-scale space station. But maintaining the Saturn series was tremendously expensive so by cutting them out, NASA's access to space was suddenly reduced to only four manned missions beyond Apollo. NASA's power base was in large part eliminated. "Well, I discussed this with Jim Webb quite a few times and he keeps asking the question, Why did we give up the Apollo-Saturn so damn fast when we really had such a tremendous capability? There isn't any very good answer to that except that it cost money, I guess," says Bob Seamans. When Paine agreed to cancel the Apollo program before it was finished, he was only beginning the retrenchment of NASA that has continued for a generation. Today, Webb believes the loss of the Saturn capability was a tragic mistake.

Paine thinks there was a downside to Kennedy's pledge. ". . . And then I think . . . we began to see the negative to Kennedy's great positive. . . . Remember the way Kennedy put it when he selected Apollo. What he said was it is absolutely essential that this nation lead in the exploration of space. That we be the preeminent power able to navigate the

President Kennedy congratulates Alan B. Shepard, Jr., first American in space, after his ride in Freedom 7 *spacecraft. Between them is James Webb. (NASA)*

James Webb (NASA)

Hugh Dryden (NASA)

Keith Glennan (NASA)

Robert R. Gilruth (NASA)

William E. Lilly (NASA)

(Opposite) *The Apollo/Saturn 502 spacecraft mated to the Service Module and Spacecraft Inner Module Adapter is moved into the Vehicle Assembly Building at Cape Kennedy for mating to the Saturn V booster in preparation for the second Apollo/Saturn V unmanned flight. At right is a facilities verification vehicle. December 1967. (NASA)*

Robert Seamans, Jr. (NASA)

Paul Dembling (NASA)

David Williamson, Jr. (NASA)

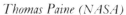

Thomas Paine (NASA)

(Opposite) *Skylab space station cluster in earth orbit photographed from the Skylab 3 Command/Service Module. Note missing solar "wing" from solar array system (SAS). (NASA)*

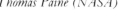

ASTP Saturn 1B launch vehicle sitting on the "milking stool" during pre-launch testing at Kennedy Space Center. (NASA)

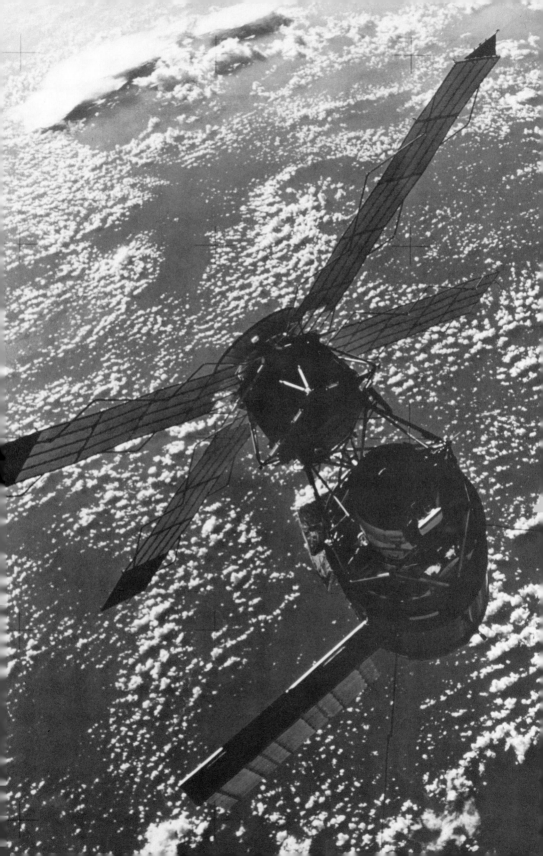

John F. Yardley (NASA)

George M. Low (NASA)

new ocean of space, and, therefore, that we go to the moon in this decade. . . . Okay, we're leading in space, he was absolutely right. That demonstrated to the Soviets and the rest of the world, not only were we leading in space, but obviously all the technologies required to do it, we were leading in. . . . You've demonstrated you're superior. That was the objective. Now, what do you do with this tool you have created? And there we weren't so smart. We didn't know," Paine admits.

In fact many at NASA did know. Wernher von Braun built enough Saturns to continue exploration of space between earth and the moon. Many at NASA proposed permanent bases on the lunar surface. According to Webb, von Braun and Mueller wanted to send two six-man ships to Mars in the hope that one of the ships would successfully make the arduous journey. Paine, realizing that Marshall had no immediate future, decided after talking to von Braun's wife, Maria, to bring von Braun to Washington, despite the political consequences. "He had really fulfilled his life's ambitions," observes Paine. "It was very clear that the only real strong motivating force left for Wernher was the Mars mission. Now that we'd been to the moon, let's get started. He wanted to push for it. And I wanted to push for it too. But I was pretty doubtful that we were going to be able to sell the Mars mission. The only way we were going to sell it is if we had one hell of an attractive mission. And at the same time [I] really felt we needed to upgrade our staff work and long-range planning. And of all the people in the world, nobody had demonstrated a better vision for the future than Wernher. He had consistently, decade after decade, said what was going to be important in the next decade, and then been right."

Paine confides that Webb wanted to keep von Braun out of Washington. "I think Jim had the feeling that, well, the Jewish lobby would shoot him down or something. The feeling that basically you were dealing with the Nazi party here.

And you could get away with it if he were a technician down in Huntsville building a rocket, but if you brought him up here and let him see the public and them him. . . . Furthermore, Wernher had an attractiveness about him with the rugged good looks and the German accent and that charismatic thing."

Paine feels that Webb's fears were groundless. "I think most people felt that he had a damned unfortunate past and nobody liked a Nazi . . . but he had kind of paid his dues and that he really helped us get to the moon in developing the Saturn V and showed himself to be a worthy citizen of this country, and while we won't exactly forgive and forget, politeness dictates, at least, we won't get into a disgraceful knock down and drag out. So it was sort of a neutral thing. He was neither the terribly charismatic or popular figure Jim feared, nor was he the great target of the anti-Nazis who very properly would object to having a prominent member of the Hitler regime ensconced in Washington in a policy area."

NASA was changing under Nixon. Paine agreed to accept political appointees to take over the NASA legal and legislative affairs offices. After that he found the White House pushing for more and more political appointees. The missions went on. Alan Shepard, the first American in space, stuck around long enough to make it to the moon. He had to struggle to learn to fly the lunar module, but for Gilruth and the veterans at NASA, there was no one more deserving of the assignment. Gilruth's fears of losing a crew were growing and he expressed them to Paine. "The lunar sites we were going to were turning out not to be all that different. And every one of them [the lunar missions] was a hazard to the three astronauts involved and eventually we would have lost a mission. We had a lot of single point failures and everything is never perfect. So when we made the decision, and this really started when I was the head, that Apollo XVIII was probably about as far as we should go, Bob Gilruth was very concerned about that decision. . . . Bob thought, gee, Apollo XIV is plenty. After Apollo XIII Bob was very nervous about the missions," reports Paine.[13]

Nixon appointed Spiro Agnew to head a task force that would determine the future of NASA. Paine felt it was vital for NASA to win the loyalty of that group so he began a campaign to win Agnew over. "His principal interest was in playing golf with the astronauts. Nevertheless, we had this darn thing and it was important that NASA capture the Space Task Group and, essentially, retain its own control over its destiny and not let it turn into a Rogers Commission type of thing," Paine says.

As did his predecessor, Paine faced an uphill battle with the Air Force. The Air Force attempted to renew its manned space program, but it paled in comparison to what NASA had already done. Paine thinks, "We then had all the capability that we needed to go ahead and put up a real space station using Apollo components at a fraction of the cost to the country and it became very clear that the things we could do in such a system, with an X-ray telescope, with astronauts going EVA to recover film plates, real time, hands on looking at what was happening to the sun, that the NASA program was superior."

The Air Force wanted MOL as a manned spy platform, and actually *launched* a full-scale wood and plastic mock-up in 1966. But American optics and sensors for military satellites made them far more efficient and secure. A new generation of CIA-designed satellites could raise and lower their own orbits and could send back either digitally transmitted, real time images or videotaped images. Sources at the CIA indicate that much of the MOL funding in the last few years of the program in reality went into unmanned "look-down" technology. With the lifting power of the Titan III in hand, the Air Force could send up huge automated spy platforms. But man was no longer needed for the Air Force's space program. McNamara had won. In August 1969, the Nixon administration finally killed MOL.

McDonnell Douglas Astronautics, the same company that lost the MOL contract, was given the contract for what became an orbital workshop. Using a Saturn V third stage as its shell, the workshop had the volume of a house. A large airlock module and a telescope system were also built along with a device called the multiple docking adapter that would allow several Apollo spacecraft to dock with the station if a rescue attempt had to be made. All told, the space station weighed in at 168,000 pounds and was eighty-four feet long and twenty-one feet wide. It was four times larger and far more sophisticated than the Soviet Salyut stations. Paine, tired of the name Apollo Applications, redubbed the orbital workshop Skylab. According to Webb, George Mueller had first sketched the workshop on a cocktail napkin on an airplane flight years before.[14]

One impetus for Skylab's political support was the increasing Soviet volume of spaceflights. Three different Soviet crews flew in earth orbit in October 1969. In April 1971, the *Salyut I* space station was orbited. In June, the Soviets occupied the world's first space station for twenty-two days. But on June 30, when Georgiy Timofeyevich Dobrovolsky, Vladislov Nikolayevich Volkov, and Viktor Ivanovich Patsayev landed, their recovery team found them dead in their Soyuz. The environmental control system failed during reentry.

Apollo XV was the first of the sophisticated "J" missions that carried the lunar rover and a larger experiment package. The crew spent eighteen hours on the moon and brought back 173 pounds of rocks from the surface. But for the American public, interest in the Apollo program was beginning to evaporate. Paine accepted it. "Kennedy being assassinated. The Vietnam war. The rebellion in the schools. And so the decision not to fly for a long period of time was one that didn't turn a hair on the American people. They didn't give a damn. By then, hell, we had been to the moon. What do you care if we fly another orbital flight or not. We know we can do it." Paine preferred to think far ahead. He was thinking of a painting of space in a 1953 *Collier's* magazine where a space telescope, a Space Shuttle craft, and a space station loomed over the earth. Von Braun wanted all three systems. A shuttle, that would give what Paine calls "reliable, low-cost transportation to a working space station to launch future missions, manned and unmanned in deep space had to be the goal."

The shuttle Mueller, von Braun, Day, and others recommended was huge. Its booster was totally reusable. Powered by heavy rocket engines and air-breathing jet engines, it would launch the shuttle and then return to earth. The orbiter section was the size of a 727 airliner. It, too, would have rocket engines to complete the boost phase and achieve very high orbits, as well as air-breathing jet engines for reentry. That was the system Paine tried to sell before he left office. It would cost between $10 and $12 billion. Because it would require little refurbishment, its cost per launch would be about one tenth of Apollo's cost. In the naive hope of getting the money from the Nixon administration for the system, Paine went along with massive cuts in the Apollo schedule and agreed with the budget office's decision to end all Saturn procurement.

For Paine there was no other choice. "If we cut out four missions, that is [a saving of] $6 billion [in today's dollars]. That's half the price of the shuttle. So I think it made sense in the 1970–71 era of the space program to start saying let's invest money in the next generation." Paine believed his shuttle would have fit in perfectly with what Agnew's task force would recommend. But he was wrong. Agnew's task force made three recommendations to Nixon each with its own price tag. Option A was a $10 billion a year effort by 1975 that would be only limited by technology. It included a manned mission to Mars, orbiting lunar and earth space stations, and the Space Shuttle. Option B recommended ending all manned spaceflight by 1974 with a modest $3 billion spending level for future development. Option C suggested a program that called for $5.5 billion funding that would include Apollo applications and $10 billion to fund a Space Shuttle. Even the hapless Agnew, who said on national television that Nixon would approve a Mars trip, was embarrassed when Nixon selected Option B, the option calling for an end to all manned flight by 1974. For Paine the decision reflected what he had already discovered, that although Nixon officially named him administrator of NASA, he was, in fact, an outsider in this administration. And so was space.

Paine was an optimist who believed that reason and goodwill would always win out. But his gestures at cutting out Apollo and cooperating with Agnew did not pay off. For Paine the revelation left only one alternative. "I sat down with Nixon always under rather formal and stilted circumstances. But he gave every appearance of listening and interacting and I would say, looking back on my interactions with the White House at that time, that I finally left because I really didn't think I could deliver to NASA the kind of relationship the head of NASA really ought to deliver."

5

Shuttle

LeRoy Day watched his creation blow apart on
television. At first he thought it was the liquid engines. They
had always been a problem. So much was demanded of those
three engines. When he found out it was the solid rocket motor that failed, it reaffirmed the main rule about manned flight
in space. It is dangerous and always potentially deadly. As he
saw his beloved machine destroyed, it renewed that awful
awareness that the NASA launching *Challenger* was not the
same NASA he went to work for a quarter of a century earlier. Roy Day left his job working on naval weapons systems
to work on Project Gemini where he met George Mueller, the
hard-driving boss of Apollo. After the military, the NASA he
came to work for impressed him "by the different level of care
and discipline that NASA put into hardware and procedures." Day labored on Apollo for a while. Then Mueller

ordered him to help create the shuttle. Day lived with build-ing the shuttle for almost ten years.[1]

In Mueller, Roy Day worked for perhaps the most com-plex man in all of NASA. Mueller was devoted to the explora-tion of space. Like von Braun and Gilruth, he intuitively understood why man had to keep looking. Mueller was con-vinced that exploring space was his generation's destiny. Be-cause so much of Mueller was always on the line, those who worked for him developed a tremendous loyalty. Mueller's staff enjoyed coming to work. Because of Mueller there was a lot of hope and excitement for post-Apollo NASA among Day and his colleagues. That hope made what happened to *Challenger* all that much harder to bear.

Mueller had a volatile but successful career at NASA. Bill Lilly, who would later control the financial end of the majority of NASA's programs, believes that Mueller was NASA's unsung hero during the shuttle planning. "He never got the credit on that thing. . . . George is one way in terms of moving in space. Even his Christmas cards were always space oriented."[2]

When Mueller assigned Day to help create a shuttle, they did not know that for the first time NASA would be design-ing a politically acceptable machine as well as a technically sound spaceship. This time the presidential support that had always been there was gone. One by one the visionaries at NASA were removed from power. At first they were "pro-moted" to meaningless jobs in headquarters. Then they were ignored. Forced into a retirement by neglect, the giants of the agency, von Braun, Gilruth, and Mueller, were rendered im-potent. They no longer had their "marching army" to lead. They no longer had a mission.

During the Nixon administration, people looking for po-litical jobs had to be more than true-blue Republicans. They had to be Nixon loyalists. These true believers of the Nixon administration had a deep distrust of bureaucrats, especially bureaucrats so openly associated with Democrats. The elitist attitude and esprit of NASA's top people did not endear them to the White House staff. Nixon placed as many mean-spirited Schedule C political employees in as many government agencies as he could. NASA was not exempt despite Paine's best efforts. When partisans had been sent in by earlier administrations, the space agency took special pride in converting them. When the White House staff complained that James Webb was doing favors for conservative Democrats, Webb urged President Kennedy to put anyone he selected in NASA to watch his actions. Richard Callaghan was chosen: ". . . At the time Kenny O'Donnell . . . was looking for someone to go over there. He asked me to go over to at least one other agency where they had, you know, no plant, no stool pigeon. And I wasn't interested in that, and then they asked me if I'd consider going over to the space agency. . . . They were concerned down at the White House. It had been implied, if not alleged, by people in the aerospace industry, that Bob Kerr and Clinton Anderson were having their way with the agency. Mr. Webb had been involved with Senator Kerr. So the people who weren't getting the contracts were the ones, you know, who were making these kind of innuendos and they were people . . . who had provided financial support in the past, so, you try and do what you can for people who have helped you. . . . But it was just a concern, you know, that the Kennedy element may not be in control. . . . So I went over, if you will, just to be an observer. Mr. Webb knew why I was coming over . . . and he made it possible for me to be involved as an observer in all that went on."[3] Within weeks, the quest of the lunar landing goal captured him. "And in the five years that I was there, it really was a tightly run operation and there was nothing political about it at all," Callaghan remembers.

According to Willis Shapley, one of the top men inside NASA at the time, Paine was kept on as administrator for only one reason. "They realized that this moon program was coming to fruition and it was a Kennedy program. . . . Also it could be the world's biggest disaster . . . so therefore, it was very important to let a New Deal Democrat like Tom Paine be administrator so you could lay it all at his feet," Shapley asserts. Paul Dembling, who was NASA's general counsel, has a different view of Paine. "Let's face it, Paine was in a real tough situation. He was a Democrat. He had run the Scientists' Campaign for Johnson-Humphrey on the West Coast. . . . Nixon was looking around for a guy, but he couldn't get anybody. And the reason he couldn't get anybody was that everybody he asked to run NASA asked what kind of commitment are you going to make to me to run NASA. And Nixon said, 'I don't know what we're going to give to the space program,' and that's why he couldn't get a Republican administrator."[4]

Inside NASA, the lack of presidential leadership was changing the agency. NASA was so geared up for the Apollo effort that few people had any idea what would happen when it was over. Few could imagine that the technology, the idea of exploration of the planets, of perhaps going to Mars, could just be put aside. Many of them had never worked harder in their lives. For Paine it was much like his experience as a World War II submarine commander. "I think we all tend to operate at about one percent of our capacity. But, by god, when you get in a wartime situation . . . or into something like [the] moon program, then you begin to operate at maybe 110 percent of your capacity. It really brings out the best in people, having tough and challenging things they have their heart and soul in. And that is the kind of operation NASA was. So even the ordinary people at NASA began to be giants in that era. And the difficulty was when the era was over. We really hadn't built a system that when the challenge was gone, it was ready to revert to an everyday government agency."

First the remarkable contractor team of 410,000 was allowed to dwindle. And the hopes and dreams that NASA employees shared began to turn to memories. Apollo, which for so many was the gateway, would, in fact, be as far as man would go. For men like John Naugle who helped run NASA's science programs, what was most remarkable about Apollo was that it was done at all. For Naugle and many of his contemporaries, the age of Apollo was a blessing, an easier time than his colleagues who are being recruited for Star Wars have now. "I never wanted to work on the bomb. I never wanted to build ICBMs. And I was lucky enough not to have to make my living that way. . . . It was, in a sense, a miracle. On the other hand, to me it's a much more logical thing to do than build 10,000 warheads." That type of attitude infuriated the Nixon White House. NASA was Kennedy's agency and Nixon would give it as little support as he could get away with politically. [5]

If manned spaceflight were to continue, accommodations with the Nixon White House had to be made. Deals had to be cut. NASA, constructed largely to carry out the lunar mission, had no leader powerful enough to articulate a new mission and get the support necessary to carry it out. Without a Webb to shield the shrinking agency from the reality of Washington, the wolves who were always at the door were now getting in.

Apollo's success made it impossible for Nixon to cancel a manned flight program altogether. Kennedy had succeeded in convincing most Americans that the future was in space. The polls, which meant so much to Nixon and his staff, demonstrated that to abandon manned spaceflight would be a political disaster. Because of the lead time needed to design and develop new programs, Nixon would reap no political benefit while in office from efforts like a Mars mission. The Russians had already orbited a space laboratory. But a Space Shuttle had the benefit of being practical and it could be funded sparingly. No one could accuse Nixon of killing manned flight, nor would he have to drain the treasury to build it. And the Pentagon could use it.

A key decision Paine made just before he left NASA would change the destiny of the space agency. In an effort to create a new NASA program that would be comparable in magnitude to Apollo, Paine concluded that the shuttle should be a "national vehicle" that would serve the purposes of the military as well as the commercial, civilian, and scientific communities. Paine regarded a "NASA only" shuttle as a political impossibility. "I didn't even regard it as political reality. To me it was very clear that the launch vehicle program for this nation has got to be able to serve both military and NASA's mix of science and commercial payloads," Paine insists.[6]

Dr. Robert Seamans, one of the three top NASA officials during Apollo, returned to Washington. But he did not go back to NASA. He was now secretary of the Air Force. While some in the Air Force wanted to develop the shuttle as an Air Force project, Seamans wanted no part of it. "We were getting lacerated for the F-111 and the C-5A. During the four years I was there in the Air Force we started . . . six or seven pretty major programs, including the B-1 and we just didn't want to take on anymore," Seamans recalls.[7]

As a member of Agnew's Space Task Force, Seamans recommended that NASA study and do limited testing on a space transportation system. "I believe we should not put a rigid time constraint on this objective," he wrote Agnew, "but rather embark on a flexible program where various alternatives are investigated."[8] Seamans believed that another crash program like Apollo was foolish. He felt that NASA had to define the needs before pursuing the goals.

Paine, convinced that the only way the shuttle could be sold was as a "national vehicle," pushed ahead without a firm commitment from Seamans and the Air Force. To get just a lukewarm commitment from the Nixon White House, Paine made several compromises before his resignation, including allowing the Air Force to set specifications for a shuttle system it made no commitment to support. At that point even Paine realized that "after a lot of negotiating, they put conditions on us [which] I think they thought we couldn't fulfill."

Among the requirements the Air Force originally requested was a crossrange landing capability of 3,000 miles so a shuttle carrying secret cargo could not be forced down in communist territory. The Air Force also wanted communications and avionics aboard the shuttle that were eavesdrop-proof and immune to the effects of a nuclear explosion. But for George Mueller and LeRoy Day, the last straw was a request that the entire shuttle development program be classified. "They told us everything to do with the shuttle [from] here on in was to be classified," Day recalls. "Of course this was ridiculous. You couldn't do that. . . . Thank goodness we had George Mueller along at the time. He's a very capable, diplomatic guy. He doesn't come on with a big stick, normally. . . . In nice talk, not only did he say, 'No,' but 'Hell no, we will not do that.'"[9]

Paine inflicted on NASA a program that would be in part dictated by the Pentagon. And the Air Force had the best of both worlds. It could make demands, but not be responsible if they failed. But of all the fears of building a joint military vehicle, none caused greater concern than the fear that NASA would lose its reputation for openness. Nearly everyone of the old-line NASA veterans brought these concerns to

Paine. People in NASA's vast international programs reminded him that during Gemini the Mexican government threatened to withdraw Guymas, Mexico, as the site of a NASA tracking station if announced military experiments were carried aboard. They asked Paine who would have command over the missions, NASA or the military? Paine thought these concerns were all too premature to worry about at that time.

Today, Roy Day's den is filled with models of shuttles that were never built, including the giant reusable shuttle that Tom Paine had envisioned. After Paine left, George Low, a gifted engineer, became acting administrator of NASA and Dale Myers became head of manned spaceflight. Low had neither the political clout nor savvy of any of his predecessors. But he did have a burning desire to keep NASA in the manned spaceflight business. To do that he began to make a series of deals. One of the first was to agree with the Nixon budget office to an unrealistically low figure for shuttle development. This budget doomed Tom Paine's reusable and operationally economical shuttle.

Tom Paine's exit from NASA in March 1971 was marred by the behind-the-scenes battle over his shuttle. Paine is critical of Low's actions. "Our feeling was that this [$10 to $15 billion] was the lowest operation cost system that we would achieve. Now, as the fellows got into it, they struck a bargain with the devil that it would be an $8 billion development and they locked themselves in. See, they got in a syndrome when Jim Webb said Apollo would cost $20 billion. So later I was able to make big speeches about, my God, we did it on time and within budget. We did it in budget because Jim multiplied by two. I didn't add that. Jim was a very wise fellow. He knew about these things and he did exactly the right thing."[10] Paine complains that NASA was believing its own press releases when it agreed to the $8 billion development figure with the Nixon White House. "I think that for one reason or another the budgets got more restricted. And I think the world would have been quite different if somebody had multiplied the $8 billion by two and we'd gone in for $16 billion. Then we would have had a shuttle come out that probably would have had a substantially lower operating cost."

Paine believes that the seeds for the destruction of the shuttle program were sowed in what seemed to NASA management at the time like a small series of compromises to keep manned flight going. "The road to hell is notoriously made small step by small step. The devil always has a very tiny bargain. Just move over here a little bit, and well, gee, you are not going to quit. . . . You wanted the shuttle for $8 billion and you got 5.2, well, gee, you are not going to quit over that. My God, you got the little thing and it's very exciting and now let's go. . . . And then you get that last-minute call from the White House and the president wanted to tell you that we're gonna have to take another $75 million out of NASA . . . and then next year another $120 million. It goes on and on," says Paine.

At what was now called the Lyndon B. Johnson Space Center in Houston, engineers and management requested permission to begin designing a small-scale vehicle before embarking on a full-scale shuttle. There were so many unknowns in the shuttle design, especially in the areas of computer-controlled aerodynamics and thermal protection. A smaller-scale engineering version of the shuttle seemed only sensible to Houston. But for Paine and then Low, there was no choice politically. They understood the only way the United States would be flying men, would be with a full-scale program. They both expressed the fear that anything smaller would be too easy not to fund. A small program would not develop enough of a political base to survive a budget attack.

By 1971, the only portion of the shuttle project that was approved was the engine development program. One of the most difficult parts of Apollo was developing the Saturn V engines. With a reusable spacecraft, the same engines would have to work again and again. The turbopumps and other elements of the engine would have to withstand enormous heat and stress. And they would have to be of a compact, integrated design never before tried. Rocketdyne, which built the Apollo engines, was awarded the shuttle contract over Pratt and Whitney. When Pratt and Whitney officially protested the award, the engine program came to a halt pending an investigation. For NASA, now politically leaderless, the engine fight was a nightmare. Willis Shapley remembers, "It was a terror. They brought out all sorts of political guns. We invited GAO [the General Accounting Office] to referee this and they did. And the finding sustained the original selection. But we had lost a year on the program." [11]

In the trenches, Roy Day was part of the team trying to redesign a shuttle that the military could live with and NASA could build with quickly declining budgets. The military wanted a 60-foot-long-by-15-foot-wide cargo bay. While NASA at first balked at the size because of the extra cost, Dale Myers decided to go along with it because the capacity could be used by NASA later to launch a space station and multiple satellites. In 1971, the shuttle fleet was to include seven vehicles. Just how they would be divided up between the Air Force and NASA was not decided. There was vague talk that the Air Force would buy several shuttles of its own. But Day thinks NASA kept it deliberately vague to keep control over the vehicle. NASA refused to agree simply to assign shuttles for exclusive Air Force use. "Well, there had been talk about doing something like that, but I think a little bit of the provincial part of NASA came into it. They were afraid they might lose control of the thing if they had somebody else running a program," Day says.

NASA, the most innovative and exciting of government agencies, now had managers who were devoting their time to just keeping the agency alive. They were left with a vehicle rather than a mission. To the public, nothing was amiss in NASA. The NASA public relations mill had endless grist from the continuing Apollo flights. After it became clear that Apollo was a success, the Nixon White House needed someone at NASA they could trust. A search for an administrator began in earnest. Any hope George Low had of becoming administrator ended with the appointment of Dr. James Fletcher in 1971.

Jim Fletcher had strong Republican credentials, but he was no White House insider. A Mormon from Utah, Fletcher had the prerequisite distrust of the bureaucracy. But those he was about to lead hoped that Fletcher would have the political clout with the White House to stop NASA's decline. Fletcher came to NASA after a long career in industry, as a physicist and as president of the University of Utah. But Willis Shapley remembers his biggest problem with the Nixon administration. "He devoted a great deal of effort just trying to figure out a working system in the jungle of the White House staff and other power centers around town." Shapley says that Fletcher had a problem selling anything in manned flight to the Nixon administration.

When Fletcher first came to NASA, shuttle official Charles Donlan says he was cool to a new manned vehicle. Donlan says he even found himself defending the fact that the shuttle had wings on it. Fletcher told Donlan the only reason the shuttle had wings on it was because its designers came from an aeronautical background and wanted an excuse to fly men. To prove him wrong, Donlan authorized a study to see if a wingless shuttle could be parachuted to a landing.[12]

Fletcher recalls the early decision period. "Basically the president through Peter Flanagan and John Erlichman said, 'What should we do as a follow on to the Apollo program in manned space?' And I had all this stuff before me. The analysis of the shuttle. Even had a space station study which was around, but that people before me had been told wasn't going to fly. So we had a choice of the Space Shuttle which finally materialized or the other big competitor was Big G, Big Gemini. That was a Titan III with another Gemini on top of it. And it was pretty obvious to George Shultz and Peter Flanagan, and John Erlichman that the only way to go was some sort of a shuttle. Now the question is how to pay for it? That's what the big argument was."[13]

The redesign for a cheaper and cheaper space transportation system accelerated. Fletcher and George Low began to put a strategy together to make certain that the shuttle system would be sold to the Nixon White House. They proposed two sizes for the Space Shuttle, a 45-foot-long cargo bay and a larger sixty-foot-long version. The administration was interested in cost-benefit justification for all its projects. After consulting with Princeton economist Oskar Morganstern, George Shultz, then head of Nixon's budget office, opted for the bigger version. The new shuttle configuration sacrificed little of the orbiter element that Paine envisioned. But the reusable manned booster system was abandoned as too costly to develop. Although a hybrid launch vehicle of solid fuel attached to a liquid fueled system would cost far more to operate over the long run, the reusable launcher was sacrificed to satiate OMB's never-ending demand for budget cuts.[14]

Fletcher defends the decision to abandon the completely reusable shuttle. "That was simply a matter of cost and time. It would have taken longer to develop and would have cost about double what the current shuttle cost." But for oldtimers like von Braun, the decision to save money on the shuttle by using solid rockets was a very dangerous one. Solid rockets were used in manned flight only for emergency escape systems and braking rockets, never for powered flight. If anything went wrong in flight, they could not be shut down. Further, the new shuttle design contained an element that shocked and surprised Gilruth and his former colleagues at Houston. Because the shuttle was to be built as a spaceplane, not a capsule, there were no plans to blast the passengers free of a vehicle facing a catastrophe. To include an escape system would have increased the cost, estimated by Bill Lilly in 1971 to be down to $6.2 billion.

To Gilruth, the lack of an escape system on the shuttle violated everything NASA stood for. The combination of solid rockets and the lack of an escape system terribly distresses Paine to this day. If only he had not insisted, over the objection of von Braun and others, that NASA keep its facilities open in Florida, which conducted studies of solid rocket technology.[15] Von Braun insisted that the technology was simply too dangerous for manned flight. But politically it didn't matter. Von Braun and Gilruth would soon be out of NASA. Von Braun would go to work for Fairchild Corporation and Gilruth would retire.

Others at NASA like Gilruth's former deputy Charles Donlan believed that the solids were hampering the shuttle's future. He pushed with von Braun and his former colleagues at the Marshall center for a pressure-fed liquid system that was both more powerful and easier to control. Officially the decision on whether liquid pressure-feds or solids would boost the shuttle into orbit was not made until after a January 1972 meeting with Nixon and Fletcher in San Clemente. Many in the shuttle program are convinced that the commitment to the solids and thus a cheaper shuttle was made months before. In the end, the shuttle that was approved could only reach orbits of 600 miles carrying payloads between 30,000 pounds to polar orbit and 65,000 to equatorial orbit.

Fletcher says what convinced him to go for the solids was the performance of the Titan. "In retrospect maybe it was a questionable decision, but up to that time they were extremely reliable and the cost per flight was low. And we knew how to recover them because the solids had already fallen off the Titans and were floating in the ocean. So it seemed like a reasonable thing to do as far as recovery is concerned. Whereas we really were not sure how to recover liquids, that had never been tried," Fletcher points out.[16] In fact, the Titan solids had never been recovered and were only a fraction of the size of the solids that would be built for the shuttle. But plans went ahead to build a solid rocket motor that could be refurbished and reused. The big liquid fuel tank for the main engines of the shuttle would have to be replaced each flight.

By the time NASA went for final approval for the shuttle program, the Bureau of the Budget had been transformed into the much more powerful Office of Management and Budget. The faces in the past had been tough, but friendly to NASA. But now on the other side of the table was Donald Rice. Rice lived in a world that was alien to NASA. Projects he approved had to be justified by cost and operational modeling. Although NASA was about to build a fourth-generation space system, Fletcher and Low found themselves trying to justify its cost as if they were running a passenger airline: ". . . Before this you never really expected to get your money back on Apollo or Skylab or anything like that. This was pretty well accepted as a charge, a national thing you should do," Shapley recalls.[17]

In the past NASA used predictions of mission modeling to work with the scientific community in scheduling experiments. Several years earlier Lockheed, Aerospace Corporation, and a Princeton organization called Mathmatica were given contracts to prepare cost-benefit studies for the shuttle. Lilly says the original intent of the studies was to show reluctant scientists, who like to control their own rockets, that the shuttle would allow more funding for their projects. "You have got to bring in these scientists and you have got to convince them that you can do these missions on the shuttle. They are better. They are cheaper. Because left to their own devices, these scientists would have rather had a vehicle they could own themselves and play with," according to Lilly.[18] These new economic justifications, however, created the temptation to cajole as many other people as possible who had authority over payloads to commit their missions to the unconstructed, unproven, and unfunded shuttle system.

NASA based the models on the flight rate of the early 1970s, a flight rate that was on a steep decline because NASA simply did not have the funds to buy the payloads. Even the military flight rate was exaggerated. The Department of Defense refused to tell NASA the nature of its missions, so NASA hired Aerospace Corporation because of their knowledge of DOD missions to build mission models. The military's primary use of the shuttle was to launch large spy satellites, like the planned Keyhole 12, designed by the CIA. The flight rates were based on current satellite designs. But one of the main purposes of the shuttle was to put up much larger satellites that could be refurbished and refueled in space. The fact that fewer of these satellites would be needed was not taken into account in the studies.

When Fletcher became administrator he decided to use these studies for quite another purpose. He told Lilly he needed the studies to sell the shuttle to the White House, something Lilly was not comfortable with. "It made me nervous, and I didn't like it, that we were selling it on the basis of a cost-effective system for all flights. . . . I didn't like that at all. We had lots of discussions on that. And Fletcher became convinced, and I couldn't really argue that much, that he wasn't right, but he said he knew he couldn't get it approved at the White House without that kind of thing. And then that's when we got the outside consultants." [19]

Fletcher denies he misused the studies. "I did not do that. NASA was asked by OMB . . . to make a cost-benefit analysis and we picked the best guys in the country to do that. Aerospace and Lockheed were picked because we needed some kind of model for missions that were going to be flown over the next twenty-five years and it was a guess. Mathmatica was only involved in estimating what the cost-benefit analysis was." [20] But according to Lilly and Willis Shapley, the only way Fletcher could convince the White House to approve funding for the shuttle was if it had a launch rate high enough to justify the cost of its development. Fletcher says this "is absolute baloney." But those who worked for him paint a different picture. They say Fletcher and Low sold the shuttle by using studies that showed the shuttle would be the cheapest way to put anything in space *if* the flights were frequent enough.

Soon the mission models began to take on a life of their own at NASA. At first, in congressional hearings NASA officials mentioned the cost justifications of the shuttle as an afterthought. But as the popularity of the idea of the shuttle paying for itself grew rapidly on Capitol Hill, more and more NASA officials began to imply that the shuttles could replace all expendables in the NASA fleet. "There was no great scheme at that point to get rid of the expendables," Lilly said, but the pressure on NASA to live by its mission models was beginning to be applied by both friends and critics. Fletcher and Low wanted the shuttle at any cost. According to Lilly, once Low was convinced that getting rid of expendable rockets was the only way he would get the shuttle, that policy became the mandate at NASA. NASA was caught in the cost-benefit trap.

The most frequently cited study by Fletcher was the Mathmatica study put together by Dr. Oskar Morgenstern and Dr. Klaus P. Heiss. It predicted the shuttle could orbit payloads for as low as $100 a pound. The study was finished in January 1972 to coincide with the public announcement of the shuttle. Dr. Hans Mark, who then headed NASA's Ames Research Center in Mountain View, California, remembers a presentation made by Heiss. "I remember that we gave Heiss quite a going over during his visit because the flight rate he was projecting implied an enormous budget for space activities to pay for all the payloads he was proposing to fly. Many of us were unhappy with Heiss' conclusions because we could not honestly reconcile ourselves to the launch rates that he was projecting," Marks writes in his unpublished manuscript titled *The Space Station—A Personal Journey.*[21] Fletcher and the NASA public relations machine quoted that cost-benefit study so often that it became a NASA in-house joke. Lilly said the whole premise was based on flying all four shuttles at the absolute capacity of 65,000 pounds at sixty flights a year. NASA public relations people became a problem. "Yeah, they would go out and become real salesmen on the thing. You couldn't keep track of what they were doing," recalls Lilly.

The OMB demanded that the shuttle be proved economical and that's just what NASA did. "You see we had to do a silly thing to start with by proving the shuttle economical in a comparison with current systems, which you couldn't do. So you had to develop an expendable and say here is what it would take to give it shuttle capability and compare and cost the things out. And so, it was a false study. There wasn't anything to compare the shuttle to," Lilly said.

To Seamans and the Air Force, the push to put every-thing on the unproven shuttle was dangerous. Despite pres-sure from Fletcher, Seamans refused to begin construction on a West Coast launch facility for the shuttle at Vandenberg Air Force Base. Seamans says he told Fletcher "we're not going to commit ourselves to a billion dollars worth of facilities until we know how this shuttle is going to come out." Seamans just did not understand the need for a manned vehicle for every launch. "I said, 'I can't believe that it's economical to have to put men up there every time you put a simple-minded satel-lite in orbit.' I said, 'There is risk involved every time you do it. It's bound to cost more because of all that life-support equipment you have to truck back and forth.'"[22]

At NASA headquarters final preparations were being made for Fletcher's trip to San Clemente in January to make the formal pitch to Nixon for the shuttle. George Low, who had a history of technological honesty, was now preaching an unheard of frugality at NASA. Willis Shapley remembers, "He said, 'We came from the Apollo program where costs were no object.' He said, 'The idea was that we had to re-orient the agency to being cost-conscious. We can't let the people at Marshall and Houston solve all their problems by calling up the budget office and saying they were going to let out another contract for $10 or $15 million.'" Some thought that Low's new devotion to frugality did not square with his push for a shuttle program that was really another crash de-velopment program like Apollo. The shuttle was not an evo-lution of Apollo, it was a leap ahead. Houston's desire to build a small-scale test vehicle to make certain NASA had all the technology in hand before building a full-scale system continued to be rejected.

Seamans was convinced that Fletcher decided to make the shuttle his Apollo program. In Seamans' view Fletcher was committing a kind of bureaucratic suicide by crashing the shuttle program and doing it underfunded. On a winter weekend in 1971 in Washington, Dale Myers, the associate administrator for manned spaceflight, began to put together the final figures for Fletcher's meeting with the president. The bottom-line estimate to build the scaled-down system was $4.85 billion.[23] Fletcher added his "administrator's discount" and brought the figure to $5.5 billion plus a twenty percent contingency for unknowns. Fletcher told Lilly and Shapley that he had persuaded the OMB in preliminary meetings to agree to a $6.5 billion development budget.

With the numbers in his briefing book, Fletcher went to San Clemente to see Nixon at what Fletcher thought would be a pro forma meeting announcing the $6.5 billion budget. Lilly told Fletcher the only way NASA could do the job was if annual funding stayed at the current $3.4 billion level, with an adjustment for inflation. The president was presented with a model of the shuttle and the public announcement of the new "national space transportation system" was made. It would cost $5.5 billion with a twenty percent contingency. When Fletcher returned to headquarters, Bill Lilly remembers the scene. "Shultz was on the phone to Fletcher raising hell. Where in the hell did that twenty percent come from? That wasn't part of the deal at all. Shultz may have been honest . . . or he may have been pushed by somebody else, but he took a really strong position on it and Fletcher finally said, 'Well okay, we'll try it.'"

Shultz ordered NASA to withdraw all press releases indicating the $5.5 billion figure.[24] Early editions of the *Washington Post* and *Wall Street Journal* contained announcements with the larger figure. Shultz said the White House only agreed to a $5.1 billion shuttle with no contingencies. For Shapley the $5.1 billion commitment was no surprise. "They used to write budget commitments in disappearing ink in that administration," he recalls. But for Lilly the numbers were ominous. As NASA comptroller, Lilly realized that the shuttle project was starting off with a twenty percent budget overrun courtesy of George Shultz.

Shultz's decision may well have forced NASA to go with the cheaper solid rockets. A decision Fletcher seems to now confirm: "The configuration we presented to the president in January 1972, they were liquids. But we told the president we really hadn't decided between solids and liquids and so the solid decision came after the decision was made for the shuttle. . . . It was partly cost, and partly because they had shown extreme high reliability compared to the liquids." In fact, according to Lilly and Shapley, it was strictly economic considerations that put the solids on the shuttle. Many NASA experts preferred an all-liquid system, including shuttle designer Max Faget. But the $5.1 billion budget precluded building the all-liquid system Donlan was pushing. Donlan, a gruff and direct man who had been a top Gilruth aide, believed the decision to build the solids was bad economics. A liquid system using fuel fed to the engines by chemical pressure, rather than pumps, is what the tighter budget eliminated. The pressure-fed system would have meant a more powerful shuttle system that would be able to lift heavier payloads into higher orbits.

Lilly believed "if worse comes to worse we could blow the whistle" on OMB reneging on the planned shuttle budget. Lilly felt there was a slim chance that the program could be done for $5.1 billion if nothing further went wrong. That would mean that Nixon would have to keep his word and fund NASA at the $3.4 billion level for three years plus an adjustment for inflation.

Traditionally, George Low asked Lilly to write down in his own hand some ground rules for a program that absolutely could not be broken to complete the program successfully. Lilly was one of NASA's most reliable barometers for program troubles. He wrote his concerns down and Low locked them in his safe. Lilly wrote that the avionics and the heat protection system—the tiles—were of real concern. And then he added one more item to the list. "I stipulated that for the solid rocket that there would be a single contractor to do the total, not to break it up into a booster and so forth." Lilly wanted a company capable of building *every* system for the 149-foot-long rockets, from the parachutes to the design for recovery and refurbishment. But the net effect could be costly when problems arose during development. Leery of the solid design, Lilly was adamant. "I stipulated to Low and Fletcher both . . . was look, goddamn it, don't break that thing up." Lilly also listed other stipulations and warned Fletcher and Low, "You have a reasonable chance of doing it for $5.1 billion without any contingency, but it isn't very likely. If you had any trouble, any deviations in this thing, you were probably dead."

Fletcher had other problems. The OMB was recommending that the Marshall Space Flight Center be closed. To save it, Fletcher ignored Lilly's warning and gave the very center that had vehemently opposed any use of solid rockets for manned flight the assignment of assisting in the development of the solids. Lilly was out of town when Fletcher broke up the components of the solids for separate bidding. Lilly described his meeting with Fletcher when he returned. "My point was, goddamn it Jim, I leave town here for a week and you go and screw the whole goddamn thing up. You are going to double the price of the solid."[25]

Because of the lack of aerospace work, the government had fallen into a pattern of breaking up contracts into smaller and smaller segments to spread business around. The net effect of not putting the entire system up for bids was to take United Technologies Corporation (UTC) out of the running. UTC built the large solids that were closest to what the shuttle project would need—the solids on the Air Force's Titan III launch vehicles. Without one company developing all the systems, the better bid on paper came from Morton Thiokol, coincidentally in Fletcher's home state of Utah. Thiokol, to the chagrin of Lilly and others in NASA, got the lucrative contract. Fletcher says of his decision, "Hey look, I knew all those four contractors very well. Very well. All except for Morton Thiokol. But none of them really had that kind of capability. . . . They had been used to building small rockets. The only one that had built any large rockets of this sort was UTC and they just were not competitive with Thiokol on cost."[26] The solid rocket capability Fletcher's decision was supposed to give Marshall turned out in Lilly's view to be non-existent. "As far as I am concerned they never did develop any capability. They spent a lot of money but they didn't do anything." Lilly clearly believes that UTC should have gotten the contract for a total system. But once Fletcher decided to break up development of the booster, then Morton Thiokol, free of many of UTC's union problems, offered a cheaper price.

As the shuttle debate continued, Apollo neared its end. On April 16, 1972, Charles Duke, Thomas Mattingly, and John Young took off for the moon. The mission included twenty hours on the lunar surface, and another 208 pounds of lunar rock were brought back. For NASA, Apollo XVI was a public relations disappointment. The ratings were dropping on each successive Apollo flight so the television networks reduced their coverage. The networks now debated whether to even cover the final lunar mission, Apollo XVII. Gilruth, who had been transferred to Washington and replaced in Houston by his deputy, Dr. Christopher Kraft, recalls NASA's astounding solution to the lack of television coverage of the last Apollo flight. "You know we had to pay the networks to cover the last landing on the moon. . . . We thought

. . . it would be good, this is the last flight and the last return from the moon . . . the networks were not going to cover it." [27]

As the sparring between NASA and OMB on shuttle program costs continued, the clock struck midnight for Apollo. On December 7, 1972, a cold front cut across the Cape just a few minutes before lift-off. Apollo XVII was different from all the previous missions. This last trip to the moon was to leave at night. After a brief delay, the lift-off came. From the press site three miles from Pad 39A, three thousand correspondents were stunned by what they witnessed. The power of Saturn turned night into day. The Apollo team could not have ended the lunar program on a more moving or dramatic note. Some reporters wept at the sight. As the light and noise receded, the Saturn became a speck of light. The last lunar voyage ended five days before Christmas, nearly five years after Frank Borman read Genesis from lunar orbit.

Three miles from Pad 39A work went on. Only one more mission remained in the budget for von Braun's moon rocket, the Saturn V. Saturn's last flight would be to loft NASA's new space station called Skylab into orbit. Inside the Vehicle Assembly Building (VAB) welders were constructing a fifteen-story "milking stool" to sit astride the mobile launcher so a Saturn IB could launch astronauts to the new space station using the bigger Saturn V launchers. After the Skylab program the smaller shuttle would be based in the sixty-story VAB. But with the shuttle at less than half the size of the Saturn V, everything would be reduced in scale. The budget cutbacks had now reached Florida and were sweeping over the Cape. Engineers and technicians trained to send men to the moon found themselves delivering telephone books and pumping gas to survive. The dream was dying very hard in places like Titusville, Cocoa Beach, and along the rest of the spacecoast.

For John Naugle, a cancer began to spread in NASA as Fletcher's intentions with respect to the shuttle became clear. Fletcher came from the old world of Thompson Ramo Wooldridge, later known simply as TRW. His view of space was from the "black" or secret side, given his experience with numerous military space programs. "So, Jim was suspicious of the bureaucracy, in contrast to Webb, who knew the bureaucracy, knew its strengths and weaknesses and knew how to use it. That was one of his strengths. See, he [Webb] had been at OMB, he'd been up on the Hill . . . Webb had all of that [experience]. He also knew how the system worked and how people would respond and, in addition, he had a tremendous personal intelligence and energy. He could get things done."[28] When Fletcher began doctoring the figures to sell the shuttle and made his subordinates join in the myth of the economic shuttle, the erosion of what Webb labored so hard to build began in earnest. "That was the fact that the perception that we had to argue that it [the shuttle] was cheaper. It would be cheaper than the expendable launch vehicles. It would be better than all the expendable launch vehicles. That it would replace all the expendable launch vehicles. . . . Well there was a feeling that we were on the razor's edge. That if we said a wrong thing, or anything like that, the shuttle would be killed," Naugle remembers. At NASA the perception was growing that the only thing keeping the agency alive was the shuttle project. And Naugle went along with it because not to have gone along would have endangered his beloved space science. "Maybe it sounds cynical, but my view of life was that first of all I could conceive that after Skylab there could be no manned flight program. You know, I could imagine what that would be. And what I saw there was that NASA could lose a lot of its leverage around town if you lose that program. Secondly I could see that things like Viking, things like the Space Telescope . . . would then be targets . . . instead of people taking off on the manned flight program."

Naugle found NASA getting in deeper and deeper. In order to get the launch rate up to justify the shuttle, Fletcher "created a very large-scale science program and then showed you could cut substantial money out of that program—like a $14 billion program for $7 billion" by using the shuttle. In reality the NASA science budget was only in the $750 million range. According to Naugle, Fletcher pushed for larger and larger scale projections of scientific use of the shuttle to justify the program. "We put together a major program in the area of Spacelab. If you go back and look at those economic studies you will find that there is a large number of Spacelab missions in there."

A space laboratory was to be built by a consortium of European countries to fly on the shuttle. It was, in effect, a mini-space station that gave scientists a pressurized, shirt-sleeve laboratory in the shuttle's cargo bay accessible from a shuttle hatch. The Europeans had invested a billion in Spacelab. The collapse of the shuttle program resulted in the cancellation of eighteen planned Spacelab missions. The Europeans actually spent more on their contribution to the shuttle than the Department of Defense. Naugle says Fletcher's motivations were clear. "I think Fletcher felt sincerely that if he couldn't justify the shuttle economically, he couldn't make it go. And that was where my feeling was that if he had gone back to Nixon and said, 'There is no way José that I can justify this economically; we either do it as an R&D program because it ought to be done, or we go out of the manned spaceflight business.'"

Fletcher did not go back to Nixon and tell him the shuttle had to be justified as a research and development program. Instead Naugle was ordered to put *all* future scientific missions on the shuttle. One mission he was most concerned about was Galileo, a twin probe designed to explore Jupiter by having one probe orbit the planet and another land. Galileo was dependent on the position of the planets for a successful launch in the spring of 1982. Naugle knew that any delays would risk the loss of the mission. He pleaded with Lilly and others to allow him to store a pair of Titan-Centaurs for the launch. The cost of storage and maintenance was viewed as too high and his request was denied. Fletcher told Naugle that NASA was not about to pay such storage costs and he should plan launching his probes out of the shuttle's cargo bay on a solid booster called the Interim Upper Stage (today called the Inertial Upper Stage or IUS), which the Air Force was developing as a solid booster to achieve higher orbits from the shuttle. When NASA was in a more favorable budget climate, it intended to develop the Space Tug. The Tug would be the ultimate upper stage, one that would stay in orbit, be refueled and launch payloads into higher orbit.

Naugle was more than dubious. He reluctantly ordered the Jet Propulsion Laboratory to begin redesigning Galileo so its twin probes could be launched on the shuttle. The plans called for two IUS stages to be lofted into orbit along with the Galileo probes. The astronauts would combine the stages and launch it out of the cargo bay. The redesign order raised the cost of Galileo by tens of millions of dollars. Naugle faced meeting a deadline with a launch vehicle that was not even built, using an upper stage that Boeing had yet to develop for the Air Force.

More than a decade after he ordered Naugle to launch Galileo from on shuttle, Fletcher says, "I started the Galileo program. It started just the year I left. I think it is a fascinating program. It just broke my heart every time they changed the configuration."[29] When asked why Galileo was forced on the shuttle and off Titan-Centaur, Fletcher says, "There were not [any] Titans big enough to carry Galileo . . . the original Titan-Centaur would not carry Galileo." In fact, Galileo aboard the Titan-Centaur and Galileo aboard the shuttle using the IUS had equal propulsion according to Naugle and others connected with the program.

For the first time Naugle began to feel that Fletcher had gone too far. "Up until that era there, I never worried about saying what I felt. I always felt my bosses . . . while they might not agree with me, they might slap me down, they might quarrel with me, but they were not going to throw me out just because I brought them bad news. And somewhere between the time Fletcher came on board and the time he left, I no longer felt that way. They [NASA personnel] felt the technical conscience of the agency had been compromised." [30]

6

The Dark Side of Space

As NASA dazzled the American public by pulling off one spectacular event after another, another equally massive space program was taking place out of the public's view. What is known as the "black" space program became equal to NASA in dollars and by the late 1970s surpassed the civil program in spending. David Williamson, who had the job of NASA and DOD liaison, estimates that more than half of space activity is secret. "You simply cannot write about it because they will put you in jail."[1] But enough information about the programs has emerged to give American taxpayers an idea of where their billions have gone. In the past NASA refused to participate in secret joint NASA-DOD programs despite continual attempts by the Department of Defense and the intelligence agencies to use NASA and to make a grab for its budget. Those attempts did not become successful until NASA traded its independence from the DOD for what turned out to be very indifferent and tentative support of the Space Shuttle from the Pentagon.

The civilian and military programs merged closer and closer together after NASA agreed to develop the shuttle as a military vehicle. The relationship between NASA and the military-intelligence community is long-standing and sometimes hostile. At its heart is the openness of a civilian agency versus the national security responsibilities of the intelligence and military services.

Over the years NASA's civilian programs would inevitably clash with the military. Disagreements about the use of remote sensing devices caused severe strains on the agencies. Major battles occurred over how much resolution NASA's imagery satellites would be allowed. The intelligence community was concerned about the ability of the Soviets or Chinese to obtain NASA satellite pictures of U.S. strategic sites on the open market. Many in the Pentagon wanted the resolution kept in the range of hundreds of meters. With the intervention of the White House, thirty-meter resolution was agreed as acceptable. Later it was reduced to ten meters. There was no public debate over this controversy. NASA and the military have succeeded in keeping most of their battles secret until now.

The satellite that caused one of the first battles was called GEOS-A. Its purpose was to measure the earth's irregular gravitational field down to a ten-meter level of accuracy. For the first time, mapmakers would be able to determine the interrelationships of the different continents. Weighing in at only 385 pounds, this small man-made device became the scourge of DOD. In the fall of 1965, GEOS-A was perched on top of a Delta rocket ready to begin measuring the surface of the earth. But the launch was postponed two weeks because the Department of Defense insisted that the data not be made public because it could endanger national security.

DOD was afraid that GEOS-A would allow Soviet ballistic missile-carrying submarines to hit their targets more accurately. The Pentagon argued that the Soviets could not launch accurately because their submarines did not have the ability to punch detailed gravitational measurements into their missile guidance systems. They charged that the information from GEOS-A would correct that deficiency.

When the delay threatened to go beyond Thanksgiving 1965, Congressman Joe Cox of Minnesota asked the Pentagon to open the secret committee sessions to the public and show why GEOS even should be classified. When the Pentagon did not give Cox a satisfactory answer, he legislated the program from DOD over to NASA. The result was a huge success in correcting the world's maps. Some map locations were thirty miles off. According to Williamson, GEOS found out that an acre in Vermont is smaller than an acre in Florida.

Williamson had the unenviable job of negotiating between the needs of NASA and other civilian agencies for data and the DOD's need for secrecy. He maneuvered on the thin line that delineates the interests of open civilian programs and the often excessive demands of the Pentagon. While he was working in this capacity in the late 1960s, a report came in that sailors had been injured on a Japanese freighter close to Soviet territory near the Kamchatka Peninsula. The ship was hit by space wreckage, but there was no record of a satellite launch to explain the accident. Within hours of the incident the CIA learned that the freighter was struck by the wreckage of a prototype of a frightening new Soviet weapons system called FOB—Fractional Orbiting Bomb. What made this new weapon so dangerous was the way it flew. Once the rocket was launched, instead of going into a full orbit, it flew below the radar range and dropped on its target seemingly out of nowhere. This method of surprise attack did not give the opponent the normal fifteen to eighteen minutes of warning from a conventional ICBM launching.

The Soviets turned to FOB out of desperation. The United States' lead on warhead design had not narrowed, and the Air Force was secretly deploying the first generation of multiple independently targeted reentry vehicle (MIRV) warheads. This new generation placed several warheads on one rocket and each warhead could be individually aimed at special targets for destruction. For example, three warheads could be set for a simultaneous air burst over Moscow. However, to make certain that a suburban fallout shelter known to contain the leaders of the Soviet Union was destroyed, warheads off the same rocket could be programmed for ground burst to destroy that site as well.

The Pentagon explained to NASA that the Soviets were not interested in launching FOBs from the north where U.S. early warning systems are formidable. But during that era U.S. radar defenses were weak from the south. The intelligence experts knew that for the Soviets to hit any target with reasonable accuracy from that distance, the warhead would need a tracking update. This update did not have to come from an elaborate ground station. It simply needed a fixed point of reference on earth to allow the warhead to recalibrate its position. "The only place, the only possible place in the world where the Soviets could perform this function was on Easter Island," according to Williamson.[2]

To complicate matters further, the Soviets were participating in the "one world geodetic data system" where nations would use data from GEOS to develop a more uniform world mapping program. The Soviets were desperately trying to persuade the Chilean government to agree to a joint scientific project using GEOS data on Easter Island. "So here's Easter Island with the Russians kind of mumbling let's put a geodetic tracking station up there and everybody is smart enough to understand that that's a lot of hogwash. So the NASA people said why don't we lend them [Chile] the equipment and let them participate in the international program themselves," Williamson said. "And that's what happened. You lend them [the Chileans] some equipment, $15,000, $20,000 . . . and you let them take some leisurely readings. And so officially everything has been met . . . and what you have done is to beat a very serious Soviet attempt to create relationships with a whole set of countries in a chain that would allow them to form covert stations for updating."

The relationship between NASA and the residents of Easter Island grew over the years. In the early 1970s, when there was fear in Washington that the new Marxist Chilean president, Salvadore Allende Gossens, would turn over the facility to the Soviets, NASA named Easter Island a shuttle emergency abort landing site. The relations between the islanders and NASA technicians on the site became so amicable that the islanders presented a petition to then Ambassador Edward M. Korry requesting that their island be annexed as a U.S. territory.[3]

According to Williamson, the space agency was used when a satellite relay and tracking station was needed in the middle of Australia near Alice Springs to accommodate the increasing flow of information from intelligence satellites. "Everything is used. NASA gets used, excuse me, NASA gets misused. A bunch of people were stomping across Australia saying we are from NASA trying to locate a tracking station. Actually it was the initials, they were from NSA (National Security Agency) and they got us into deep trouble because we didn't know about it," Williamson says.

A number of secret military sensors were tested aboard NASA's "Explorer" series of satellites in the 1960s and 1970s. But when Williamson would try to do the Pentagon a favor by getting a program manager to make room for a military experiment, he often ran into opposition at NASA. NASA Comptroller Bill Lilly sometimes wondered if Williamson were working for NASA or the Pentagon. "Williamson used to try to get me to go along and not fight on flying different things that the DOD or intelligence people wanted without any charge," Lilly said.[4]

Programs in killer satellites, early ballistic missile warning satellites, and military communications satellites have gone from generation to generation in the Pentagon. But it is in the area of spy satellites that the Air Force and CIA's efforts in space became nothing short of remarkable. Its "lookdown" satellites launched on behalf of the CIA entered a new era with "Big Bird." Launched aboard McNamara's big Titan III, these "broad coverage photo reconnaissance satellites" began service in June 1971. Orbiting at 100 to 150 miles, the Big Bird not only sent back film cassettes, but real-time television pictures as well. A "Low Bird" version would orbit for short lengths of time at 80 miles and send back radio transmissions and high-resolution photography shot at an angle. Satellite picture readers could then combine the various angles and give strategic planners three-dimensional views of targets.

In 1971 the CIA and Air Force began designing the Keyhole or KH series of spy satellites. On December 19, 1976, the first Keyhole was launched. These satellites could remain in space for two years before running out of fuel. As they orbited they devoured through their sensors information covering 185-mile-by-275-mile sections of earth. They return their pictures to earth by digital transmission. Their resolution was so superior that license plate numbers on parked cars could be clearly read. Further, the satellites were used to photograph Soviet spacecraft in orbit and strategic bombers in flight. Spectrographic instruments on board the satellites could help intelligence experts look into the past by detecting residual heat, left by troops and equipment.

While Seamans was secretary of the Air Force, a full commitment to the shuttle was withheld. But in 1973, John J. McLucas, who succeeded Seamans, agreed to pay for the conversion of what had been the launch facility for the now defunct MOL program at Vandenberg Air Force Base to a West Coast shuttle launch facility. He also agreed that the Air Force would pay for the development of the solid fuel Inertial Upper Stage (IUS) for the shuttle. These commitments were the only two Air Force financial contributions to the shuttle program. There were supposed to be three. "The third thing that they agreed to do, but never in writing, was to buy the fifth and sixth orbiters," Fletcher says.[5]

Under the Nixon administration the military space budget increased. But the Air Force did not indicate publicly any interest in paying for Space Shuttles. The commitment to refurbish Vandenberg for the shuttle that Fletcher was so proud of became an inside joke in the Air Force. Fletcher failed to realize that by negotiating with the Air Force a long-term construction schedule for the California shuttle facility, he gave them, and their supporters in Congress, a threat to hang over NASA's head. Any pullback from the Vandenberg facility would look like a Pentagon pullback from its commitment to the shuttle. It was a threat the Air Force would use repeatedly for more than a decade.[6]

A major concession Fletcher did get from McLukas and the CIA was that they would design a new generation of spy satellites that would be launched from the shuttle's cargo bay. For the first time since the ill-fated MOL, the Air Force would reluctantly rely on a manned vehicle for its intelligence missions. By 1973 the KH-13 was being designed for the Space Shuttle. It would be the world's first spy satellite that could be *refueled* and refurbished in orbit. Sensors could be updated and replaced by astronauts. The planned cost of KH-13 was $800 million. It would weigh 35,000 pounds and was scheduled to fly on the third shuttle (in the proposed fleet of five) in 1981. The KH-13 would give the United States the world's first permanent spy platform. Despite security leaks in the Keyhole program, the Soviets could not come close to matching this or previous U.S. automated programs. Throughout the early 1970s, the motivation for the Soviet's long-duration orbital activity was at first thought to be solely for a future Mars mission. But by 1978 CIA experts concluded that the Soviets were in fact using manned observations posts in space to supplement an inferior network of spy satellites.

What attracted the Air Force to the shuttle were promises of a heavier lift capability than that provided by its existing rockets, including the big Titans. In addition, this increased lift capacity would be developed at no expense to the Pentagon. By August 1972, NASA had awarded all of the major shuttle contracts. Rockwell won the big one to design and develop the orbiter, with its subsidiary Rocketdyne continuing on the main engine program. Martin Marietta's Denver facility would design and fabricate the big external tank with Morton Thiokol building the solid boosters. Against the advice of old NASA hands, Fletcher decided to divide the management of the program among the various NASA centers. The Johnson Space Center would take the lead with the shuttle, thus removing effective control and accountability from Washington. Marshall would handle all propulsion. The Ames Research Center would develop the thermal protection, and the Kennedy Space Center would perform the final check-out and launch of the shuttles.

Just as Fletcher was facing the difficulty of developing the shuttles for $5.1 billion, the reality of dealing with the Nixon White House hit NASA. The promises of an inflation-adjusted $3.4 billion level of funding for the space agency never materialized. Willis Shapley recalls the agreement NASA had with OMB. ". . . Despite how much the shuttle really ends up costing, we [NASA] are contracting with you [OMB] to run a . . . total space program . . . for $3.4 billion per year in 1972 dollars. What the deal was if there were any overruns in any of the projects in either the shuttle side or any of the other, it would be our problem to manage the program within the total. . . . Well, in the very next budget round they cut us back [by] something like $100 million. . . . They'd say, 'Can't you just spread the schedule and take a $100 million [cut] there,' which from their standpoint of fighting deficits— my God, they were facing a deficit of $8 billion per year— . . . wasn't unreasonable, but it really screwed up the program. Well, this happened year after year, year after year. . . . The point of all this isn't the numbers. It's that you can't expect anybody to maintain a good long-range planning . . . program," Shapley remarks.[7] Fletcher did not have enough clout within the Nixon administration to stop the cuts despite his knowledge of the pain these cuts would inflict on NASA. "Well it hurt enormously and also hurt the rest of NASA because basically we had the first cut that we took and we had to slip the shuttle by one year from '78 to '79. And the second cut we just ate and tried not to slip it. . . . But we increased the overall costs . . . on the second slip. . . . To some extent we took it out of other programs," says Fletcher.[8]

The Nixon budget cuts took their toll. From the start, NASA managers fell behind in all major areas of shuttle development. Not enough funds were budgeted for the main engine program at Rocketdyne. Things were going no better on the Inertial Upper Stage being managed by the Air Force. Charles Donlan was given the responsibility of overseeing the IUS for NASA. He found that while the IUS supposedly had the power to boost 5,000 pounds into geosynchronous orbit, there were increasing problems with reliability. The weight limitation of IUS was also a growing concern since many payloads for that altitude were in the 10,000-pound range. Yet despite Donlan's reservations, Fletcher and his subordinates were scheduling missions on the IUS. To some at NASA Fletcher's actions seemed a little like an airline booking seats on planes that hadn't been built yet.

For NASA comptroller Bill Lilly, the IUS troubles were not surprising. He knew the fight with the Pentagon boiled down to two main questions. Who would pay for the increasingly expensive changes the Department of Defense wanted on the shuttles, and how much control would the Air Force have over the civilian agency? Lilly believed that Fletcher and Low lost control of the program in exchange for the Air Force's support in the Congress and with OMB. "So it was to our advantage to keep them involved. The difficulty of this process is how do you keep them from taking over. Unfortunately, I don't think Fletcher did. I think Low was too willing to make agreements just to keep it going," Lilly admits.[9] He viewed the military's role in the shuttle with a built-in caveat. "I always started off with the assumption, in dealing with the DOD and these military people, that their mentality is to never tell the truth anyway. They look down on civilians. In one sense, they are not to be trusted. . . . It's their own playpen and they want to keep it."

Despite the slippage, Lilly still believed the shuttle program could be brought in for $5.5 billion. His view of how NASA should interact with the contractors was the key to making the program a success. Lilly held one contractor's feet to the fire during an incident involving Rocketdyne over a small-engine test stand contract in California. Lilly's representative said that Rocketdyne was insisting that the contract would run over budget. "I sent my guy out there [and] told them this is the goddamn position and this is what is going to be done. And I said they are going to accept that contract, at the price that's in there now. There will be no overrun costs. . . . Well they hemmed and hawed . . . so I cut all payments not only for Rocketdyne but for Rockwell, the parent company," Lilly says. Six weeks later Lilly succeeded in getting them to finish the contract at the original price. He found with the shuttle program that "you had to keep doing it to the bastards. . . . It takes a lot of goddamn work and a lot of unpleasant work."

But as the shuttle program progressed Lilly discovered some other unpleasant side effects to doing business with the Pentagon. Budget cuts forced NASA to begin relying on Pentagon inspectors at various facilities. NASA soon found out that what was acceptable to DOD inspectors was *not* acceptable to NASA. And Lilly, who was accustomed to a free hand within NASA in dealing with contractors, was learning that contractors were beginning to use the same revolving-door practices at NASA that they used for years with the Pentagon. Despite the new shuttle program, the lack of funding catapulted large numbers of NASA employees from public service into the private sector. NASA workers soon found themselves facing contract employees who were former colleagues as they tried to conduct oversight of the shuttle program. Lilly realized that the old NASA that would not tolerate conflict of interest was gone. Also gone were the civil service exemptions that differentiated NASA from other government agencies. "I don't think they were abused either. They disappeared more because of [NASA's] inability to defend them," explains former Administrator Paine.[10]

At Johnson, Lilly was finding it harder to tell "where Houston left off and Rockwell began." Lilly believed that NASA field centers and contractors were growing "too cozy. . . . You have to be very careful with this kind of thing. I think they got real lax in the real checks and balances, the adversarial relations, really challenging and not taking their word for it. Making people prove what they said." What became especially distressing to Lilly was how field centers like Houston and Marshall would fulfill work proposals by headquarters with material directly prepared by contractors. "Hell, you'd put out a requirement on Houston to come up with something and on some of the damned information that they would come up [to Washington] and present, they wouldn't even mark off Rockwell's insignia on the goddamned stuff . . . and it wasn't unusual at Houston or Marshall. . . . They became dependent on the contractors. They couldn't do it without them and they relied on them too closely," Lilly states. The quality control that Glennan demanded and the technical expertise that Webb insisted on were also fading from NASA.

Lilly's relationship with the contractors was legendary. "I would never let a contractor into my office. I mean I would never put up with them. I would go through the thing where if some guy wanted to come see me for a little while to give me a pitch on something, fine. But no lunches, no anything, with anybody. I never went to any of their things. You just couldn't afford to get into that, you know, trusting them and getting on a social basis with them," Lilly says. In the 1960s he was respected for his stand. But by the late 1970s, contractor lobbying offices were interceding with congressmen on NASA's oversight committees to overturn Lilly's decisions.

On May 15, 1973, the last Saturn V lifted off with the unmanned Skylab. The mission was almost lost when a meteorite shield and solar electrical panel were ripped off the space station during the launch. But Houston planned a rescue mission and Skylab was saved using a parasol installed by the first Skylab crew. The parasol protected the station from being overheated by the sun. While the Soviets had earlier orbited a space station, theirs was less than a quarter of the size of Skylab. In July and November, two more crews would bring the total time aboard Skylab to 172 hours between May 1973 and February 1974.

For Robert Aller, one of the program's managers, what the crews left behind "was a real space station" and NASA began to make plans to reactivate Skylab as the core of a major station after the shuttle began flying. In the meantime, the NASA budget precluded astronauts from returning to Skylab aboard Apollo capsules. The most sophisticated laboratory ever put in orbit was shut down. Instead Aller was reassigned to the Apollo-Soyuz Mission, a project that had questionable value to some at NASA and that would use up the last of the Saturn IBs—equipment that could have been used for another Skylab visit.

For Aller that was not the end of Skylab. He pioneered a program to develop with Martin Marietta a bold solution to build a remote-controlled device to raise Skylab's decaying orbit and save it as a long-term space station. To deliver the device to the Skylab, Aller needed the shuttle. When NASA began the contract with Martin for what came to be known as the "teleoperator," Aller recalled that the shuttle manager "was saying that he would deliver the shuttle to meet that mission." Aller remembers, "We wanted to fly out of the shuttle and dock it [the teleoperator] to the docking port in Skylab, stabilize Skylab and fly it to a higher orbit." [11] If Skylab proved too far gone by 1979, when the mission was planned, then the 100-ton space station could come back into the atmosphere in a controlled, but safe, reentry. Nothing as big or as well built as Skylab had ever reentered the earth's atmosphere. NASA believed that large heavy sections could survive and cause damage or death in an uncontrolled reentry.

As the Skylab missions ended, the scheduled launch date for the new shuttle was extended. Wounded by smaller and smaller budgets, NASA's aeronautics and scientific programs took a beating to keep the shuttle going. Although the beginnings of the rampant inflation caused by the Arab oil embargo were evident, OMB continued to deny NASA any budget increases. The few major scientific programs that survived were kept going largely because they had received the majority of their funding during the halcyon Apollo days. The Saturn boosters were turned over to space museums around the country.

Morale in NASA was plummeting. Lilly was faced with angry scientists tired of having their programs decimated by the shuttle. "We were having our own fights with our own scientists in the agency who didn't like this business either." The same arguments the Air Force had made against the shuttle were now increasingly being heard inside NASA. Fletcher's enforced coalition was already in chaos before the shuttle was even built.

As the scientists rebelled, Lilly found that the Air Force was using its support for the shuttle as leverage to force more and more out of NASA. The Air Force demanded secure communications facilities at all NASA shuttle control centers. After the launch towers and orbiter processing facilities were designed and fabricated, the Air Force told NASA it had to have the ability to change a payload on the launchpad at the last minute. That added yet higher costs to the facilities at Kennedy. Lilly said the logistics of removing a payload while the shuttle was erected on the launchpad were nightmarish. But in some ways Lilly did not blame the Air Force: "I don't know if they had a defined need at this point for the shuttle's capability. The blue suiters and the others were really forced on this thing. And as far as they're concerned, in the types of payloads that they have, they have never had one yet that required all the capabilities of the shuttle."

To compound NASA's troubles, the communications staff began to realize that the old-line NASA tracking system would not handle the vast amounts of data that the new shuttle system would be sending back. This problem would be especially acute when the shuttle was carrying the European Space Agency's new laboratory with a full complement of experiments. Further, the Department of Defense was demanding that NASA encode and encript all of its communications data from the shuttle. For years NASA had wanted to close down its expensive and antiquated manned spaceflight tracking network around the world and replace it with a new satellite system called the Tracking and Data Relay Satellite System or TDRSS. The TDRSS satellites, placed in geosynchronous orbit around the world, would allow the shuttle to remain in touch at all times by automatically relaying its signals from satellite to satellite and back to the ground. The satellites could handle not only voice and data, but also television and encrypted military transmissions.

While the shuttle itself could operate using the old system, TDRSS was needed to complete all the missions for which the shuttle was advertised by NASA. But NASA's budgets barely allowed development of the shuttle itself, much less a new, sophisticated communications satellite system. With NASA cutting back many of its established programs, they knew they could not go to the administration or Congress and ask for millions of dollars for this new project. NASA concocted a scheme of going to the Federal Financing Bank, part of the U.S. Treasury, and being the guarantor of loans to a contractor to build and buy the system. Through lease payments, NASA would pay back the contract and pay off the loans. After ten years the entire system of six satellites would revert to NASA. Since NASA was signing a lease, OMB would not have to pass judgment on the new satellite system. Lilly was dubious. But NASA had already waited two years too long to begin on the system and no other way was known to get it.

When NASA put the system out for bids, the space agency had a rude awakening. Only Western Union and RCA expressed an interest on "bidding" for the system. Bill Lilly recalls there really was not a single "real bid for it. I mean it made the government really put up all the costs for it." Western Union began the project and TRW ended up building the very complicated satellites. Lilly says NASA figured the payments on the TDRSS could be made from the savings from closing the tracking stations. What NASA had not counted on was massive inflation and huge cost overruns on TDRSS, largely due to constant changes in communications design brought on by the Pentagon. Now NASA was committed to paying off a loan with interest that threatened to top a billion dollars—nearly the cost of an entire space shuttle. For NASA's Tracking and Data Acquisition Division, TDRSS would symbolize how high technology and too little money took NASA down another primrose path.

Many at NASA were still plagued by safety concerns for the shuttle. Rocco Petrone, a huge man of Neapolitan heritage, who contributed to NASA's early successes, was brought to Washington by Fletcher and Low to be a technical general manager for manned spaceflight. Petrone, like Gilruth, had respect and concern for the people who developed and operated NASA's space machines. He had nightmares over every possible fault in the shuttle system. He knew that if one of the solid rockets ignited just one second before the other, the entire shuttle would lift-off and tumble end over end into conflagration. He worried that the solids could not be shut down so the orbiter could escape the stack if there was trouble. But perhaps his most nagging worry was whether NASA really had enough experience to build a new space transportation system without an escape device for the crew. Was NASA really so much more sophisticated in its development of this fourth-generation vehicle, or was it just arrogance that was showing? Was NASA sacrificing safety to keep within the Nixon administration's tight budgets? Available to Petrone was the 1971 Rockwell study on ejection systems for the shuttle. The open ejection seats that were planned for the first orbiter added only $10 million to the development costs. A small escape capsule for a two-man crew could be bought for $7 million. But the only system that would work for the entire shuttle crew was a crew compartment escape system that the study projected would cost $292 million. Fletcher decided NASA could not afford the additional cost.

For Gen. Jacob Smart, who played a major role as a NASA-DOD liaison, it was all a matter of money: "There were all sorts of shortcuts that were taken. . . . And you've read recently how foolish NASA was to have discarded all those redundancies that was the soul of the space program. NASA didn't do it because it was stupid. They did it because they were forced to do so. . . . We can never be perfectly safe and it's always a human decision as just how much is enough. But in this case how much was enough was not determined by the scientists and engineers but by the politicians. . . ."

According to Smart, NASA needed alternative means to launch various payloads to take the pressure off the shuttle program, but these arguments were tossed aside by Fletcher. ". . . We were not in the mood to be sensible or conservative in our construction program. So everybody had to stand up and swear that the shuttle would do everything, you see, would replace women and whisky and all those other good things," Smart adds. [12]

Although Petrone was supposed to be in charge of manned shuttle flight, he confided in David Williamson [13] and others during 1978, that Deputy Administrator George Low was bypassing him in the decision-making process on the shuttle. Low would deal directly with shuttle director John

Yardley without consulting Petrone. Low angered Petrone by isolating him in his job and by Low's interference. "Petrone was really pissed off at Low and Fletcher. But they misled him. . . . They brought him up here to be a general manager type in the technical program, but Low would never let him operate . . . ," says Lilly.[14] Low's genius for spotting problems before they got out of hand in Apollo simply did not seem to work in the shuttle era. Because Low so weakened accountability, it became more and more difficult to reward good staff members or replace the incompetent ones. Low was also changing the character of NASA. David Williamson recalled that Low illegally classified technical data on the Apollo heat shield. "Most of our stuff was by law available to everyone," insists Williamson.

Fletcher now faced a troubled shuttle program and TDRSS. Both programs were behind schedule and over cost, which led to growing management problems. Deputy Administrator Low continued to deliberately weaken his associate administrators in Washington, the men who were supposed to be in charge of the programs, and work directly with Houston and Marshall. Dale Myers ran the shuttle development program in Washington and worked closely with his old friend Christopher Kraft in Houston. But, according to Lilly, "Low started weakening the whole process. Low felt we didn't need a lot of the reporting . . . also Low started the business of weakening the associate administrators like Dale Myers and others." At NASA headquarters, tensions were rising.

Troubles began almost from the start as the shuttle's main engines went through development nightmares. These liquid-fueled engines called SMEs had to last over fifty missions and had to be stopped and started with total reliability. They had to fly into space and be able to withstand the rigors of reentry only to fly again. Although not nearly as powerful as the big F-1 (the Saturn V engine), the 375,000-pound-thrust SMEs had to perform flawlessly for eight and a half minutes on every flight. The cluster of three engines had to be constantly cooled by their hydrogen fuel or the entire cluster would melt from the high operating temperatures. The engines had to be gimballed and throttleable for the computer-controlled ascent. During the first few years of testing, one engine after another melted down and exploded. At Rocketdyne and on the test stands at the Bay St. Louis facility, engines were blowing up only seconds after ignition for too many different reasons. Cracks in the pump blades and other failures kept hampering the program and slowing the shuttle.

To make matters worse, the man in charge of shuttle development had had enough and quit. Dale Myers, who promised Fletcher that he would stay at NASA through the first flight of the shuttle, didn't and in 1974 left. "Fletcher was really pissed off at Myers, because Myers went back on his word. Apparently, he had given Fletcher his word that he would stay through the period of development but he didn't," Lilly recalls.[15] Ironically Myers would return to NASA as an associate administrator with Fletcher after the *Challenger* tragedy.

To run the troubled program, Fletcher brought in John Yardley. Yardley had a reputation for being tough and for learning enough about every phase of a development project so almost no one could snow him. Lilly says "his type of management was that he had very strong opinions and he dealt with his organization in such a way that when they came to him with anything he would berate them and in essence, embarrass them."

According to Lilly and others at NASA, Yardley did not tolerate sloppy work, an attribute that was getting rarer and rarer in the NASA management team. But Yardley shared with Low and Myers the fault of bypassing headquarters management and dealing directly with the field centers. Eventually Yardley was performing direct engineering on the shuttle instead of supervising others' work. When Yardley worked as a contractor with McDonnell Douglas, he pushed for the liquid-solid configuration. Now he had to live with the consequences. By the time he started heading the shuttle program, he found Bill Lilly's worst fears about the solids were coming true. "Well, I have worked with most of the solid contractors over the years," Yardley says. "Thiokol built our initial Mercury retro-rocket. They build the Gemini retro-rockets. And I was comfortable with them. What I didn't really realize until I got working closer with them is they are not an aerospace engineering firm. They just don't have the depth and strength you would expect in a real aerospace firm."[16]

For Yardley what started off as just a simple engine contract turned into a logistical mess. Yardley had to depend upon engineers at the Marshall Center who had fought solid propulsion as part of their tradition. In the end, Marshall went outside for assistance in engineering and designing the solids. Just as Lilly recommended from the beginning, Marshall gave the contracts to United Technologies Corporation. The 149-foot-long, 12-foot-diameter solid rockets weighed two million pounds each. Yardley finally solved the problems of the divided contract by letting Thiokol do little more than build the motor itself. "It really wasn't a booster contract at all. Marshall did the booster in-house and then they got United Technologies as a support contract and gradually transitioned most of that to them. But they [Marshall] actually bought all the stuff, specified, and did the engineering. But they did worry about the motor. And the big thing that got to us is the segmented booster," Yardley says. The 149-foot solid booster had to be put together in four segments. Designing the joints to make certain they did not leak was proving a formidable task.

For all of NASA's experience in moving big rocket stages by barge and specially modified aircraft, its handling of the four-segment solid rocket almost defies explanation. Precise and extreme care was practiced in moving the elements of the Saturn V moon rockets. But Morton Thiokol, which never built anything on a large scale prior to the shuttle solids, apparently put little effort or thought into the problems of shipping damage. Since the solid rocket motors were so heavy, some at NASA pushed for the contractor to locate its facility right at the Kennedy Space Center. But what seemed practical in the age of Apollo was impossible now. It was a clear-cut decision for Yardley. "You know, to build them in one piece takes a hell of a facility investment . . . plus we had a great precedent with the Titan and they followed that design. . . . They had to ship it horizontally and they were not smart enough to make sure it was supported in a manner that it would stay round," Yardley says. He also explained that in the early and mid-1970s, there was little worry about the effects of temperature on the rocket joints.

By the summer of 1974 the average age of a NASA employee was increasing. The space agency was not hiring at a rate fast enough to replace the veterans who were leaving. Lucrative aerospace industry jobs were taking more and more NASA employees from the ranks. The country had little interest in NASA that year. The nation was sitting on the edge of its collective seat wondering if Richard Nixon would leave us in peace or pull the whole system down with him. For Willis Shapley no president had been less accessible to the NASA administrator. "Nobody ever went to see the president unless he was giving out medals or things like that. It simply didn't work that way. The point is you had to find out who was going to make the decision. You had to get as many people on your side. You had to know how to operate in the generally indifferent and hostile environment. . . . Well, the administration was hostile to almost everybody, frankly. I mean we always felt that we were being persecuted a little bit . . . ," says Shapley.[17]

Fletcher signed on to NASA to put his mark on the agency. He followed a road that the most successful of his predecessors had warned against. He went after a big program with neither the Congress, the military, the scientific community, nor the White House behind him. It was a big risk and he was paying for it. All he received from Nixon was a small piece of detente for Henry Kissinger. The White House instructed NASA to conduct a joint manned flight with the Soviets. The Apollo-Soyuz mission involved the launching of the last Apollo and Saturn to mate and dock with a Soyuz. The only new engineering required was an adapter which would demonstrate the potential of international space rescue. The demonstration had little real meaning since NASA would have no more Apollo hardware to fly after the test. OMB had removed it all from the budget. The mission ordered by Nixon would be flown under Ford.

By the time Richard Nixon flew to the El Toro Marine Air Station as an ex-president, James Fletcher really understood how little interest Nixon had in spaceflight. Fletcher's inability to sell NASA to Nixon was reflected in the numbers. NASA had never been at a lower ebb than in August 1974. What seemed especially frustrating to the NASA veterans was that it had only been five years since Apollo landed on the moon. And the program was in shambles. The careful relationship of trust Webb crafted with the congressional oversight committees suffered under Fletcher. The political appointees he brought into NASA's general counsel and congressional relations offices at NASA did not help either. Nixon made a former law partner's brother-in-law the NASA general counsel, the first such political appointment to that sensitive position.[18]

Gerald Ford's brief presidency gave Fletcher and the shuttle program a respite from the budget pressures. For the first time Fletcher had genuine hopes of seeing the shuttle through to flight. Fletcher remembers that "President Ford strongly supported the space program. . . . It was such a brief period, but he didn't make any cuts and we were optimistic that if we needed more money, we could get it under his administration." [19] Ford was a Washington insider who knew how to work with the various government agencies. NASA rewarded Ford with its first manned flight in two years. Deke Slayton had waited sixteen years to fly. He was one of the original Mercury astronauts and was approved for flight by one medical specialist after another. But Jim Webb had bumped Slayton from the second manned orbital mission because of Webb's fears that if Slayton's minor heart ailment flared up during flight, it could damage NASA's reputation for safety. [20] But as Slayton commanded the Apollo-Soyuz test mission, his irregular heartbeat worked well enough. Slayton, Tom Stafford, and Vance Brand docked in space and shook hands with Aleksey Leonov and Valery Kubasov.

The last mission involving the Apollo hardware nearly ended in tragedy for the American crew. After reentry the crew opened a pressure release valve to equalize the command module atmosphere with the earth's atmosphere. But the reaction control rockets failed to shut down and deadly nitrogen tetroxide oxydizer gas entered the cabin's breathing air. The crew survived the incident, but some at Houston and in Washington wondered if the layoff from manned flight hadn't put the crew at risk. NASA learned little about the Soviet program from the flight, except that the Soviets built spacecraft that were neither as capable nor as sophisticated as our own. Soyuz had little of the redundancy of Apollo. According to Bob Aller, the Russians learned much more about NASA. "They got a terrific exposure. . . . An awful lot of

Soviets got exposed to what it is like over here . . . but we didn't get involved in their technologies and they didn't get involved in ours. The only real interface was the modular docking collar that was built for the two vehicles." A new era in space cooperation might have opened up, except NASA had no manned vehicles available. Any possible future cooperation with the shuttle program was eliminated when program managers reminded the international affairs office that the shuttle was a military vehicle.

On a hot and muggy August 20, 1975, a month after the Soyuz test flight, a "Jim Webb bonus" called Viking left for Mars. Webb managed to wrangle enough money for Apollo to make certain that a major series of scientific unmanned explorations would be assured in the 1970s.[21] Of all NASA's unmanned missions, none had more effect on the world than Viking. After Paine approved the project in November 1968, the Jet Propulsion Laboratory finally decided to apply all its hard-earned engineering lessons into a very special machine. Looking like real flying saucers, the Viking probes featured an orbiter that would circle Mars. Undocking automatically from the orbiter would be a lander with descent rockets and parachutes to make use of the earth-like Martian atmosphere. A second Viking took off in September.

The goal was to discover if there was life on Mars. *Viking I* went into orbit around Mars on June 19, 1976. The celebration of the two hundreth anniversary of the United States began on the fourth of July with the tall ships in New York Harbor. Now the celebration turned to the stars. To many within NASA everything seemed possible again on July 20, 1976, when Viking soft-landed on Mars. For the public, the color pictures of the rust-colored Martian landscape coming back were a reaffirmation of what NASA was so unfailingly able to do. For men like Lilly and Naugle, it was a reminder of Jim Webb's foresight. In Houston, where plans were being formulated for the first atmospheric flights of the shuttle, everyone knew that Viking landed seven years to the day that *Eagle* dropped to the lunar surface. In September the second Viking lander dropped to the Utopia Planitia. Although no life was found on Mars, the Viking probes sent back tremendous amounts of information which are still being examined.

But Martian landings and national celebrations could not convince the United States electorate to forgive Gerald Ford for pardoning Richard Nixon. NASA's stake in the 1976 election was enormous. James Earl "call me Jimmy" Carter's running mate, Walter Mondale, was a sworn enemy of NASA. In the Senate he had unsuccessfully tried to chop away at the shuttle. To make matters worse, Carter was running against Washington. He was running against the people at NASA who spent their careers ensuring a successful American space effort. Even though most of his cabinet appointments were hardly strangers to Washington, the effect his campaign had at NASA was devastating. As members of a government agency, NASA employees did not consider themselves to be the problem. Now, after a hostile Nixon administration and a brief respite with Ford, NASA faced Carter with trepidation.

Nineteen seventy-seven was a very important year for the new space transportation system. At Rockwell's Palmdale facility, a non-space flight version of the shuttle, dubbed *Enterprise*, was rolled out. It presented an amazing sight. The size of a DC-9, *Enterprise* weighed 149,600 pounds. It looked like a killer whale with its black-and-white surface gleaming in the desert sun. NASA's tireless public relations staff helped the event get substantial media coverage. But most of the press failed to note that this shuttle could never fly in space. It was designed to test the whole ability of the shuttle craft to glide to a landing. Later it would be used to test launch facilities and equipment. It had no tile heat-protection system, and it had no engines. It was just as well. Neither did NASA.

James Fletcher's resignation as NASA administrator became effective on May 1, 1977. He left a legacy that kept manned spaceflight alive. But he also left another legacy. The constant underfunding of the shuttle put it years behind schedule. When Fletcher left, none of the shuttle management team believed a shuttle could fly for at least two more years. Jimmy Carter, a quasi nuclear-engineer, did what John Kennedy failed to do; he took his science adviser, Dr. Frank Press, seriously. Carter appointed Press' friend Dr. Robert A. Frosch as NASA's fifth administrator.

Frosch was a weapons scientist with a background in physics. His speciality was nuclear bombs. Starting in the early 1970s Frosch became involved in the United Nations environmental programs and then became associate director of the Woods Hole Oceanographic Institution. Frosch had never met Carter when he was summoned to the White House. "I was, in fact, interviewed by the president for this job. I wasn't the only one interviewed . . . ," reveals Frosch.[22]

Frosch was different from any of the earlier NASA administrators. He was a Jew. He had a laid-back management style. And despite his political loyalties both in the Washington and scientific arenas, he could be fiercely independent. Among his first actions at NASA was to look at the funding commitments for the shuttle. After reviewing the documents, Frosch understood what the agency had been through. "It was obvious the right number was $6.5 billion. And all they got was $5.5 billion and a long silence. That's the nth attempt I know of somebody trying to build a sensible contingency for such a thing. You know, in my mind . . . the program started with a twenty percent overrun from day one."

When NASA announced that the aerodynamics of the

shuttle would be tested in August 1977 by mounting *Enterprise* on the back of a specially equipped Boeing 747, there was an uproar. Some critics predicted the shuttle would slide into the tail of the 747 and doom both aircraft. "We had a lot of flack on that. All the dire predictions were that this was going to wipe the tail out. . . . Uninformed expert opinion I call it," former shuttle manager Charles Donlan remembers.[23] On August 12, the biggest aircraft combination in history rolled down the runway at Edwards Air Force Base. Astronauts Gordon Fullerton and Fred Haise sat in the crew compartment at the controls. The first unpowered tests of the shuttle would determine if all the engineering and planning was correct. Would the unpowered shuttle fly, or drop like a stubby-winged rock as some of its critics predicted? Although this shuttle was incapable of spaceflight, it was real enough to indicate that manned flight would never be the same.

The crew compartment featured three levels. The mid-deck was where the astronauts would enter the craft. It featured sleeping and eating facilities and the first genuine attempt at modern earth-style sanitation, as well as a galley and access to an airlock leading to the huge cargo bay. Downstairs was a storage area for the shuttle's life support system and complicated avionics and electronics. But the flight deck was what made the big difference. Configured like an airliner, the flight deck had room for four seats. The pilot and co-pilot had cathode-ray tubes so they could monitor the four IBM computers that managed the residual energy of the shuttle returning from space. It was the proper management of that energy that determined if a shuttle was going to land or crash. Because there was no money to give the shuttle air-breathing engines, once it reentered the atmosphere, the shuttle became the heaviest glider ever built, with only one shot at landing.

Although Max Faget and scores of other engineers and designers said it would work, none of the astronauts thought this bizarre looking spaceship was of much use in the atmosphere. When *Enterprise* reached 28,700 feet, the 747 released it. As expected it swooped up and away from the 747. Fullerton and Haise were surprised at how well the control surfaces reacted. The gravity-fed landing gear dropped down, and *Enterprise* landed. The shuttle program had its first success.

Frosch learned quickly that he worked for an administration that was trying to free itself of the evils of the past. Every program had to be examined with the view that if it wasn't worthwhile and cost efficient, it should be eliminated. Carter called it zero-based budgeting. He said this approach worked well on the state programs in Georgia. But to people like NASA Comptroller Bill Lilly, "it was just more bullshit, like cost-benefit analysis."[24] In 1977, during one of Frosch's first meetings with the president, Jimmy Carter asked his new NASA administrator to examine the shuttle program to determine if it should be shut down.

To Frosch it was a serious question. "You know part of the problem is that even for me the strong arguments for the manned systems are long-range arguments. I am yet to be persuaded by the materials-in-space argument. There isn't any evidence. There ought to be something there, but not much has turned up yet. There are certainly lots of payload delivery things that can be done unmanned. . . . In the end, the real argument for me is if we are going to want to explore the solar system and use it. That is not going to mean just machines. . . ." Frosch had received his first assignment. Now he would determine if NASA would continue to send men into space. Within a few weeks he made his decision.

7

Carter—
The Man Who
Paid the Piper

IT WAS A TYPICALLY COLD JANUARY DAY IN DETROIT. DR. Robert Frosch was at the airport grabbing a quick bite at a stand-up coffee bar while waiting for a flight to Los Angeles. He stood next to two ground crewmen. Their conversation caught his attention. "They were saying, 'Wasn't that a terrible accident.' And so I figured an airplane had gone down some place. So I said, 'What accident?' And they said, 'The shuttle just blew up.'"

It happened five years after Frosch left NASA. But for him it was "the 3:00 A.M. nightmare. Not the nightmare you expected, but the ultimate nightmare. Oh, I had a whole string of nightmares. The one I would have given highest probability was probably a liquid engine going out, stopping, or blowing up at the wrong time," Frosch recalls.[1]

Frosch had one private dread after another about this shuttle he was destined to build. "I would have thought of a computer problem that made reentry computation difficult or something like that. Or the landing gear not coming down." There were others. But for Frosch none of the nightmares matched the reality of trying to get the shuttle into space.

Frosch spent a good many of his waking hours wondering if the shuttle's main engines could ever be made to work without exploding or melting. The SMEs were beginning "all up" testing during his first year at NASA. Because of budget shortfalls, "we were chronically short of engines for tests," Frosch remembers. "There were things we wanted to do, and we had to combine tests because we did not have enough engines standing in line." A shuttle engine is not like a car engine where something could malfunction and the car would still run. If a part failed in the shuttle, the engine would blow up or simply melt. For Frosch, each engine loss was a procurement disaster. "I concluded the troubles we were having were system troubles. They weren't component troubles. And we could rig test components until we were blue in the face and the first time we hung the engine together, we would still have system troubles because the key characteristic of the engine is that it is an integrated engine," Frosch explains.

The shuttle's main engine (SME) operated on liquid hydrogen and oxygen propellants. No rocket engine ever built for manned flight could develop more thrust-per-pound of fuel. There was no way to test the engine part by part. When the engineers had trouble it was when the entire engine was fired. The SME had to fire for at least eight minutes in flight and they were melting down after only a few minutes on the test stand. Because the shuttle would have no escape system after the first few test flights, the engines *had* to be reliable.

Frosch succeeded in keeping the shuttle program alive in the Carter administration. But to Willis Shapley, who had been connected with NASA throughout the entire history of the agency, the Carter years were the most difficult he had witnessed. "The Carter administration was really the first time that the basic policy was that if something in technology was worth doing, the private sector should do it. . . . But Bob Frosch, I know, was very much frustrated by the . . . policy slant against applied research. . . . From a standpoint of somebody in an agency where you do an awful lot of applied research . . . such as going to the planets, it's sort of an absurd position. If the research you are doing is worth doing, stop doing it."[2]

Frosch found himself at odds with Science Adviser Frank Press and the administration's bias against applied research. And the shuttle made a big target. Hans Mark, then the Ames Research Center director, recalls, "Jimmy Carter was not [a space enthusiast]. And more important, Frank Press was not."[3]

Shapley had been called out of retirement to come back to NASA to try to figure out why the costs kept outpacing the budgets. He concluded that NASA would assume the most optimistic events in shuttle development at the beginning of each year to plan the budget. "Then they would find out they didn't have enough money, so some of the requirements slipped forward to the following year. But meanwhile they had already had to justify the budget for the following year. . . . So their requirements kept pushing ahead into the amount of funding. . . . Nobody had been able to rise above the whole problem to see [what] they were doing. It wasn't that they were going to get more money in total no matter what happened. I mean, the front office was fighting to get every single dollar they could by hook, crook, or any other way . . . ," says Shapley.[4]

NASA faced a new nemesis at the Office of Management and Budget (OMB). Walter Mondale, who waited for more than a decade, finally got his chance to do serious damage to NASA. Mondale, who understood a great deal more about how Washington worked than Carter, placed some of his operatives at OMB. For Bill Lilly, the tenor of the budget sessions changed dramatically. Lilly found that Carter officials were taking the stand of an angry contractor who did not like NASA's position. For the first time Lilly believed that NASA's independence was in real danger. "In the old days you could rely on the people at OMB because, while they were hard to deal with, they were honest. They would deal straightforward with you. You knew where they stood and you could do your job. You could fight and argue, but you didn't believe they would go and screw you on something. That they would be devious about it. It got to be a time when they would let contractors start coming over there to make pitches. And you had more and more political people over there in the White House and in OMB with backgrounds in these areas. But, shit, you'd get asked questions that you knew had to come from the contractor."[5]

For the first time contractors were pressing some of the politicians they supported to go after NASA in OMB. Instead of being asked to justify budgets for reasons of national interest, NASA program people were being asked questions that affected the well-being of contractors. For a time Lilly ordered his program people to stop talking to OMB budget examiners. Lilly says, "And then you would find out through the grapevine that 'such and such' a contractor had been over there pushing."

Although NASA had trouble with OMB, Carter was not openly hostile. "The interesting thing about Carter is that I think he was genuinely interested in the program and excited by it and excited by the science. He was relatively easy to talk to because he did have an education as a naval engineer and had no difficulty with the technical concepts," Frosch recalls. Just how valuable Carter's understanding of celestial physics was, became clear when the General Accounting Office

(GAO) questioned the need for both the new Vandenberg launch facility and the Kennedy Space Center.

"Aside from the usual foolishness of, can you really run a civil, not to say a military program with only one launch and landing site, they insisted on being very pigheaded about the question of polar orbits and equatorial orbits. And they wanted us to launch out of Kennedy to the north. I just didn't think the jettison point for the external tank should be over Siberia, and that this device, with some of the stuff still burning, should go over New York or Atlanta. I don't remember the trajectory but it was all pretty dumb. They wanted to dogleg it and they didn't understand the energetics of having to go off in one direction and turn this monster," states Frosch. When he appealed to Carter, the president quickly dismissed the GAO effort. But the "dogleg" launch plan would come back to haunt NASA.[6]

While Carter had a fascination for NASA's science programs, down to what experiments were going on certain flights, manned flight was another matter. "It worried him. I guess he was a little bothered by the idea it's all a big expensive show kind of argument, which may have stemmed from Mondale . . . ," Frosch recalls. Lilly had mixed feelings about his meetings with Carter. "I would say that he was one of the more open presidents in the sense . . . of listening to you. . . . You [could] go in and have a chance to argue your case."

Frosch felt that the early design and development work on the shuttle's various systems was flawed and NASA was paying the price. Engineering on system after system was still being done long after production commenced on the first orbiter. One of the major concerns was how to bring back an object the size of a DC-9 through reentry. "We knew it would fly, but can we control it?" Frosch wondered. For all of NASA's experience in manned spaceflight, the biggest object that had ever been brought back through reentry was the twelve-foot Apollo cone. Although Apollo and the other programs gave NASA a background in the range of twenty-two times the speed of sound, there was no experience in bringing back anything this big and heavy. While ground controllers or an astronaut could bring in a crippled Apollo, Gemini, or Mercury spacecraft, the pilot of the shuttle did not have the ability to perform "seat-of-the-pants" maneuvering. Without the four computers and the fifth back-up machine, the shuttle simply could not fly through reentry. And once the craft was through reentry, to make certain the one and only shot at landing worked, the computers had to determine how to manage the residual energy to deliver the vehicle back to earth.

As the shuttle team grappled with getting beyond *Enterprise*, the unspaceworthy test orbiter, Frosch realized that the probability of getting the money to finish the shuttle program was looking grimmer and grimmer. The cost overruns were growing. But Frosch seemed to have a friendlier Pentagon to deal with than his predecessor. The new secretary of defense, Dr. Harold Brown, was the former president of Cal Tech and he backed the shuttle program to the chagrin of the uniformed Air Force. Brown tapped Dr. Hans Mark, the director of NASA's Ames Research facility, to be undersecretary of the Air Force. One of the main responsibilities of this position was control of the Air Force's space program. Mark, a German Jew who immigrated to the United States as a teenager, always had a fascination with spaceflight. But his background as a physicist had much more to do with nuclear weapons than a civilian or manned space program. His mentors were men like H-Bomb developer Edward Teller.[7]

Mark's enthusiasm for the shuttle seemed unbounded. Robert Seamans recalls that Mark, more than any other Pentagon official, committed the Air Force to the shuttle. "Hans Mark really bought the thing, absolutely hook, line, and sinker. And he felt very, very strongly that there should be a national commitment. That DOD and NASA should go right down the line. And this should be the launch vehicle of all time," Seamans says.[8]

Despite Mark's enthusiasm for the shuttle, high-ranking NASA veterans like Comptroller Bill Lilly were more than a little leery of him. "I wasn't a NASA proponent. I was a shuttle proponent," Mark asserts.[9] But Lilly remembers that Mark "was so . . . pro-military. He had been quite open for years in some circles that the only justification for NASA was to support the DOD. There wasn't any reason for it otherwise. You could fly its science missions when there was room available. You know, no real justification. He was always so convinced that the Russians were coming. That there was a spy under every tree. . . ." But Lilly's biggest problem with Mark was personal trust. "Hans, you just couldn't trust him. The son of a bitch was devious. He would undercut you. He would undercut the agency. He would lie. He would do anything, mainly because of his own feeling of what was important for the country," Lilly explains.[10]

During the shuttle development, NASA was not only at the mercy of its own oversight committees, but also its tough-minded Appropriations Subcommittee chairman, Congressman Edward Boland (D-Massachusetts), who became chairman of the House of Representatives' Intelligence Committee. He took his intelligence position very seriously. And because that role included all Air Force activities, including those on the shuttle, Hans Mark kept Boland constantly briefed. According to Lilly those sessions were closed to NASA but dealt with military applications of the shuttle. "Well Hans was over there [on Capitol Hill]. And he sure as hell wasn't doing us any good at all. And he was selling Boland and others . . . ," Lilly remembers. Boland would not try to deliberately damage NASA. But when it came to a decision that Boland perceived as a battle between the military and the space agency, the record shows that Boland sided with the Pentagon most of the time. To Lilly and others at NASA, Boland was particularly impressed by Mark's advice.

To keep Air Force support for the increasingly costly shuttle, Frosch found himself making the same kinds of deals with the military that Fletcher had made. As Lilly witnessed it all, his frustrations grew. "Frosch was not a big lover of DOD, even though he had come from over there. He gave me support at times fighting them, but it kept getting pieced away. . . . I was anti-military because I didn't like many of the military people in NASA. I wanted an open program. I wanted a civilian program. I could see in my mind there was no advantage for DOD. To me, it was inconceivable to think they would have their whole launch system for their missions, their intelligence missions, dependent on NASA," Lilly comments.[11]

To advance the argument for the shuttle as the only national launch vehicle, Mark reminded Boland of Fletcher's and Low's promises of how inexpensive shuttle flight would be. As the Appropriations Subcommittee chairman, Boland began to press NASA to eliminate expendable rockets from future NASA budgets. Frosch and Lilly realized that because of Mark, they were being pushed down a path where there would only be the shuttle: " . . . The idea was that nationally one could certainly manage to continue some kind of an ELV [expendable launch vehicle] program even using those that had been built or continuing some production lines. That wasn't all that expensive. . . . But there was simply no way in which you could construct such a program politically," says Frosch.[12]

Within the Air Force, Mark urged that payloads being planned in the future be solely designed for shuttle launch. Mark needed a supporter of manned spaceflight from the uniformed military, and so he appointed Maj. Gen. Tom

Stafford, the highly successful Gemini and Apollo astronaut, to his staff. According to a draft of Mark's unpublished manuscript, *The Space Station—A Personal Journey*, Stafford's assignment was to develop a report called "The Utility of Man in Space." Unfortunately for Mark, the report was issued just as cost overruns and further delays caused even more doubts about the shuttle program.

But the shuttle was not the only NASA problem. A little-known NASA project called SEASAT was to monitor the temperatures, wave topology, and other features of the oceans. SEASAT was perhaps the most impressive in NASA's growing line of environmental-intelligence satellites. John Naugle recalls how the program was promised by Goddard for $49 million. "But Goddard snowballs everything . . . but in this case we beat on them and beat on them and they said they would do it for $80 million . . . so Low said, 'No way José, you told me it would cost $40 million. . . .'" To save money the program was moved to the Jet Propulsion Laboratory. But then came more cost overruns.[13]

To add to Naugle's problems, the Navy objected to information SEASAT could make available to the Soviets. The Navy feared that SEASAT would be able to pinpoint for the Soviets the location of the U.S. fleet at any given time. Further, Navy officials feared that SEASAT's very powerful imaging radar might be able to trace the so-far-untraceable U.S. nuclear submarine fleet. "The question was the more you find out for pure science, a lot of it is very important to missile navigation and things like that. . . . There were real questions. . . . And there were real fights. Boy, there were tough fights. . . . These were substantive questions which had to be solved, many of which don't have a very good answer. . . . But perfectly good logic coming this way meets perfectly good logic coming this way, and it doesn't add up," Shapley remembers.[14] Once the heated arguments cooled down, the satellite was launched on June 26, 1978, from Vandenberg on an Atlas F. For one hundred days the satellite sent back remarkable information in greater amounts than any other environmental-intelligence satellite. And then the satellite failed. The investigation board discovered that the entire satellite shorted out. The most sophisticated of all the resource technology satellites never had a chance for long-term operation.[15]

The Carter administration further blurred the line between the civilian and military programs with a series of National Security Council documents on space detailing how the civilian shuttle could be used for intelligence gathering. The documents made many at NASA uncomfortable because, while they discussed civil space, they were classified. It was becoming obvious that NASA would continue to play second fiddle to the military. A document signed by President Carter and drafted by Science Adviser Frank Press set out, according to David Williamson, the interrelationships between space and the various government agencies in a series of top-secret reports. For the first time space policy of a civil and military nature was being officially integrated. Williamson conducted those relationships for twenty years without a written presidential policy. "I had been doing it at the interagency level, without presidential sanction, without presidential signature, for twenty years but Carter wanted to sign it. The trouble is he would only read half the report. The report is about that thick [two inches]. There is a copy of it in the world today where Carter's marginal comments stop halfway. . . . The cover memo that he signed approving it deals with material unread. Fact! Beyond that evidence I am not going to argue. But that's how the science adviser wiggled his 'technically trained' president into doing things. Swamp him at the front end and time forces the president to rely on the science adviser's advice and interpretation of what he thought was right and good," Williamson says.[16]

One such document, circulated by Science Adviser Frank Press in September 1978, was called PD-42. PD-42 outlined a U.S. space program that emphasized national security and took a direct shot at NASA. The report stated that "it is neither feasible nor necessary at this time to commit the U.S. to a high challenge, highly visible space engineering initiative comparable to Apollo." Over at the Air Force, Hans Mark got a copy of the document and seethed. According to Mark's manuscript, on a sailing trip with Press on the Chesapeake Bay, Mark protested the idea of announcing what you were not going to do. But Press,[17] long considered by NASA to be an antagonist to manned flight, argued that "he wanted the statement of policy because he was concerned about the continuing commitment to the shuttle. He said that President Carter was a frugal man and that he was afraid that if the shuttle did indeed get into technical difficulties, the President might be tempted to cancel the program," Mark wrote. While Mark disagreed with his sailing companion, others in NASA knew what was coming. The planned seven-orbiter fleet was first trimmed to six and then five. Now there would be an attempt to slash it again.

October 1, 1978, was a beautiful day at Cape Canaveral. It was also Jimmy Carter's fifty-third birthday. Frosch worked for months to get the president to demonstrate publicly his support for the civilian program. Finally Carter's staff agreed to a birthday trip to the Kennedy Space Center. But instead of dwelling on the benefit to mankind from the civilian program, Carter shocked and surprised the audience when he proclaimed that photoreconnaissance satellites were the heart of his arms control program. NASA officials were dumbfounded that the president would select a civilian space agency function for the first public acknowledgment of such

U.S. activities. In Carter's effort to ratify the second Strategic Arms Limitation Treaty (SALT II), he did not tell his audience, or the Senate, that the Soviets had purchased detailed plans to our most sophisticated satellites, the KH-11, Argus, and Rhyolite.

In California, Christopher Boyce and Andrew Daulton Lee conspired to steal and then sell the operational manuals of Keyhole, Argus, Rhyolite, and other spy satellites to the Soviets. To make matters worse, a high-ranking CIA official, John Paisley, who was investigating the intelligence loss, disappeared under strange circumstances. A body was recovered from the Chesapeake Bay and identified by the CIA as Paisley's. However, the body turned out to be four inches shorter and thirty pounds lighter than Paisley's official CIA physical description. CIA Director Adm. Stansfield Turner began, in the opinion of some, an inept and embarrassing coverup of the Paisley matter and the Boyce-Lee case. But the damage was done. Turner and Carter had presided over the biggest intelligence loss in American history just as they were trying to assure the Senate that our ability to verify Soviet compliance with SALT II was assured.[18]

Although Carter made a lukewarm endorsement of the shuttle program in his speech at the Kennedy Space Center, the PD-42 document was, to the pleasure of Frank Press, accepted as White House policy. Frosch, who was happy just to have Carter pay attention to NASA, extravagantly promised that NASA would have a very special present for Carter's fifty-fourth birthday, the lift-off of the first shuttle.

On the fifteenth anniversary of John Kennedy's assassination, NASA Deputy Administrator Dr. Alan M. Lovelace and Associate Administrator for Manned Flight John Yardley informed Mark that more development troubles would push back the first shuttle flight until beyond the 1980 election to early 1981. According to Mark, a week later, on November

28, 1978, Acting OMB director James McIntyre called a meeting about the shuttle with CIA director Turner, DOD secretary Brown, and Air Force undersecretary Mark. McIntyre offered three options for the shuttle. The first was to keep five orbiters and both the Vandenberg and Kennedy launch sites in the budget. The second was to convert the shuttle to a purely experimental program and cut back the fleet to three orbiters with only Kennedy as a launch site. And the third option was to build four orbiters and leave the question of Vandenberg to a later date. McIntyre argued for the second option. Two weeks later in a second meeting, Harold Brown contended that the OMB proposal was unacceptable to the Pentagon. Brown argued that because the first two production shuttles from Rockwell would be heavier than the second-generation shuttles, their capabilities to launch spy satellites into polar orbits would not be as great. Brown also reminded McIntyre that the Vandenberg launch site was absolutely necessary for the polar orbits. In the end Vandenberg survived OMB, but NASA lost the fifth orbiter.

Mondale's people at OMB succeeded in getting Carter to reduce the orbiter fleet from five to four. For NASA it was a devastating blow. Lilly says that Mondale did everything he could to derail the civilian program. "He was the biggest enemy NASA had in that period," asserts Lilly. Frosch found Mondale frustrating to deal with because he would never simply say he was opposed to the program. "He appeared less as a direct enemy than a guy who refused to play. . . . Mondale's people were in the OMB and elsewhere and they were some of the direct people we had to deal with. I kind of got annoyed at the fact that it was clear he was against the whole thing, but he wasn't willing . . . to participate. . . . You had the feeling his people were always working in the background," says Frosch. The loss of the fifth orbiter was something Frosch thought he could reverse once the shuttle flew. "I was trying to sell them on buying another sample of something that hadn't been demonstrated yet and that's a poor position for a salesman of any kind," Frosch explains.[19]

On a hot, spring morning in Palmdale, Rockwell rolled out the world's first reusable spaceship. The rollout of *Columbia* was greeted with the extensive media coverage and public excitement that NASA missed during this lull in manned flight. Unlike *Enterprise*, which had no tiles and no engines, *Columbia* was the real thing. She was dubbed "the flying brickyard" because of the uneven appearance the more than 30,000 tiles gave her skin. But the euphoria over her March 24, 1979, debut evaporated very quickly when the 747 with *Columbia* on top landed on the shuttle strip at the Kennedy Space Center. *Columbia* looked like a toothless old maid. The wonderful Reusable Surface Insulation System—the tiles— had broken off during the relatively smooth airplane flight. The media speculated what would have happened had it experienced the much rougher launch into space. The troubled shuttle program was now getting public treatment usually reserved for military projects that went sour.

For Frosch, the "great tile caper," as he called it, was an awful experience. More than all the shuttle nightmares of engines, flight controls, and boosters, none was more frustrating than the so-called reusable thermal protection system. NASA's Ames Research Center had the tile responsibility. According to Mark, as early as 1972 Ames' scientists warned NASA headquarters that plans to glue the tiles to the shuttle could lead to real trouble. By 1978 the trouble became evident. It was trouble that went all the way up to the administrator. "The biggest problem with the tiles was not solving the material problems with the tiles but trying to decide . . . what the actual flight forces the tiles would have to undergo. It wasn't that we didn't know what it took to pull a tile off. It was that we didn't know what the forces would be in actual flight. See, the problem is you've got this flying machine which is behaving aerodynamically so you have all the drag and lift forces. It's sort of twisting a little bit. . . . It's vibrating. So you have got those forces. In certain parts of the regime there are shock waves. . . . You have thermal forces including the fact that the whole machine is breathing a little. You don't know how to add those forces up because they come slightly differently at different points in the flight. . . . So some bright fellow, me at one point, says, 'Let's design for the worse cases.' . . . And if you do that you would never get the machine off the ground. It would weigh too much. So you don't do that," says Frosch.

Frosch continues, "There was a lot of foolishness about the glue. There was never a problem about the glue. There was a problem with the strength of the tiles." The tiles were not glued directly to the aluminum skin of the orbiter, but to a kind of felt-like material called Nomex. " . . . Felt means something specifically. It means that you have a non-woven mass of fibers. One of the processes that finishes off the non-woven thing so it will adhere is called felting." In this process masses of needles are applied to fabric so the threads create a surface for the glue to stick to. Unfortunately, NASA did not foresee that whenever the needle went through the fabric, an unevenness developed in the felting. In those places, once they were glued, extra stresses were put on the inside of the tiles. The result was that the "glue from the Nomex did not give way. The tile would break just inside where it was glued to the felt . . . so you would get this white gap," concludes Frosch.

But Frosch did not know that there was deliberate sabotage to the shuttle at Rockwell's Palmdale facility. NASA, renowned for making certain that contractor personnel who had access to life dependent systems had full background checks, no longer had the funds to make such checks. But no one at the space agency ever believed that ex-convicts would be assigned to install tiles on the space shuttle fleet. According to Frosch's assistant, David Williamson, that is exactly what happened. In a community good-citizens effort, Rockwell set up a small program to hire ex-cons on a part-time basis to install tiles. To the horror of NASA officials, random quality-control inspection revealed puncture holes in the installed tiles. In order to extend their employment, the ex-cons attacked the very fragile tiles with sharp tools. It was later learned that the perpetrators believed that damaging the tiles would not really hurt the shuttle since, from their viewpoint, they were put "on the orbiter." All they were trying to do was create make-work to keep their jobs. But, it took months to resolve the tile problem.[20]

When the engineers finally figured out a way to prevent the tiles from breaking, each tile had to be reinstalled with several people crawling all over *Columbia* overseeing each other. Because of money shortages, NASA management put together a crew of tile-setters that Frosch concedes were "a very good crew but not anybody's long-term employees." Frosch says, " . . . I got nervous about it but the conclusion was there wasn't any such thing as a skill. You didn't go out in the market and say, 'I am going to hire an experienced shuttle tile-setter.'" The publicity NASA received for using a crew of low-paid college students to help build a $2 billion spaceship was not very complimentary.

For NASA, little went well in 1979. Nature and an underfunded shuttle program conspired to cheat the space agency out of the opportunity to rescue the long-dormant Skylab space station. Intense solar activity was causing the earth's atmosphere to expand and the orbit of Skylab to decay much faster than anticipated. " . . . I got involved in trying to save Skylab," Bob Aller, the former Skylab program manager, recalls. "We were going to build a teleoperator and fly back to Skylab from the shuttle. . . .

John Yardley was saying he'd deliver us the shuttle to meet that mission . . . and the crew would have flown the shuttle right up next to Skylab, deployed this thing . . . that would move the vehicle into a higher orbit. . . . Well, as all new, fast programs, we got into funding trouble on this thing . . . and Yardley says, 'No, we're going to cancel it because of your cost overrun.' . . . And why he was cancelling was because the shuttle was never going to make it. . . . We could have had all the teleoperators in the world built and there was not going to be any shuttle to carry them up there and that was the difficulty," explains Aller.[21]

The second week in July proved to be a nightmare for NASA management. They attempted to explain to the world's press that there was an excellent chance that pieces of Skylab big enough to kill people were going to land someplace on earth and they really had no idea where. On July 11 the 170,000-pound space station entered the atmosphere over the Indian Ocean and the bulk of its wreckage fell harmlessly across the Australian desert. But NASA lost what some in the agency hoped would be the very reliable core of a big space station. And the public was laughing at them.

Morale was a continuing concern for Frosch. He called what many of the NASA veterans suffered "nostalgie de Sputnik." According to Frosch, its symptom was wondering "why everybody doesn't love us anymore." But, during 1979, the Voyager I and II fly-by of Saturn and Jupiter helped agency morale. The spacecraft, launched two years before, returned unbelievable images of stormy chemical atmospheres on Jupiter and revealed details of Saturn's ring structure that caused scientists to totally recast their ideas about the planet. Both Voyagers continue their endless exploration that will eventually take them out of the solar system.

In April 1979 Hans Mark was appointed secretary of the Air Force. He now had full Air Force authority over all shuttle decisions. In August, Mark met with Williamson, who was handling liaison with the DOD for NASA. Williamson informed a shocked Mark that cost overruns on the program were approaching $500 million. Lilly, shuttle designer Max Faget, Yardley, and others all told Mark that the cost overruns of the program would be a billion 1972 dollars. Lilly had been right. His original estimate was $6.2 billion. The runout costs to "operational" status were now approaching $6.2 billion. Mark found that his position as a shuttle defender within the Pentagon was under heavy attack. He wrote in his manuscript, "I had numerous discussions with many people in the Air Force about the question of manned spaceflight during the four years I served in the Pentagon and I failed to make any significant headway in persuading people of the military value of manned spaceflight."

While NASA was continuing to have troubles with shuttle development, the Air Force was not doing much better. The Vandenberg facility was also experiencing massive cost overruns. Mark blamed NASA. "Some of these problems were caused by a faulty relationship between NASA and the Air Force at a time which did not give the Air Force enough management freedom to do the job properly." In reality, NASA was largely kept out of the Vandenberg operation. Attempts by the leadership of the uniformed Air Force to remove money from the budget and end the Vandenberg construction effort were stopped by Mark. Frosch knew what many in the Air Force were trying to do. "Well, we had to battle like hell with them to get them to build Vandenberg. There was a point where Vandenberg kept falling out of the budget. . . . That was the real way they tried to get rid of the shuttle was by not building Vandenberg . . . ," Frosch remarks.[22]

"The Vandenberg shuttle launch facility thus became my 'gold watch,' which is Pentagon jargon for any program that is imposed on the military establishment by a member of the civilian hierarchy," Mark wrote. Lilly charged all along that Mark's intention was to get control of the shuttle for the Air Force after NASA funded and built the system. A reflection of Mark's feelings about that appear in his manuscript. "Even more important than the question of what people could do in space is the matter of who controls the launch vehicles. This was, and still is, a primary motivating factor in the thinking of many senior Air Force people both military and civilian. The fact that the shuttle was not under management control of the users concerned many people. Specifically, they were worried about NASA's ability to meet Air Force schedules and particularly to carry out some launch-on-demand type missions that the Air Force might want to execute. There was not much I could do directly about this as long as the Shuttle was (and is) operated by NASA. What I could do (and did) was to develop the idea of dedicated Air Force missions in which the Air Force was in complete control of the mission even though NASA actually owned the vehicle."

Mark wanted an Air Force control center because he worried about NASA being vulnerable to sabotage. One reason Mark opposed Houston controlling the missions was the vulnerability of Houston as a control center. "I worried about Johnson for a number of reasons. One is that it is on the coast. You know you can stand a ship offshore and lob shells into it. It has hurricane problems. You know, it can be basically shut down by a hurricane."[23] In reality the Houston center controlled several flights when hurricanes hit the Texas coast.

The Air Force and DOD hierarchy, now fully committed to the shuttle because they had no other launch options, would push for more and more control over the program as NASA came to the Pentagon for support for its money problems with OMB and the president. The administration approved a request from NASA for a supplemental appropriation for the shuttle. Bill Lilly did not like to ask for supplemental appropriations for NASA programs, but the due bill for building the shuttle had to be paid. President Carter was furious when he learned that a second supplemental would be needed to get the shuttle finished. Mark remembers the incident. "Well, I lobbied Harold Brown. But Hell, without Brown's support, the [shuttle] program would have died. I went to Harold and said, 'Look we need this bird,' and he agreed with me pretty much immediately. . . . No question he was in favor from the very beginning. And the problem was . . . we had this overrun that Frosch had surfaced . . . I think the problem was that NASA did it in two steps rather than one and so everybody got pissed off at them. . . . They had to go back twice and the president got all upset and said, 'Let's kill it.'" Mark and others say that it was largely Defense Secretary Brown who saved the shuttle program from being totally cancelled.

On November 14, 1979, President Carter met with Frosch who convinced him to continue the program and fund the overruns. Carter called a meeting for later in the day with Frosch, Lovelace, Yardley, and Lilly from NASA, McIntyre and his deputy from OMB, Frank Press from the White House Office of Science and Technology, and Mark from DOD. At the meeting that afternoon Carter told them that the due bill on the shuttle that had been building for three administrations would be paid. Frosch remembers Carter then asking detailed questions about the engines and the tiles and other technical aspects of the shuttle.[24]

In exchange for his support in the White House and Congress, Mark and his Air Force extracted concessions from NASA. In a memorandum of understanding negotiated by Maj. Gen. James Brickel for the Air Force and Philip E. Culbertson for NASA, the space agency relinquished more of their control over the shuttle. NASA agreed to allow the Air Force to bump *any* NASA or commercial payload on national security grounds. Mark proudly boasted that this gave the Air

Force what he liked to call "assured access to space." In their own defense, Frosch and Lovelace argued that the agreement would not lead to the militarization of NASA, but they demanded and got a proviso that in any disputes the final arbitrator would be the president.

Frosch and Lovelace did not foresee that the shuttle would soon have competition for commercial satellite customers. The French were already beginning to market their Ariane expendable booster, and no government agency could bump their paying customers. Frosch and Lovelace did not realize how much damage this concession did to attracting paying clients to the shuttle. After signing the memorandum of understanding, Hans Mark ordered that the necessary steps be taken to end the Air Force's procurement of expendable launch vehicles (ELVs). Although he felt a combination of shuttles and ELVs was better, Frosch was forced into the same position.

By late summer 1980 Frosch began to realize some of the problems he would face in running an operational shuttle system. The Air Force's contribution to the shuttle, the Inertial Upper Stage (IUS), was proving to be a very expensive lemon. Frosch began to worry about how payloads were going to get into higher orbit. "The Air Force never turned up with the IUS properly and there was one point where I got paranoid enough so I began to think it wasn't accidental that they were having all that trouble," comments Frosch. He had good reason to be suspicious.

Since the decision was first made to build the shuttle, the General Dynamics Corporation had been lobbying NASA's Lewis Research Center and headquarters on a shuttle version of its Centaur upper stage, which had been flying on the Atlas for years. General Dynamics was beside itself over losing the sale to NASA and the military of its potentially explosive liquid hydrogen–fueled upper stage. But NASA's safety people at Houston said that carrying a liquid-fueled Centaur aboard the shuttle was the equivalent of putting a bomb in the cargo bay. When Mark was director of the Ames Research Center, he witnessed the origins of the Centaur upper-stage debate. "The guy who really started the notion was Bruce Lundin, who was then the director of the Lewis Research Center. He thought it would be a good idea to put the Centaur on the shuttle, and so did I, because I thought it was the highest-energy upper stage we had, and that we would need it for the various things we wanted to do. . . . So I supported him. . . . I remember Chris Kraft, who had just become director of the Johnson Space Center at the time, saying, 'No way, it's unsafe.' . . . And so we got outvoted."

With the IUS faltering, General Dynamics convinced Frosch's deputy Al Lovelace that the Centaur upper stage for the shuttle should be built. General Dynamics' interest in the project was hardly altruistic. The Centaur program was a big money-maker for the company and even a small-scale program could add up to a billion-dollar contract. Frosch and NASA wanted a more sophisticated reusable upper stage known as the Space Tug. This device would be parked in orbit. The shuttle astronauts would then refuel it, attach it to a satellite or probe to be launched to a higher orbit or out of the earth's gravitational pull, and send it on its way. When the mission was accomplished, the stage would automatically return to a lower earth orbit.

But General Dynamics had a lot riding on the Centaur production line. Already faced with losing sales of its Atlas to the military and NASA when the shuttle would replace all such expendable launchers, the world's largest defense contractor began a campaign to sell the upper stage that has yet to be duplicated in NASA contractor history. James Beggs, a former NASA associate administrator, was hired by General Dynamics as general manager. Beggs urged Frosch to buy the Centaur for the shuttle. GD, as the company is known, drafted a report for officials at the Lewis Research Center[25] that made a case for NASA giving General Dynamics the upper-stage contract without going out for competitive proposals and bidding. A company report was submitted to headquarters *as if it were a NASA report*. Doggedly, Lovelace, according to NASA officials, kept Centaur alive despite the safety objections of Frosch and his Houston team. Kraft, who made his dislike for Lovelace crystal clear, absolutely refused on safety grounds to consider putting such a device in the cargo bay of the shuttle. Kraft raised enough technical questions to win the support of Frosch. But both Kraft and Frosch would not be with NASA much longer.

But before he left, Gilruth protégé Kraft butted heads with Hans Mark again and again. Mark wanted Kraft to ease flight requirements for shuttle astronauts so he and other private citizens could fly on the still-unproven system. Kraft told Mark in no uncertain terms to forget about it. But Frosch agreed to allow the Air Force to come into Houston and rebuild the complex to prevent eavesdropping by the Soviets. This especially upset Kraft. In order for the Air Force to have secret communications with the shuttle on military missions, tens of millions were spent on the Johnson Space Center (JSC). Copper was installed in walls and floors. The Air Force was given their own shuttle-control facilities. What had been the showcase for civilian manned flight was now effectively being turned into an Air Force fortress.

Carter's budget commitment put the program back on track and Frosch began planning the first shuttle mission. Unlike any previous manned vehicle, the shuttle would not be tested dozens of times and then be dubbed "man-rated." It would have to work the first time out. Frosch was not entirely comfortable with this prospect. "Yeah, I was very nervous. I guess my private feeling was that the chances of doing the whole launch without some glitch, not a catastrophe, but some major glitch, was not better than 50–50. If we got through that launch the next one might be 3–1 and 10–1."

In the fall of 1980, Carter and Frosch met to discuss the upcoming first flight. The president was not comfortable with the shuttle either. Carter asked Frosch if *Columbia* could be converted to a completely automated launch vehicle. He wanted to know if the shuttle could be launched and landed without a crew.[26] Frosch told him that in principle the ship could be flown that way, but major changes would have to be made and they would be very expensive. At the same meeting Frosch told the president that he wanted immediate and direct access to the president throughout the flight. "He wanted to know why this was. And I said, 'You know, we don't know what is going to happen. We think we are all right, but it is a risky business. If something goes wrong, you better not find out about it afterwards. You better know about it immediately and I want you to know about it from me . . . ,'" Frosch recalls. Frosch came back to Carter and confirmed that an automated system could be designed but that it made no sense. *Columbia* was almost ready. Frosch personally met with John Young and Robert Crippen whom he approved to fly the first mission. Young had more hours in space than any American astronaut.

According to Lilly, Frosch felt that the new space transportation system would not be truly operational for many years to come. Frosch did not intend to succumb to economic pressures to force the development of the shuttle. "He thought they really intended to have an operational kind of thing. He also did not believe that it was going to be operational for a long, long time. I know I used to tell him as far as being operational, Frosch, that son of a bitch [the shuttle] is going to be R&D on out into the year 2000. . . . He said, 'Hell yes!' He agreed. That didn't mean you couldn't do more and more. But in my mind, the thing is such a complicated business that it takes the complete dedication of people at all times . . . ," Lilly states.[27]

Despite Mark's support of the shuttle, he had few real friends in NASA and fewer at DOD, especially in the uniformed Air Force. According to Mark's manuscript, his preoccupation with space caused one colleague at DOD to suggest Mark move to a job at NASA in Carter's second term. Mark, disenchanted with Carter, had far more ambitious plans. Mark, always politically alert, was cultivating both Republicans and Democrats. Mark writes that in the summer of 1980, he told associates that he was having "doubts" about Carter's ability to get reelected. He was particularly disturbed by Carter's famous "malaise speech" in July 1979. But his actions as Jimmy Carter's secretary of the Air Force were incomprehensible to some. A senior vice president for Hughes Aircraft, Arthur Wheelon, was working in former-Governor Ronald Reagan's presidential campaign. Wheelon asked Mark to brief the Reagan staff on the shuttle. By the end of August 1980, Mark became so convinced that Reagan would win, he secretly arranged a meeting in September. Mark never informed Secretary of Defense Harold Brown. At the Metropolitan Club, just a few blocks from the White House, Mark met with Richard V. Allen and Clay T. Whitehead of the Reagan staff. Behind the back of his boss, Harold Brown, and his president, Mark hedged his bets with Reagan. In an admission of some guilt in the matter, Mark wrote, "I salved my conscience by writing out a letter of resignation which I resolved to send to Brown in the event that President Carter won reelection. As things turned out I could have saved myself the trouble. . . ."[28]

On November 4, 1980, Hans Mark went to vote. "Here I was a member of the Carter Administration, and I voted for Reagan because I thought Carter was incompetent," Mark admitted in his manuscript. Mark's instincts were right and the strange interlude of the Jimmy Carter presidency ended, but not Carter's personal agony. For more than a year he had been preoccupied with getting the hostages out of Iran. The Shiites had, in effect, taken his presidency away. Carter suffered every humiliation to save the hostages.

Worried about his job prospects after the Carter administration, Mark applied for a civil service position at Ames Research Center, which he had headed until 1977. The man who originally recruited him into NASA was James Beggs. Beggs served in 1969 as associate administrator for advanced research and technology, not a high-profile position in the space agency. When Beggs left the space agency during the Nixon administration to be Secretary of Transportation John Volpe's undersecretary, he was instrumental in transferring NASA's brand-new Electronic Research Center in Cambridge, Massachusetts, to the Department of Transportation.[29] The head of that center was Mark's old friend, James Elms, who, according to Mark, thought it would be a great idea if Beggs were to be Reagan's administrator of NASA with Mark as his deputy. Elms, according to Mark, persuaded Governor John Volpe to recommend the pair to run NASA. While all these political machinations went on, Mark continued as Carter's secretary of the Air Force.

Mark used such Reagan favorites as Edward Teller and Wheelon to push for his appointment. Mark also got two DOD and NASA contractors, Robert Anderson of Rockwell, the prime shuttle contractor, and Tom Jones of Northrop, to support his nomination. NASA former-Deputy Administrator George Low was now working on the Reagan transition team. Ironically, on the seventeenth anniversary of John Kennedy's murder, Low called Mark at the Pentagon. "Specifically Low wanted to know whether I would accept the job as NASA administrator," Mark wrote in his manuscript.

Mark told Low that he would prefer, given the political circumstances, to serve as Beggs' deputy.

While Mark was plotting his political future, a worried
Bob Frosch was still agonizing over the first shuttle flight.
Frosch wanted to leave NASA at the end of the Carter administration, but he did not want to "walk out and leave this thing
[the shuttle] sitting there on the pad." After a discussion with
his deputy, Al Lovelace, Frosch made his resignation effective January 20, 1981. They decided that Lovelace would offer to stay at NASA until after the first shuttle launch. Frosch
explains what Lovelace told him happened next. " . . . The
Reagan guys were doing interviews for people who wanted to
stay on and so they told him to come over. And . . . some guy
. . . said, 'Well, what do you want?' And he said he's the
deputy administrator of NASA and there's this crucial launch
coming up and he would be interested in staying on to oversee
that if he can be useful. Well, he got a kind of, 'Oh, you
bureaucrats just want to hold on to your damn jobs' and he
[Lovelace] nearly walked out. But apparently cooler [heads]
prevailed. . . . Otherwise, I don't know what they would have
done with somebody who walked in off the street."

The space agency that was a remarkably effective and
very special organization continued to deteriorate during the
Carter years. By the end of 1980, NASA's capability to technically verify any contractor's work had all but vanished. By
the end of 1980, the NASA that was once the toughest quality-control operation in or out of government was now
depending on the military for many of its inspections. And by
the end of 1980, the NASA veterans who fought the hardest
for safety were leaving. It had been eight years since Fletcher
flew to San Clemente to get the shuttle approved. Now there
would be no more excuses, no more delays. That spring,
Columbia was scheduled to fly.

8

Fly Now, Pay Later

In politics, success is dictated by timing. Ronald Reagan has great timing. The hapless Jimmy Carter succeeded in getting the hostages out of Iran. But their imprisonment helped end his chances for a second term. Jimmy Carter, with eyes wide open, paid the shuttle cost overrun bills with his own limited political currency. And Ronald Reagan, as Richard Nixon did with the lunar landing, was destined to get a free political ride from the new shuttle.

As Reagan took office, workers at the Kennedy Space Center were busy getting the *Columbia* ready. NASA was in the final months of preparation for the first test flight of the nation's new Space Transportation System. After nine years of short-changed budgets, a long hiatus in manned flight, horrendous problems with tiles, engines, and contractors, *Columbia* was preparing for an early spring lift-off. Jimmy Carter would no longer have to bear the responsibility for the lives he so worried about losing in a test flight.

By the time Ronald Reagan was sworn in as the country's fortieth president, no decision had been made on who would run NASA. Hans Mark was still conducting an aggressive campaign for the job. But Reagan's staff was in no hurry to see the president tie his name and mandate to a shuttle system that was about to be tested for the first time. Just as Richard Nixon waited for Apollo to prove itself before appointing Fletcher, Reagan would wait to see if *Columbia* proved successful. At least for the first few months, NASA would be left to its own devices. Frosch's deputy, Dr. Alan Lovelace, became acting administrator. He hardly behaved as a caretaker. One of his first actions was to reverse Frosch's decision on General Dynamics' proposal for the liquid-fueled Centaur upper stage for the shuttle.[1] While General Dynamics' lobbying had been rebuffed by Frosch and in Houston on safety grounds, Lovelace wrote to Speaker of the House Tip O'Neill notifying the Congress that NASA intended to reprogram funds to the Centaur.[2] He did this despite concerns from Bill Lilly and others that NASA's Lewis Research Center and General Dynamics were woefully underestimating the cost of turning Centaur into a high-energy upper stage. The reaction at the Johnson Space Center was outrage.

Frosch was known as a relaxed, accessible manager. NASA Center directors could pick up the phone and contact him directly. But unlike Frosch, Lovelace had a reputation for being a very tough manager who was not in the habit of tolerating dissent. Frosch readily admits using Lovelace when something difficult had to be done. "Well, Alan had a little bit of the reputation of being kind of tough . . . and he and I used to play good policeman, bad policeman very effectively," Frosch notes.[3] Lovelace succeeded in selecting the Centaur over the solid-fuel IUS because NASA was in full transition.

The old-liners from the Apollo days were all but gone. Chris Kraft, disgusted by the whole situation, retired. Bill Lilly was considering leaving. Among the most honored of government employees, these two men at times both felt like outsiders looking into the manned-spaceflight program. Lovelace convinced the shuttle managers in Houston to support Centaur. For Lilly it was an amazing turnaround for the manned-flight people at Houston. " . . . They completely came around [as if] all the safety problems had been solved . . . and everything was fine, and no problems," Lilly says sarcastically.[4]

For Lilly, the NASA he knew and helped build was in final convulsions in 1981. His view of the responsibility of public service was straightforward. Beginning with Adm. "Red" Rayborn and the Polaris program and later with Jim Webb, Lilly learned to ride herd on contractors and double-check everything his program people told him. Nobody at NASA accepted anything from contractors, not drinks, not lunch, and certainly not jobs. All that began to change after Webb left.[5] For Lilly, the ascendancy of Lovelace was a problem. "Al had a background in the military and I used to have to try to stick a lid back on all the time because he had too much of a military background and was too easily convinced in negotiations," Lilly recalls.

By March, Mark's lobbying of the new administration paid off. According to his unpublished manuscript, Mark got a telephone call from the White House personnel office informing him that he was being nominated for deputy administrator of NASA. Pendleton James, then head of political patronage, told Mark that his boss would be James Beggs. Beggs had a history quite different from his predecessors. He was a Naval Academy graduate who went on to Harvard Business School. Beggs' business career soared. He was with Westinghouse Electric for thirteen years. He spent a year at NASA under Webb. Beggs' wife Mary remembers Webb introducing them to President Johnson. "Jim was a Republican in NASA and they knew it. Jim Webb knew it. . . . He [Webb] said, 'I want you to know we look for people who can do the job in NASA, and we don't look for party affiliation,'" Mrs. Beggs remembers.[6] But the Nixon administration did look for Republicans. And Mary Beggs was a Republican chairman in Howard County, Maryland, and a strong Nixon supporter. Bill Lilly says, "I always had the feeling that the real politician in his family was his wife."[7] So it is not surprising that Beggs was offered several jobs in the Nixon administration, including head of the Federal Aviation Administration. He left NASA to serve the Nixon administration as undersecretary for transportation. Beggs then went to Howard Hughes' super-secret Summa Corporation, which built the Glomar Explorer for the CIA. In 1974 he joined the world's largest defense contractor, General Dynamics.

In 1977 Beggs headed a study team looking at how NASA should operate the shuttle. His conclusion was that a company like the Communications Satellite Corporation (COMSAT), with some U.S. government representation on the board of directors, should be formed to operate the system. Beggs quickly gained the confidence of General Dynamics' controversial chairman, David Lewis, and became a member of the board of directors as well as executive vice president. In that role he lobbied NASA to buy the Centaur upper stage.[8]

According to Mark, he and Beggs met on March 21 in St. Louis to set their priorities for NASA. The first decision was to make the shuttle a fully operational space transportation system. The second decision was to convince President Reagan to build a permanently manned space station. And the third was to acquire an upper stage for the shuttle. Considering the many problems at NASA and the Air Force's commitment to the Inertial Upper Stage (IUS), the third decision seemed an odd priority. The General Dynamics' Centaur could prove an embarrassing conflict of interest for Beggs since he lobbied his predecessor to pursue it. But they did not tell others of their priorities so the Senate confirmation hearings went smoothly.

Now Lilly found himself working in a NASA where the contractor revolving door spun around as each administration changed. For Lilly the discipline of taking nothing for granted was wearing away. Lilly was tired of the lack of vision recent presidents and administrators demonstrated in understanding what space meant for the future of the country. "I was getting pretty fed up with the whole attitude of the Carter and Reagan administrations. It wasn't worth it, you know. Because once you have been with something like NASA from the start, you hate to turn loose of it and just let it go to hell. You stay on. But I just got fed up once they selected Beggs, and particularly Hans Mark. I said, 'No way. I am leaving.' I wouldn't work for either one of them. Beggs is alright in some ways but he has no guts, no staying power with anything." Lilly also refused to work with Mark. "I wouldn't have anything to do with him." Lilly watched Mark with amazement as he tried to cultivate allies everyplace. "He struck me as a devious guy who worked behind the scenes on everything. . . . He did not have his influence at the top. . . . He would befriend a lot of low-level people at the Pentagon . . . majors and captains."[9] Lilly felt that Mark used them as his informants and spies.

Even Beggs' wife was aware of Mark's activities. "Well, no sooner was he in, than the NASA people turned out to really have a fit because they thought Hans was going to militarize space. And Hans thought he was going to be running the agency. Well, he didn't and that was his big surprise. . . . I never knew what kinds of games he was playing . . . Jim . . .

was aware of Hans' orientation," Mrs. Beggs remarks.[10] The relationship between Mark and Beggs was not one of trust. Mark was so loquacious that, according to Mrs. Beggs, he once told the administrator's driver that he intended to replace Beggs. Beggs was also warned by Bill Lilly. "I told Beggs I would help him for a while but under no circumstances be under Hans Mark. I would not do it . . . I told him half his problems were coming from the guy sitting in the other corner. I told him he is going to give this whole god-damn store away to DOD. And you're never going to make anything here of this thing. I mean you are getting yourself in a position on this damned shuttle . . . that the more you fly, the more you are going to lose. And he'd just laugh and say, 'Oh, you mean my friend over here.' I said, 'My friend my ass.' But he would laugh about it, like, yeah, he agrees with you and yet he wouldn't do anything. Then he'd say, 'When it comes to that, I'll get rid of him, you know.' But I never saw him do anything about it. Beggs was the type that had good instincts, you know . . . but he just never had the stamina or the drive to follow through on anything," Lilly contends.[11]

As NASA came closer and closer to the launch of *Columbia*, one thing was clear. John Yardley did a great job forcing the problems to solutions and getting the vehicle ready. To get his shuttle off, Yardley was operating against a political clock. Since he inherited the shuttle program, he was blamed for many of its problems. Yardley understood better than most at NASA what responsibility he faced. The Apollo 204 fire devastated him. The long hours and constant criticism on the shuttle took their toll. But Yardley was the shuttle program. The force of his personality and his demand for information kept it on track. Pressing in on Yardley was a troubling combination of events. The shuttle proved a very difficult vehicle to handle. Because of the tiles, it was the most fragile space vehicle with which NASA ever worked. And Lilly articulated another deeper problem that Yardley faced—the deterioration of the kind of management discipline that brought NASA to the moon. Lilly describes the earlier days at NASA. "Everybody was held personally accountable [and] everything had to be in writing. There was no reporting by exception. It had to be there." According to Lilly everything had to be signed and certified by those responsible. That would change drastically during the shuttle program. Paperwork was so neglected by the time the shuttle was flying it was nearly impossible to establish a clear line of responsibility. As the shuttle was nearing its first flight, Lilly says, the sense of caring and accountability was drastically diminished. While Yardley understood the shuttle system better than anyone at NASA, his habit of bypassing his deputies left the program without a management structure. Yardley was the type of engineer "that would understand everything about it and engineer it himself. . . . He was real smart. He could keep more facts and information in his head. . . . And he really weakened the organization by doing everything himself. . . . Consequently what he finally ended up with was a bunch of nincompoops over there on his staff. He kept them around but they didn't do a damn thing," Lilly maintains.

Lilly says the Carter and Reagan years shattered the sense of pride and devotion that NASA's civil servants had before presidential campaigns ran against Washington. "I don't know how others work, but I know the people I worked with. Shit, we used to work seven days a week for years. . . . You never thought about it. . . . But to be put in the same class as the Post Office Department or Agriculture or a bunch of clerks. . . ."[12] Chris Kraft, a professional and intense man, who stood up to three administrators in defense of pure civil space, was persuaded to return under Beggs. But according to Lilly and others, Craft became increasingly bitter and angry toward Beggs and Mark as one compromise after another was made to keep the military in the shuttle program.

Lilly described Beggs as "a nonentity" in his earlier stint at NASA. After all, to Lilly, Beggs was first and foremost a contractor. Unlike old NASA hands, Beggs believed that the contractor and government were a partnership and not even occasionally adversaries. Such a relationship was the ideal born out of a free-enterprise system and representative democracy. For all his experience in the business, Pentagon, and NASA worlds, Beggs was a political amateur. Beggs' exaggerated sense of his influence with both the Congress and the White House would cost him and NASA dearly. Although he worked for Reagan's election, he was not one of the new, ultraconservative Reaganite true believers. As a lifelong Republican businessman, Beggs did not realize that the conservatives' agenda was not subject to the kind of compromise that he was used to. If you were not one of them, you were against them. If Jim Beggs became an obstacle, he would be removed.

Old NASA hands wondered if Beggs was any match for the people surrounding Ronald Reagan. They had seen presidential appointees who disliked manned spaceflight, who wanted to save money, who wanted to take longer to do the exploration. But never had there been so many opposed to everything NASA stood for. So when George "Jay" Keyworth, a forty-three-year-old weapons designer from Los Alamos, became Ronald Reagan's science adviser, NASA faced a crisis of survival. He did not trust the space agency. "Of all the organizations that I have dealt with, some so wrapped up in their bureaucratic interests that they were certainly counter to the directions . . . the country was going in. Some of them filled with incompetent people. Some of them outstanding. I have only seen one that lied. It was NASA. From the top to the bottom they lie. . . . The reason they lie, of course, is

Roy Day (NASA)

Robert A. Frosch (NASA)

Alan M. Lovelace (NASA)

(Opposite) *STS-1 (Space Transportation System) on Pad A at Kennedy Space Center after three-and-a-half-mile trip from VAB (Vehicle Assembly Building). (NASA)*

Hans M. Mark (NASA)

The Space Shuttle Columbia *rises off Pad 39A a few seconds past 7 A.M., on April 12, 1981, with astronauts John Young and Bob Crippen on board. (NASA)*

James M. Beggs (NASA)

*Harold C. Hollenbeck (Courtesy
of Mr. Hollenbeck)*

"Cola star wars." (Below) *Astronaut Karl J. Henize tests one of two carbonated beverage dispensers on mission 51F aboard* Challenger. (Right) *Astronaut Anthony W. England, mission specialist, tests the other.* (NASA)

Philip E. Culbertson (NASA)

Rocco Petrone (Rockwell International Corporation)

William R. Graham (NASA)

James Fletcher (NASA)

because they are wrapped up in a higher calling. In their eyes they are white lies. They tell lies in order to do what has to be done. Because in the end the result will be for the betterment of the public. So they are not lying from evil. But, nevertheless, they are lying," Keyworth asserts.[13] He believed that the entire basis of the shuttle was a lie. "If you believe that the shuttle is going to be cheap relative to ELVs [Expendable Launch Vehicles], then I'm forced to ask you, 'Does that imply that we will spend no money to assure the safety of men on board?' And I think the answer is, 'Of course not.'"

As Beggs prepared to take over NASA, he began to realize that the NASA he knew as an agency official and as a vice president at General Dynamics had changed. The agency he came back to head was forced to go hat-in-hand to the military for support. When he returned, Beggs found a NASA where severe budget slashes had caused scale-backs in quality control and security. NASA had even turned to the inefficient and costly Pentagon procurement system. Not only was the "can do" attitude at NASA severely weakened, but so was NASA's ability to prevent being snowed by a contractor.

What James Beggs inherited was an agency that was held together under a series of administrations headed by presidents with marginal interests in space and even less interest in paying for it. As NASA's resources got smaller, the Pentagon's got larger. For Beggs it became clear that the NASA he was now running was not the agency that had put men on the moon. The youth and excitement of the space age was creeping into middle-age spread. In many ways Keyworth was right. NASA lied about the shuttle.

Hans Mark convinced Beggs that the only way to keep the shuttle program going was to force the Air Force to stay with it. Mocked by officers of the uniformed Air Force because of his mania for the shuttle, Mark was now advising Beggs on how to keep their support of the program. And "the blue suiters" used every shuttle setback to lobby to get out of participating in the program. For Secretary of the Air Force Vern Orr's deputy, Edwin C. "Pete" Aldridge, the cost of Vandenberg was becoming a problem. What was supposed to cost about $400 million had now ballooned to $2 billion and showed no signs of slowing down.[14] Several dozen big Titan rockets could have been procured at that price. From a national-security standpoint, NASA had not even flown the shuttle. Aldridge had to face the real possibility that *Columbia* could fail, and the pressure for the Air Force to go its own way would be overwhelming. The uniformed Air Force simply wanted control over their own launch vehicles and their own space program.

As preparations were underway for the first flight of *Columbia*, there was a terrible accident at the Cape. To prevent a fire, the engine compartment of the shuttle was flooded with pressurized nitrogen. Two launchpad team members went into the compartment and passed out before anyone realized what had happened. The shuttle claimed its first two lives.

For Yardley, the pressures increased. The results of a Frosch investigation into shuttle management reduced some of Yardley's power and authority. Despite the installation of Richard "Dick" Smith as the new Kennedy Space Center director, things continued to go wrong at the Cape. Yardley finally left headquarters and moved into a nearby condominium to supervise the launch preparations. But Lilly and others in NASA knew that there would be no shuttle system without him. "Because John could do more as an individual than you could do with a whole organization, I don't give a shit what it was . . . your real concern was that when John left, there was not going to be anything there," Lilly asserts. For NASA that concern was real. Yardley came back to NASA to straighten out the shuttle program. Now the long hours, the strain on his health, and the cut in salary combined to make him ready to return to McDonnell Douglas. Yardley was also unhappy with splitting shuttle management away from the rest of the responsibilities for manned flight. Yardley was convinced that problems with shuttle systems would fall through the cracks and be ignored. He would be proven all too right.[15]

What worried Lilly and many of the manned spaceflight engineers was the continuing pressure from the White House and Capitol Hill to make the shuttle economical. The Fletcher-Mathmatica models were still haunting the program. Almost everyone at NASA realized that this magnificent research and development organization had no experience in either selling commercial payloads or scheduling flights to accommodate cargo. But that worry was put on the back burner in early April 1981.

For the first time since the Apollo days, hundreds of reporters returned to the Cape to cover the first launching of the country's new Space Transportation System, STS-1. What they found was quite a shock. The communities surrounding the space center never really recovered from the loss of momentum in the program. Along U.S. Route 1 abandoned businesses and buildings were commonplace. It was like visiting the battle site of an old war fought by another generation. Across the causeway on Merritt Island and beyond the visitors center there were other changes. The openness of the facility was gone and the old lax security was now tight. One aspect that had not changed was the sometimes overconfident and overselling media office. The usual array of nature and VAB tours, films, and briefings kept the days leading up to the launch busy enough. At night there was always a party thrown by one of the contractors.

In the evening the shuttle could be seen from miles away as the xenon lights aided the pad crews. For all its shortcomings, *Columbia* stood alone the night before her launch as the world's first real spaceship. NASA had taken relatively little money and delivered late and with great pain the most sophisticated machine in the history of man. Computer programming troubles plagued the countdown. The failure of a backup computer delayed the first launch. Then on a beautiful Sunday morning in early April, *Columbia* was brought to life. The long fueling process began. The crew climbed into their ejection seats—seats that would be removed after the first few flights. In the huge external tank, 143,000 gallons of liquid oxygen were loaded into the upper tank while 383,000 gallons of liquid hydrogen were loaded into the larger lower tank. The liquid propellants weighed 790 tons. Sheets of ice formed on the upper part of the big tank. The oxygen inside was minus 297 degees Fahrenheit. The hydrogen stood at minus 423 degrees Fahrenheit in the lower tank.

On Sunday morning, April 12, 1981, nothing stood in the way of STS-1. At T minus 3 minutes the control surfaces of the shuttle were tested. The three main engines were gimballed. The test movements were felt by the astronauts. At T minus 31 seconds control of the shuttle became internal. Now the automatic sequencer, the four IBM computers, with a fifth machine as a backup, took over. The computers determined if the machine would be launched or would shut itself down. Now the water suppression system started. Thousands and thousands of gallons were pumped to help dampen the vibration from the blast of the engines—vibration that could cause the *Columbia* to break apart as it sat bolted to the pad building up enough thrust to lift-off. The water suppression system also protected the mobile launcher from the searing and corrosive heat of the solid, aluminum-based fuel. At T minus 8 seconds the cold fuels descended into the main engine preburners. This in turn ignited gases that turned the high-pressure turbopumps that injected the fuel into the engines. In the firing room, the launch team could now merely

monitor the event. At T minus 6.8 seconds the NASA television loop showed electrical igniters lighting the orbiter's main
engines. In a shower of sparks and water, each engine ignited.
Inside, the astronauts heard the noise and felt the vibration as
the thrust built. Each engine produced 375,000 pounds of
thrust before the computer program gave the command to fire
the solids. For the next six seconds the shuttle systems measured and monitored and sampled the performance of *Columbia*. Three miles away in the firing room, the engineers could
only wonder if the solids would work on a manned system.
For many of them, the thought that this system was never
tested before was pushed aside. Only the computer program
was able to start the process to ignite the unstoppable solids.
The moment of truth would be zero. Had Max Faget been
right or wrong? Would this be victory or would the dream
cartwheel into the Florida swamps? If the solids did not ignite
within a second of each other there would be conflagration on
pad 39A. The stack would go asymmetrical and *Columbia*
would be lost. At zero the solids fired. White steam filled the
horizon and the hold-down bolts broke loose. The crew could
hear the roar. They felt the swing of the vehicle and the surge
of energy.

It was nothing like a Saturn V launch. That giant rocket
rose slowly and leaned away from the launch tower and left
the Cape in thundering dignity. The *Columbia*'s solids
climbed faster. They gave *Columbia* nearly eighty percent of
her lift-off thrust. As she cleared the launch tower, thrust of
the main engines increased to 104 percent of their rated
power. The ground shook. The higher the altitude, the better
the engine performance. As fuel was used up, the vehicle was
lighter and the stack moved faster. At eleven seconds *Columbia* was rolling over in the sky onto her back before the crowd
more than three miles from the pad heard and felt the power.
At Houston, Hans Mark, as the deputy administrator desig-

nate, was a guest in Mission Control. He was captivated by the vision on the monitor.[16] Already John Young and Robert Crippen's fates were transferred to Houston as *Columbia* cleared the launch tower. Only one man had the power at the Cape to affect the mission. If he determined Houston's vehicle was out of control, then as the range safety officer it would be his job to end any danger to civilians. *Columbia* carried long-shaped explosive charges along the solid rockets and on the big external fuel tank. The orbiter itself had no explosives aboard. An arm command sent by radio would prime the explosives and a fire command would destroy *Columbia* and all aboard her if she went astray.

As *Columbia* climbed, Faget's design was next tested by Max Q. Crippen radioed that the vehicle was throttling its main engine thrust down to sixty percent at 34,000 feet. Would this bizarre looking combination of vehicle and fuel tank hold together? Crippen radioed "throttle up" and *Columbia* was through Max Q. Now the solids had to burn. When the burn pressure in the solids dropped, a ball-like socket holding them to the orbiter and external tank would build up enough force to set off eight separation motors to eject the solids away from the stack. There was no emergency escape to break the orbiter away from the solids while they were firing. Such an attempt would probably cause its immediate breakup. If the solids failed to separate, the weight would drag the shuttle back down into the sea. The main engines could not make orbit with that much dead weight. Then it happened. From the ground it seemed like an explosion. But it wasn't. At twenty-seven miles of altitude, the solids' separation was confirmed by Crippen. The fifteen-story-tall solids, looking like giant roman candles still spewing smoke, tumbled end over end until their pilot and drogue parachutes stabilized them. Three 104-foot-wide main parachutes softened their impact into the ocean. The solids landed 120 miles down range in the Atlantic. Waiting below were recovery ships to save the $20 million booster casings for another launch. All together the main engines burned for a little over eight minutes. *Columbia* achieved orbit. At the Cape the water suppression system seemed to do its job. Although Pad 39A was still smoldering, the corrosive aluminum fuel of the solids did little damage.

For the first time in U.S. history, Americans had climbed aboard an unproven rocket system and flown it. Almost instantaneously the reaction to the flight of the first reusable spaceship energized the nation. The quest for something beyond our everyday lives was touched again by NASA. What the Air Force had privately called NASA's white elephant was now in orbit. The most sophisticated vehicle ever built worked and was still in civilian hands. Beggs understood that this first flight would make the public and Congress forget about the problems that plagued the program. He saw the sixty-foot cargo bay as a truck ready to haul goods into space. It was a reality that could be driven home before the National Security Council and in the Senior Interagency Group (Space), or SIG (Space), meetings. NASA was flying again and Beggs believed that Fletcher's gamble had finally paid off.

But the color camera that showed the giant cargo bay revealed something else. Tiles were missing from the aft right orbital maneuvering pod of the shuttle. In Houston, Mark watched as concern grew. Tiles along the all-important bottom of the orbiter, which would face temperatures of 2,000 degrees, were missing. The more critical tiles had been put through a strengthening process. But the heat protection people were worried. So were Lovelace and Yardley. The Air Force offered to attempt to photograph *Columbia* with powerful new secret ground cameras. NASA accepted the offer, but the results were not detailed enough to make a judgment. The

CIA suggested using a combination of the Big Bird and Low Bird satellites for real time television transmission. But it was decided to try something revolutionary. The spy satellite, KH-11, in orbit above the shuttle would be moved in position to train its powerful sensors on *Columbia*. Crippen and Young flew with the top of *Columbia* facing earth so the big satellite had a clear shot of *Columbia*'s underbelly. The experiment had two purposes. One was to assist NASA and the other was to see how effective the intelligence agency's satellites were at observing objects in space. Although the results were top secret, NASA and CIA sources say the attempts were remarkably successful. Assured that no large sections of tiles were missing, the mission of Crippen and Young went on.

For the American public the roominess of the shuttle compared to earlier capsules was a surprise. The ship proved magnificent in space. After a little more than two days in space Young and Crippen closed the cargo bay doors and consulted their four computers to program the trip home. The shuttle's forty thrusters and main maneuvering engines positioned the *Columbia* nose forward for reentry. The engines slowed *Columbia* down and pulled her out of orbit. At 400,000 feet *Columbia* was still traveling at twenty-five times the speed of sound. The computers began to control the flight surfaces in split-second actions. At Houston and at the landing site at Edwards Air Force Base only the designers and engineers understood how much could go wrong. Nothing this big had ever been brought back to earth. As a plasma sheath of gases enveloped *Columbia*, the twelve minutes of communications blackout began. *Columbia* got hot, very hot, 1,800 degrees Fahrenheit and more on the edges of her delta wings and nose.

To dissipate the speed *Columbia* flew with its nose forty degrees above the flight path. At four times the speed of sound, the rudder replaced some of the thrusters for flight control. *Columbia* crossed the northern California coast and began the descent across the mountains into the Mojave Desert. Sonic booms were heard across the state. Hundreds of thousands of people waited at Edwards to see the world's first real spaceship return to earth. *Columbia* slipped under the speed of sound and became a glider. As her designers looked on, this unlikely airplane dropped down on to the desert floor faster than they ever imagined. At 1:21 P.M., April 14, the shuttle landed at 225 miles an hour. Engineers decided the missing tiles were caused at launch by excessive vibration. Corrections in the water suppression system were made. The first test flight of the shuttle either met or exceeded all expectations.

Two months after welcoming Crippen and Young home, and six months after Dr. Lovelace went to the congressional leadership to seek funding for the Centaur upper-stage contract for General Dynamics, Al Lovelace resigned from NASA and took a high-paying position with the defense giant. After assignments in St. Louis and Detroit, Lovelace was put in charge of Centaur development. Beggs and Mark were now in control of NASA. Another supporter of the Centaur project was brought by Beggs and Mark to headquarters, Dr. Milton A. Silveira, who would later be named NASA's chief engineer. All high-level opposition to the Centaur upper stage was now shoved aside. Beggs' and Mark's third priority was now well on the way to becoming reality.

Mark convinced Beggs to name Phil Culbertson as the number-three man in NASA. This surprised and disturbed some at the agency. Culbertson was removed during the intense struggle to complete the shuttle and forced off John Yardley's team. Instead, Culbertson was reassigned to interagency matters on behalf of Frosch. It was in that role of liaison with the military that Culbertson became close to

Hans Mark while Mark was at the Air Force. According to his book, Mark convinced Beggs that to sell a space station, NASA needed Culbertson at a high-level job.

By mid-1981 NASA faced opposition in the White House, in the Pentagon, and in the intelligence community to the proposed space station program. Keyworth says, "I will have to tell you that in spite of the fact that Hans Mark and I were sort of bred out of the same school, both close to Edward Teller, both nuclear physicists . . . Hans Mark was so oscillatory that you could only be sure of one thing. He would never take the same position twice. And I think Hans Mark became simply irrelevant very quickly. I think he was an irritant to Jim Beggs." [17]

An administration was now in power that had officials who had no use for and were openly critical of a civilian-controlled space program. One former Defense Intelligence Agency head, Gen. Daniel Graham, along with hydrogen bomb creator Dr. Edward Teller had Ronald Reagan's ear. Mark could not convince Teller to support either the shuttle or manned spaceflight aboard a space station. According to Mark, Teller told him that automated systems and robotics on an automated platform were much more useful and that man would simply be a vulnerable and tempting target in space. For Mark, who had studied under Teller, this was particularly hard to take. Shortly after taking over, Beggs was aware that the "black" Air Force was getting increasing support and attention. But he did not know that the president's commitment to space would not be to a project of peaceful exploration by a civilian agency, but to the most massive military weapons system ever conceived by man. While Beggs' people were trying to figure out how to keep a manned program of large proportions going on a tight budget, defense planners were already looking at the civil program's budget as a possible source of revenue to feed into what would become the "Star Wars" cauldron.

Just as Beggs was sworn into office, the Pentagon once again played the Vandenberg card and announced that the shuttle facility would not become operational until 1985, a year later than scheduled.[18] Beggs and Mark decided that to keep the Air Force on the shuttle, they would try to make some concessions that might garner more cooperation. But Beggs found himself hamstrung. As Beggs tried to acquiesce to the Air Force, he said he found "they kept saying, 'We want a robust system.' And I never understood what that meant. And they said, 'We want assured launch capability.' And that was a code word for having several different systems in several different places. But that is a fallacy because the problem with any of these launch vehicles is that they all sit on the coasts and that they are all within the range of a submarine or a small boat slipping in at night. Once you have erected the damn thing on the stand, it is very vulnerable. It could be knocked out in a minute and you don't need much to knock it out. All you need is a machine gun really or a high-powered rifle," Beggs explains.[19]

To compound NASA's troubles, Air Force officials now were saying that delays in the shuttle program could endanger national security. This accusation infuriated Beggs. The Air Force now wanted to keep buying their Titan rockets as an alternative to the shuttle system. There was no comparison between the shuttle and the Titan, the Air Force's principal launch vehicle. Originally the rocket was designed to be an ICBM and to launch Gemini spacecraft for NASA. Titan evolved into a more powerful booster, Titan III, with solids combined with main liquid boosters for a bigger lift capacity. But even a modified Titan with a 20,000-pound lift capacity was still a twenty-five-year-old, uneconomical design by today's standards. However, the entire Air Force space program of spy satellites was based on missiles of that same generation. The Titan was also very expensive to maintain and keeping the production line open was costly to the Air Force. But at least the Air Force had total control over Titan.

The Air Force wanted to buy the Titans, Beggs says, "so they could bail out of the shuttle. And once they were off the shuttle—and this is a very involved strategy, and I think they had thought it out—once they were off the shuttle, the program would go down the tubes."[20] Beggs believed the Air Force was convinced the shuttle's fate rested on a three-legged stool. One leg was the DOD launches, another the commercial launches, and the third was the scientific payloads. According to Beggs, the Air Force thinking went this way. "Without one of these three legs the stool would fall over. . . . You needed all three to make it economically viable. So what the military figured, if we can take all the military payloads off the shuttle, it will collapse of its own weight. Then we'll take it over. We've got to because we are the only ones. Once everybody's back on ELVs, the shuttle will be just an experimental vehicle and we'll do what we always do with NASA experimental vehicles, we'll take it over."

To get off the shuttle and still maintain their "assured access to space," the DOD needed to make the ELVs economically feasible to produce. The Air Force demanded that a "fairer" shuttle pricing policy be set, and proposed that NASA charge the staggering price of $120 million for a shuttle flight. This high price would allow contractors to build and sell ELVs for less than a ride on the shuttle. It would also bring a quick end to subsidies of the shuttle system. The DOD could then say flying on ELVs was cheaper and begin purchasing expendable boosters again. Because the Pentagon's contracts would start up the ELV production lines, the government would be subsidizing the development costs of private ELV businesses for commercial customers who wanted to put up observation and communications satellites. This action, in turn, would take commercial business away from the shuttle. The Pentagon proposal threatened not one, but two legs of the wobbling shuttle stool.

While the pricing struggle continued, Beggs tried to convince the Pentagon not to purchase the old Titan technology but to let NASA help them upgrade and modernize their booster fleet. Beggs and his engineers knew that a Saturn V class vehicle was needed and they had an answer. What Beggs wanted was an unmanned variant of the shuttle nicknamed "big dumb booster." Titan's 20,000-pound lift capacity would be dwarfed by this booster that would be able to launch 250,000 pounds to low earth orbit. The shuttle's orbiter weighed 100 tons without fuel and payloads. NASA would remove that weight from the rocket stack and replace it with a lighter, unmanned payload carrier. Since the carrier would not have to return from space or protect humans, the payload capacity would be increased to more than four times what a shuttle could carry. Because the machine would be unmanned, it was dubbed "big dumb booster." But the Air Force wanted no part of another NASA program that was out of their control. Beggs says Aldridge and other Air Force officials opposed the new booster because it would enhance the future of the shuttle fleet—something the Air Force did not want and something Beggs says he could not understand. "It has the charm of once you have designed the thing and use it, then the two systems complement each other so you are drawing off the same production lines. You can use the same launch crew and you can use the same launchpads," argues Beggs. He insists such a system would have made the entire shuttle system much more economically feasible, "and that is exactly why they did not want it."

But Beggs and Mark had other worries. The space station they were trying to sell would take much longer to assemble in space with only the shuttle to launch its elements into orbit. If NASA could build the new dumb booster, the space station could be erected much more quickly. As Beggs and Mark looked to the future they realized what Fletcher had traded for the shuttle in 1972. The giant Vehicle Assembly Building and the lunar mobile launchers at the Kennedy Space Center were converted for the shuttles. Today, at the visitors center, there is a model of the VAB with the shuttle on one mobile launcher dwarfed by the Saturn V on another. Perhaps that simple comparison sums up the downgrading of the entire space program that began under Fletcher.

But Beggs' real worries about the survival of the shuttle program centered on the White House and OMB. Pressure was coming from David Stockman to justify the shuttle system economically and commercially. The $100-a-pound launch figure that Oskar Morganstern projected was not even remotely accurate. The real costs were thousands of dollars a pound. But instead of treating the shuttle as an experimental and extremely complicated new Space Transportation System, according to nearly the entire senior management at NASA, Beggs and Mark decided to push the shuttle through its development program in only four flights. Succumbing to pressures from the White House and Capitol Hill, NASA decided to begin carrying paying customers as soon as possible. Frosch and Yardley's warnings went unheeded. Mark wrote in a draft of his book about his career at NASA, "We had to fulfill the promise that NASA made when the shuttle program started in 1972. Although the first flight of *Columbia* in April demonstrated that the shuttle was technically a success, we still had to prove it was operationally successful. This meant that we had to show we could meet the flight schedules and payload requirements demanded by the users of the launch services provided by the shuttle. We also had to learn to control the operational costs."

To appease the White House and the Pentagon, Beggs named an old associate to replace John Yardley, Maj. Gen. James Abrahamson. Beggs knew Abrahamson from his role in developing the F-16 fighter, which General Dynamics built. Abrahamson wore his military rank lightly and mixed easily with civilians. Beggs, though skeptical of the Air Force's motives, believed that if a military man were running the shuttle program, the Pentagon might be convinced of the shuttle's strategic importance. As for Abrahamson, there was no question about his interest in spaceflight. He was an Air Force astronaut in the defunct Manned Orbiting Laboratory (MOL) that was killed in large part because of NASA's effectiveness. Many of the MOL astronauts transferred to the civilian program, but not Abrahamson. His career took him in and out of the netherworld of the secret or "black" Air Force. His arrival at the shuttle program was seen by some veterans of the agency as going beyond the NASA tradition of borrowing a military man for a civilian assignment. Many old NASA hands, already fearful of flying military missions, became convinced that the manned program was now fully in Pentagon hands.

Some at NASA referred to Abrahamson as the Al Haig for the 1980s. As associate administrator for spaceflight, Abrahamson took control of day-to-day shuttle operations. For many at NASA it was simply one more concession to the military to keep the shuttle program going. But Abrahamson's appointment freed Beggs and Mark to pursue the goal of a space station. Despite growing White House opposition both men persisted. According to Mark, Beggs' strategy was to direct all of NASA's efforts to convince President Reagan personally of the value of the space station. The first opportunity for NASA to lobby the president came courtesy of Chris Kraft in Houston. As the countdown continued for the second launch, STS-2, Kraft read in the local paper that the president and George Bush would be in Houston during the spaceflight. Kraft told Mark that it would be wise to invite the president to the Johnson Space Center so that he could observe the operations during a flight and talk to the astronauts. At 9 A.M. on November 12, 1981, Joe Engle and Richard Truly became the first men to fly a used spaceship. That afternoon a faulty fuel cell caused Houston to cut the mission short by three days. The next evening the president visited Mission Control. Beggs used his flight on Air Force One from Washington as well as the forty minutes the president spent in Mission Control to lobby for the space program, especially a new space station. Reagan spoke to the crew. He seemed truly interested in space and Mark and Beggs now thought they could convince Reagan to build the space station.

While even Abrahamson could not sell the strategic value of the shuttle to the uniformed Air Force, CIA reports showed that the Soviets considered the shuttle the United States' "most important strategic space asset in terms of surveillance capability and emergency deployment." On STS-2 an experiment having nothing to do with the military would prove the Soviets right. It was added to *Columbia*'s manifest as a last-minute experiment. Its addition to the flight plan seemed like a minor event to those in the program. A group of Jet Propulsion Laboratory and NASA scientists were told that instead of flying ballast to fill the cargo bay, there would be room for an experiment. Using old electronics, some of it left over from the Apollo program, Brooten Schardie, a scientist with NASA's Office of Space Terrestrial Applications, designed the OSTA I experiment. Using a relatively primitive optical recorder, the experiment was supposed to be a simple geological survey using ground-imaging radar. The shuttle, with its open cargo bay facing earth and its optical recorders running, sent radar beams to the Sahara desert below. When the ship returned and the images of Schardie's experiments were processed, the roads and streets of an ancient city buried by the sands of the Sahara were revealed. A lost civilization was discovered. The military implications were immediate. The data collected through the radar demonstrated that the shuttle was a remarkably steady platform and that sensors and cameras mounted on the 122-foot-long ship would be free from the vibration and buffeting smaller satellites suffer. The shuttle itself, manned by a crew to control her movements, was an extraordinary observation platform more stable than even the planned $1 billion Keyhole 12 spy satellite. The reality of the shuttle's military importance was feared by the Soviets and nearly ignored by the U.S. Air Force. According to CIA sources, funding for the Soviet program increased dramatically. A copycat version of the shuttle was put into production. The Soviets, realizing they did not have the technology to build the shuttle's reusable engines, sacrificed the reusable boosters, both liquid and solid, just to get an orbiter into space. Among the information that U.S. intelligence picked up on the Soviet program was that a "big dumb booster" was being built by the Russians. For the Soviets, still lacking the ultimate in "look-down" technology, a shuttle system was extremely important.

For Beggs the difficulties with the White House and the Department of Defense were growing. Keyworth, the White House science adviser, was not satisfied with the space station as NASA's next manned space adventure. He demanded that NASA submit bigger and more challenging programs. For the preliminary studies to determine the type of space station NASA would request, Beggs called upon former NASA Administrator James Fletcher to chair the space station selection panel. As Fletcher and Low did with the shuttle, Beggs and Mark were creating a major program for NASA without benefit of national debate or presidential leadership. Beggs says he wanted to prepare real options for the president to choose from. In fact, the new administration was drafting quite a startling space policy without his help. A space policy that would tie the civil and military programs closer together than ever before.

Keyworth constantly denounced Beggs and Mark for their lack of imagination. "I think in contrast to what people say, Jim Beggs is a straightforward and honest man. But he is a man whose perceptions and strategies are designed to avoid losing and he was working for a president who only understands strategies to win. Jim came to me with Hans Mark in early 1981 . . . the only time the two of them agreed on anything. It was their notorious three ring sign. . . . They [the rings] represent one-third of the American people who believe we have spent enough in space, one-third who believe we have spent too much, and one-third who would like to see us spend less. And they said, 'This is precarious and the challenge is to keep one-third of the people in support.' And I said, 'You guys, this is nonsense. You have got a president who just believes in everything the space program represents let alone the space program itself. Opportunities are galore here.'"[21] Keyworth says he told Beggs and Mark that Americans better understood and supported technology than the three rings indicated and they were missing an opportunity for broad support. Mark denies that he ever discussed the "three ring" theory with Keyworth, but others at NASA remember similar comments from Mark. Keyworth says his concern about the space station was that it was "first and foremost a motel in the sky for astronauts. It was not a step toward something that was of comparable magnitude to Apollo. It was not something that captured a major investment or increased public support for the space program." To Keyworth the space station as proposed by Beggs was a repeat of Skylab and not a "worthy venture twenty years later for the United States of America." Keyworth says he made every effort to get Beggs to be more aggressive. "I begged Jim. I practically got down on my hands and knees. I bought him innumerable lunches." What Keyworth says he wanted from Beggs was a massive program to return to the moon with a manned base and preparations for a trip to Mars.

Beggs did not enjoy being put in the position of being negative about manned flight, but he believed that Keyworth was part of a much bigger problem in the Reagan administration. "This was all part of the original scheme of the CIA, DOD, Jay Keyworth, and quite a number of floaters around the White House who were trying to see if they could kill off any potential program. . . . And the way they thought they could do it was [to] try to get me and Hans and others to come out strongly and request some grandiose program like a Mars mission or even a return to the moon. . . . Then the president would say, 'Well, you know, price it out.' Which we would do and it would cost $50 billion and that would be that. It would be all over," Beggs explains.[22]

Beggs and Mark began a major sales effort to try to solicit support from other government agencies for a space station. "We started out that way. The strategy we employed . . . was let's try to involve the military. Let's try to get the intelligence folks interested. And let's see what we can do to stir up some foreign interest. So we had effectively three strings in the bow. And, of course, we tried to get our own scientists, our own constituency, to come along. That was a hard sell because most of the scientists who work with the agency [NASA] are not very impressed with manned activities," Beggs advises. Beggs was frustrated by the scientific community because he felt, "they don't understand the politics of it and they consider it a competitor for funds, which was unfortunate. Because the plain facts are if there weren't a manned program they wouldn't get as much as they are getting now."

Mark convinced Beggs that despite their frayed relations with the Pentagon, perhaps a space station might be more appealing than the shuttle or the "big dumb booster." But Beggs found another stonewall. "They didn't want to get trapped into the commitment again. And they looked at it in another respect. They looked at it as a competitor for funds. They said, 'If that money goes into the space station . . . if they should spend money on that, money will not be available for what we would like to do in space.' And that's bull. . . . These things aren't mutually exclusive. If NASA doesn't get the money, the money won't go to the military. And, in fact, the president made two decisions almost simultaneously. He was considering the space station and Star Wars," Beggs recalls.

The decision Beggs and Mark made to build a permanently manned space station had a profound effect on the shuttle. At Rockwell in Palmdale, California, three more shuttles were in varying stages of construction. By the end of 1981, *Challenger* was nearly complete and was only seven months away from delivery. *Discovery* and *Atlantis* would be delivered in the next two years. Rockwell would soon have to tell many of the subcontractors for the shuttle to shut down various production facilities. Congress and the Air Force expressed great interest in building a fifth orbiter before the production lines closed. Fears that one of the shuttles could be damaged or destroyed prompted much of the support. And the Air Force needed the newer, lighter-weight shuttles for most of their missions. If NASA ordered a fifth orbiter during 1982, the cost would only be in the range of $1.2 billion. But if the production lines were shut down and an orbiter was ordered later, the costs could double or triple. Rockwell, of course, was up on Capitol Hill lobbying to keep the production lines open. Many members of Congress wanted a fifth orbiter. James Abrahamson was not a happy man when he was told to stall as the Congress pressured for a fifth orbiter. Beggs wanted enough time to get approval for the space station. If he could not get the money for both, the funds needed to expand the shuttle fleet to five would be used for the space station. As 1981 ended, NASA devised a scheme to keep the Palmdale production line open by ordering spare parts for the shuttle fleet. Robert Allnut, then associate administrator for external affairs, says that Beggs and Mark never intended to build a fifth orbiter. "Beggs undertook to do two things while he was administrator. One was to move the shuttle into routine operational status and the other was to sell the space station, which meant he had to get the president to do that. So there were a series of opportunities created, media events at each of which, some while I was there and some after I left, where the profound hope was the president would end up doing this. . . . That was the real goal, not the fifth orbiter," says Allnut.[23]

Meanwhile at Morton Thiokol and the Marshall Space Flight Center, the recovered solid rockets from the second shuttle flight went through their refurbishment process. Almost as an afterthought, technicians and engineers noticed some charring of the huge rubber gaskets that help seal the segments of the giant solid rocket motors together. The gaskets were known as O-rings. Routine examination reports were filed at Marshall. Washington was not notified.

9

The Contractors and the Congress

RAY SENA WAS THE FIRST WHO NOTICED IT. HIS FELLOW employees at Rockwell were working on a military satellite system for the Pentagon. When they turned in their time cards, the hours would be charged to NASA. When he asked his supervisors about it, Sena was told that the contract for a Global Positioning Satellite for the Air Force was over budget. Under the terms of the Air Force contract, the company would have to absorb the loss. But the contracts with NASA allowed profits after all costs were added in. As later reported in the press, by charging the hours off to the Space Shuttle account, Rockwell would not lose a dime. Sena turned over evidence of the charge-offs to the FBI. Rockwell fired him.[1]

In November 1982 the Reagan administration sent a message to DOD and NASA contractors. After investigating Sena's charges, the Justice Department sent no one to jail. The government settled out of court with Rockwell for $1.5

million. But according to Sena, that incident was not the end of the scandal. At Rockwell's Palmdale facility there is a bigger production line than the shuttle's. It belongs to the B-1 bomber. In 1977 President Carter cancelled the B-1 bomber. But, mysteriously, work continued on the project. Sena wondered where the money came from to keep the line going. His co-workers told him that the work was paid for out of the Space Shuttle account. Their time cards were charged to NASA. Dina Razor, director of the Project on Military Procurement, explains what Sena says took place. "It appears the Space Shuttle money had been used to keep the B-1 bomber alive since its cancellation in 1977 and has hidden the true cost of the airplane."

Rockwell's gamble paid off. President Reagan reversed Carter's decision on the B-1. In the four years between the two decisions, major systems improvements were made on the B-1. Razor points out that the government had estimated the cost of each B-1 at $270 million. But Rockwell won congressional approval by underbidding that figure by $70 million a plane. Razor says she is convinced the lower bids were made possible by charge-offs to the Space Shuttle, charge-offs that could also account for many of the cost overruns the shuttle program was experiencing during that same period.

Former NASA General Counsel Paul Dembling says such behavior was not unusual among contractors. "I think many times it isn't even top management that tells them to do these things. I think it is a guy who had a budget [and] wants to show that he's doing a good job. This is what happens usually. And I've done enough with government contracts to see that the guy who's the project manager or the program manager . . . wants to bring stuff in under budget. He wants to show his bosses he's doing well. He makes adjustments. . . . He fudges a little. . . ."[2]

And Dembling should know. First as NACA general

counsel and later as Jim Webb's, Dembling had a front-row seat in the drama that is the politics of space. As space became commercial, Dembling became the expert. He became a hired gun. He hung out his shingle as a wizard in space law. Dembling was not seen as just a technician of law, but as somebody who knew the secrets, who understood the meaning of the answers. After all, he had worked with those who began it all. In 1982 Dembling saw NASA as an agency that had become impotent. NASA simply no longer had the money or clout that gave it the power to perform its old successes. Dembling remembers how the NASA he worked for managed the programs. "You didn't have to hire anybody at NASA. Everybody who ran those programs knew them well enough so that they could say to a contractor, 'Damn it, you're screwing up on this thing. Here's the way you've got to correct it. Or here's what you want and here's the way you have got to build it.' . . . That was the big difference."

In Dembling's day the space agency had the ability to discover contractor fraud and abuse and do something about it. NASA had the clout to threaten offending corporations with the loss of all NASA contracts like Webb did with Rockwell after the Apollo 204 fire. But under the Reagan administration attitudes were different. So many administration officials had ties to government contractors it was almost impossible to keep track. Two key shuttle allies in the White House were close to Rockwell. Then Cabinet Secretary Craig Fuller once represented Rockwell, and Michael Deaver, a top White House official who frequently discussed space matters with Beggs, also had connections with the conglomerate. In fact, when Deaver left the White House he wound up representing Rockwell on the B-1. So for the new administration, Rockwell's slap on the wrist for the shuttle charge-off was business as usual and that atmosphere seemed to be typical.

By 1982 the elaborate system that Jim Webb installed to

make certain favoritism did not affect NASA contracts was all but gone. Webb had attempted to isolate NASA's technical people from political pressure with complicated contractor selection procedures. One by one these rules were stripped away. To complicate matters, NASA executives were going into industry jobs and back to NASA at increasing rates. It became increasingly difficult for a technical person to confront a contractor when the contractor was represented by a former NASA official who could return at any time as his boss.

Beggs was just such a boss. He left NASA, wheeled and dealed when he was with General Dynamics with the people he worked with at NASA, and now he was back. Like Fletcher, Beggs wanted his name attached to a big project. In Beggs' case it was the space station. He and Hans Mark started pushing a space station design that the manned space staff in Houston called shortsighted and dangerous. The Johnson Space Center staff disliked the design because it required astronauts to work out in space for even the most routine of servicing. Extra-vehicular activity can be very dangerous. This design conflict arose because Beggs followed in the footsteps of Fletcher and Low and turned over the project to the Marshall and Johnson field centers, which had been rivals for a generation. The designs the two centers proposed were not compatible. With little management from Washington, the two centers jockeyed for power over the station.

To veterans in both centers the $8 billion figure for the huge station seemed like a fairy tale. The relatively simple European Spacelab, which remains in the shuttle's cargo bay, cost a billion dollars to develop. Now Beggs was promising the White House that NASA could develop a full-scale space station with working, sleeping, and scientific quarters, that produced its own electrical power, and put it in high orbit for $8 billion.

As Beggs was trying to get the president to endorse the space station, George Keyworth was openly attempting to force Beggs to relinquish control of the entire shuttle fleet to the Air Force. Beggs understood all too well that the shuttle represented the only power base NASA still had. But Keyworth made no secret about what he was telling the president. "I was certainly an advocate for saying that we should get the shuttle operationally in the hands of the Air Force as soon as we possibly can. . . . The main reason I had for that was simple. It is because whatever one can say about the military . . . they are good at logistics. And they are better than NASA at operational responsibilities." And Keyworth says he was not alone. "Everybody agreed. You know NASA's clever technique. Everybody agreed it should be turned over to the Air Force," Keyworth insists.[3] Keyworth describes Beggs' strategy. "NASA's approach was to say well certainly we think the Air Force should operate the shuttle. But it won't be operational until around 1988, the last year if the president were elected twice. Remember this was well before '84. So it was to delay it until it was so far down the road they did not have to worry about it anymore. Then each year they would add two more to it. So it was to procrastinate," Keyworth says.

Since Beggs was outnumbered among his political colleagues, he realized it would be political suicide to take on Keyworth and other White House staffers publicly. Beggs did not want to give his enemies an excuse to marshall more support for their position. He was already finding that the Heritage Foundation and other ultraconservative think-tank organizations were echoing Keyworth's arguments. Despite his troubles, Beggs had two things going for him. The shuttle was an enormous public success and the president of the United States liked him and liked space.

Beggs kept up his effort to sell the space station and pressured his managers to make the shuttle a viable commercial rocket system as quickly as possible. He remained convinced that a successful shuttle program would build congressional and public support for his space station efforts. Eventually such a record would force the military to cooperate. Beggs tried to help push the military on board the space station by courting the Air Force's most important satellite customer— the CIA. Hans Mark convinced Beggs that if the CIA could be persuaded to sign on to the space station as a participant, even a secret one, the Pentagon might feel obliged to follow. Beggs understood CIA Director William Casey's fascination with gadgets. And in Beggs' view there was no more ultimate gadget than the proposed space station.

But Beggs failed. "It could . . . have been a case of the bureaucrats just deciding that they didn't want to buy into this program because it wasn't their idea. You know, the CIA is funny that way. It's a big 'not invented here' house. And we tried. I spent a lot of time working on them. As a matter of fact, I took several of the astronauts out to brief them on what they observed. . . . And they would 'ohhh' and 'ahhh,' but we just never got anywhere with them," Beggs remembers.[4] Keyworth says Beggs' space observation proposals were nonsense and Casey understood that. "Anything that's manned can't give you good resolution because men move. When you're trying to get the kind of resolution that we believe in for imagery from space, you'd better not have anybody tromping around. It's got to be absolutely stable. But I don't believe Beggs ever understood the classified part of the space program," Keyworth says.[5]

While Beggs was trying a more conventional approach to bringing the intelligence community on board the shuttle, the irrepressible Mark created a minor firestorm with his sales pitch. According to Keyworth, in a visit to Senator John Warner (R-Virginia), Mark tried to demonstrate the value of men observing from space. "Hans Mark actually went around the Hill showing people a SEASAT picture of a strip in the ocean saying we see submarines. Now look, in order to hustle something in space he is willing, without any compunction, to threaten the whole U.S. submarine program. The last arm of the triad we have that is really viable," Keyworth says. Mark defended his actions. "Yeah, I thought it would be a good idea to fly some experienced Navy pilots and have them look for wakes and I did promote that."

Mark's and Beggs' third goal of building a high-energy upper stage for the shuttle began to run into problems. Beggs says he became suspicious that the Air Force, which was developing the Inertial Upper Stage (IUS) for the shuttle, was deliberately slowing the IUS program as an excuse to get off the shuttle. At the same time Mark was trying to gather support for the more powerful Centaur upper stage among congressmen and others at NASA on the grounds that it was needed for mysterious national security missions. Bill Lilly, who retired from NASA but continued as a consultant to Beggs, even got a visit from Mark in his Alexandria, Virginia, home. Mark urged Lilly to look at some secret missions for which the Air Force needed the Centaur. "I didn't look at them. I just didn't believe [him]. He was lobbying to get me to support him in this nonsense," Lilly remembers.[6] But Mark shared the Soviets' belief that a manned vehicle like the shuttle was a strategically vital deployment and observation system and he believed the Centaur upper stage would help bring military opponents around to his way of thinking.

The fight over the upper stage typified congressional ignorance of NASA's day-to-day programs. Three times in three years Congress let NASA switch between the solid-fueled Boeing Inertial Upper Stage (IUS) and the liquid-fueled General Dynamics' Centaur for their missions. For General Dynamics, 1982 was a fine time to lobby for its Centaur upper stage. It was an election year and the Centaur production line was beginning to slowly draw to an end. Unless a new shuttle version was approved, the profitable rocket stage would be eliminated. "I know that we informed people. . . . the front end of the Centaur production line had gone cold. . . . I think that there were Centaurs in the final phase of production around the time of the . . . decision on that. But there weren't many in the pipeline," recalls Chris Hansen who was a General Dynamics lobbyist at the time. Senators and congressmen up for reelection were key to the Centaur's survival. New Mexico's Senator Harrison "Jack" Schmidt, a scientist and former astronaut, was chairman of NASA's Senate Oversight subcommittee and faced a tough reelection race. On the other side of Capitol Hill, the House of Representative's Space Subcommittee's ranking member, Harold "Cap" Hollenbeck, also faced a tough campaign. Both men were Republicans and friendly to NASA, and both men were considered backbenchers in Congress.

The committees that controlled NASA during the Apollo days were led by the giants of Congress like Congressman "Tiger" Teague and Senator Robert Kerr. But with the decline in NASA's budget and influence and the weakening of the congressional seniority system, space was relegated to relatively minor subcommittees. The only senators or congressmen who sought assignments on these subcommittees were largely the ones who had either contractors or NASA facilities in their state or congressional district. Hollenbeck explains the reasons: "Teague was ailing and he let jurisdiction slip. The committee was important in the beginning when Teague had it, but it was only important because circumstances made it important, money and the visibility of the original space program. The importance of a committee is determined by what jurisdiction it has. And Teague, because he was ailing and the new, more modern legislators were coming in 1972 and 1974, lost a lot of jurisdiction to the Commerce Committee. He even lost patents to the Judiciary Committee. When I first went on the committee it was low in the pecking order. The congressmen didn't want to pay a lot of attention to it. There had been no manned flight in six years which decreased NASA's visibility. Just look at the makeup of the committee. Look how many younger guys are very senior."[7] Neither Hollenbeck, from northern New Jersey, nor Schmidt represented many NASA contractors. But Schmidt, a former Apollo scientist, owed his fame to NASA.

Schmidt garnered a reputation for not paying enough attention to local issues in his home state. His opponent's campaign slogan, "What on earth has he ever done for us?" was proving effective. It also echoed Schmidt's less well-known nickname in the Senate, "Moonrock." Schmidt's unwavering support for the Centaur drew no support from the White House or Keyworth. "We tried to resist it. . . . Any man who a few weeks before his election was frantically trying to get 90 million federal dollars for a copper mine in New Mexico. . . I guess that's the standard in politics, but I find it pretty repulsive. The guy is a flake," asserts then Science Adviser Keyworth.[8]

Hollenbeck had just as serious political problems. New Jersey lost population in the 1980 census and was losing a congressional district. Unfortunately for Hollenbeck, the Democrats succeeded in removing sixty percent of his district and replaced it with solidly Democratic towns. From General Dynamics' perspective neither man could afford not to support Centaur. Both Hollenbeck and Schmidt received large campaign contributions from General Dynamics. Centaur lobbyist Chris Hansen was even a member of Hollenbeck's reelection finance committee.

But Hollenbeck started to make waves and he made them publicly. He realized how important the civil space program was to the emotional health of the country when he saw the reaction of his son to the launch of *Columbia*. Hollenbeck began to get deeply involved in NASA issues. And he began to ask questions of his Space Subcommittee staffer, Jeff Irons. "Nineteen eighty-one was a very slow year on the subcommittee after the shuttle launch. I did not pay enough attention to the staff work. In 1982 I began to realize that instead of keeping an arms-length relationship with NASA and the contractors, Jeff would tell them everything I was looking at in advance. He was listening to them more than listening to me. Jeff always wanted to avoid controversy with the contractors. He was an engineer and wanted to go on to an aerospace job on the outside," Hollenbeck remembers.[9] But Hollenbeck did not know that Irons applied for work with General Dynamics *before* he landed a job on the subcommittee.[10]

To the chagrin of the White House, the Department of Defense, and many of his colleagues on the committee, the normally complacent Hollenbeck began demanding answers and complaining openly about concessions from NASA to the Pentagon. Hollenbeck was getting frustrated over the lack of oversight and requested a hearing on whether NASA should purchase a fifth orbiter. Hollenbeck, who thought he had a good relationship with Beggs, could not get an answer from NASA on whether they needed the fifth orbiter or not. He had no idea that Beggs was sacrificing the fifth orbiter to get the space station. On June 15, 1982, to the surprise of many, Hollenbeck asked searing questions at the subcommittee hearings, questions that neither Irons nor NASA had been asked before. "The fifth orbiter, that was the hearing where I wrote my own questions. [Congressman] Ray McGrath [R-New York] likes a fight. He thought those questions were great. I can remember the look on Abrahamson's face was like holy shit where did this guy come from. . . . And NASA wouldn't say if they wanted a fifth orbiter. They wouldn't say who would pay for one. They wouldn't say who would use it," Hollenbeck relates.

The following Saturday in Teterboro, New Jersey, Hollenbeck hosted "Space Day" for his constituents. Thousands turned out to the big Atlantic Aviation hangar. There was no question in Hollenbeck's mind where the American public stood on space. He gave a powerful speech to the unexpectedly large crowd. He said, "On next week's flight a secret military cargo aboard *Columbia* will limit the use of live television. For the first time our space program must worry about being less than open. The question of the decade may be whether we use the shuttle for peace or for war. Now that the shuttle works, the military has climbed aboard the bandwagon. The gauntlet is down. The battle will be to save the civilian agency that brought us to the moon and beyond. I promise you that there are fights ahead and unless we Americans are vigilant, the civilian space program could be swallowed up in the giant whale called the Pentagon." The Hollenbeck speech and the controversy at the hearing were played as part of an NBC report that wrapped around the coverage of the first shuttle launch with a military payload. Remarkably, few other congressmen spoke out against the militarization of the space program.

But Hollenbeck did not let up. He had waited for over a year for the new administration's space policy. Keyworth, not Beggs, was drafting it. James Fanseen, who worked as NASA's White House liaison, coordinated the arrangements for a dramatic announcement of the new policy by the president. Arrangements were made to have President and Mrs. Reagan welcome *Columbia* home on July 4, 1982, at Edwards Air Force Base. NASA went all out to provide a sensational backdrop. The *Enterprise* would be parked behind the president. And the newest shuttle, *Challenger*, would be located nearby, poised on the modified Boeing 747 to fly to the Kennedy Space Center for her maiden voyage.

According to Hans Mark's manuscript, the president's visit fit perfectly into Beggs' plan to enlist the president's personal support for the space station. But on June 30, Mark was informed that the president would not endorse the space station in his space policy speech at Edwards. According to Keyworth, Beggs had angered the White House by telling reporters that the president would announce the space station in his speech. "The president was angry. Ed Meese was angry. Jim Baker was angry. Mike Deaver was angry. I was angry, and Bill Clark was angry. You don't function very well when you make everyone angry," observes Keyworth.

As scheduled, on the Fourth of July, Beggs introduced the president and Reagan made his speech. The speech was full of generalities. Simultaneously the White House press office made public the new (and mostly classified) space policy.[11] In retrospect Keyworth believed the Reagan space policy that his office drafted was a failure and there was little need to make much of it secret. But Keyworth is proud of the damaging blow to Beggs that he succeeded in incorporating into the new policy. For the first time in almost a decade, Keyworth managed to get expendable launch vehicles (ELVs) inserted into official policy as an alternative to the shuttle. He claims he did it because it was obvious what could happen. "We don't talk about these things publicly, but . . . we perceived that someday someone could very well be killed on the shuttle. . . . And we knew that despite all the critical military assets that we needed to put up, we were not going to send up a shuttle [after an accident] until we've analyzed [it] twenty-five times over. We had estimated a minimum of a two-year delay."[12]

Keyworth kept the door open for the Air Force to buy

Titans and Beggs lost another round to the military. The Pentagon by keeping ELV production lines open presented another problem for Beggs. The contractors could also sell their rockets to private businesses for civilian commercial use. Two of the three strings in the shuttle bow—military and commercial payloads—were beginning to unravel after the July fourth policy statement.

In Congress, Hollenbeck was furious when he learned of the new policy. He asked California Congressman George Brown to request full committee hearings on the new space policy. On August 4, 1982, the hearing room was packed. George Keyworth was the lead witness. Alabama Congressman Ronnie Flippo chaired the hearings. After brief opening remarks, Flippo yielded to Hollenbeck. No one expected Hollenbeck to take a tough stand. The crowd sat in silence as Hollenbeck said:

> NASA, with its rich history, its great accomplishments has been turned into a situation-comedy father. Like its TV counterpart, it is snickered at because its wallet is bled by ungrateful children, but its quiet good nature seems endless. The tragedy is the American people are not aware of the politicizing and militarizing of the civilian space agency. The Congress and the press have failed to do their jobs. How depressing it is to know that America's space policy for the 1990's is classified "Top Secret." How frustrating it is to know that we have made the decision to cloak space in national security. We have abandoned openness and now we take the policy of the Soviet Union as our own. We now hide a program that made its reputation in front of the eyes of the world. . . . The arrogance of this administration, of the military, and of some of the contractors

toward a civilian agency that accomplished so much does not go unnoticed . . . I speak for a strong civilian space program not simply to annoy those that now run NASA, but because it was a civilian-run team that put us on the moon, that did it in budget, and that made damn few excuses. I, for one, do not want a gold-plated space program that is part of some Star Wars Pentagon. . . . I can only hope the next generation of Americans will not look back upon those of us here today as the leaders who sat in silence as America turned a noble endeavor into an interstellar war machine. President Kennedy was once asked the difference between the Atlas rocket that could destroy Moscow and the one that orbited John Glenn. He answered: "Attitude." We went into space as a new frontier and now we drag the hate and the bitterness of earth into the heavens as if it is the right of man to make war everyplace. We need a good and brave leadership who will stand up and say, "Enough!" The greed machine of contractors, revolving-door jobs, the endless excuses to build more military hardware now is being applied to virgin territory. What we are talking about is not national security. What we are talking about is big bucks. Big bucks that can be spent without the glare of the press or congressional oversight because the government can invoke the magical phrase, "national security." The space policy of the Reagan administration is a national tragedy. It is ill-conceived and endangers our children's future. How pathetic our oversight has been. We fall short in our ability to get the truth. The goodwill that was space is gone. The NASA that set sail on this new sea is a romantic memory.[13]

But Hollenbeck paid the price for his outspokenness. That month the United Nations was holding a conference on space in Vienna, Austria, called Unispace. Hollenbeck explains what happened. "The United Nation's Conference on Space was on the peaceful uses of space. And ordinarily the delegates would be the top two members of the Science Committee and then sort of down the pecking order in terms of seniority. One day at a hearing Larry Winn, the top Republican on the committee, came to me and said, 'I'm not going to that U.N. conference so you would be next in line.' And I didn't say anything. I didn't commit or anything like that. So then a couple of days later he came back to me and he said, 'Well, listen, I've got to talk to you man to man because you're next in line to go to the Unispace thing. Now if you want to go I think you ought to go to [Congressman] Bob Michael [the Republican leader of the House of Representatives] and I think you ought to raise some hell . . . because you got blackballed. . . . The administration doesn't want you to go.' And I said, 'Well, why not?' And he said, 'Apparently because of your views on the peaceful uses of outer space,' which were to use it peacefully, right? [Winn continued:] 'And because of speeches you made about the Pentagon.' And I said, 'Who are they going to send?' [Congressman] Ray McGrath [R-New York] and [Congressman] Bill Lowery [R-California] were on the Space Subcommittee with me. And I said, 'Are you going to send one of them?' And he said, 'No, Bill Carney.' [Congressman] Bill Carney [R-New York] [while] on the committee itself at the time, was way, way down in seniority. He wasn't even on the Space Subcommittee. And, of course, Carney was a supporter basically of weapons in space. And he went. But at any rate that's the first time I guess you would say you knew you were blackballed. I was disgusted by the whole thing," Hollenbeck recalls.

The Republican leadership had good reason not to want

Hollenbeck at the U.N. meeting in 1982. According to those who attended the Vienna conference, while foreign delegations discussed the peaceful uses of space in the official meeting rooms, secret rump sessions were taking place in restaurants and hotel rooms. Representatives from contractors were lobbying for a space-based weapons program. For the first time the "Star Wars" idea was being internationally floated by the contractors.

But Hollenbeck ignored the snub and continued to cause problems. If a single issue galvanized him, it was the Centaur upper stage. Two things bothered him about the Centaur. He agreed that NASA needed a high-energy upper stage for the shuttle. But he did not want to give General Dynamics a sole-source contract for billions of dollars to build an upper stage with old technology. The second concern was that experts at NASA and Rockwell had argued for years that the Centaur was fundamentally unsafe in the shuttle. Hollenbeck decided that the best approach would be for NASA to hold an open competition for a high-energy upper stage with new technology that would be safe to fly in the shuttle. He decided NASA could use the Air Force–developed IUS until the new upper stage was ready.

Hollenbeck's position angered General Dynamics. Chris Hansen, then General Dynamics' Centaur lobbyist, argued that they had more experience in high-energy technology than other contractors. He said there was no time for a competition because there were payloads that needed the power of the liquid upper stage by 1986. He said it would take too long to compete and then build a brand-new upper stage. The troubled IUS program strengthened General Dynamics' hand. The Air Force was complaining about contractor troubles and cost overruns. According to Tom Brownell, who worked on the IUS project, "the initial studies showed that the IUS would be $7 to $9 million each." But these estimates were for a relatively simple vehicle with no backup systems in guidance and communications. The ceiling was lifted twice as the Air Force gold-plated the small solid stage. The military made change orders that drove the price up to $50 million each. Now NASA would have to pay for the increased costs when it purchased its stages. The delays and the costs gave General Dynamics and NASA's Lewis Research Center an excuse to push again for Centaur. John Naugle and NASA's science staff were beside themselves. Naugle had been trying to get his Galileo Mission scheduled for years. Now after a twin launch was designed and planned aboard a planetary version of the IUS, the Congress was debating dropping the IUS in favor of a Centaur stage that had not even been built.

General Dynamics was unrelenting in its lobbying effort for the Centaur. But what angered Hollenbeck was not the heavy Political Action Committee (PAC) contributions that were being liberally spread around Capitol Hill. Instead of lobbying Centaur on its merits, General Dynamics succeeded in convincing Intelligence and Appropriations Subcommittee Chairman Ed Boland that the Air Force needed the Centaur for important national security missions. Tired of General Dynamics' heavy-handed lobbying, House Science and Technology Committee Chairman Don Fuqua complained to veteran General Dynamics lobbyist Moon Mullins. Fuqua asked him what was going on. Mullins told Fuqua that it was Boland who was asking for the information and they were just supplying it.[14]

But what bothered Chairman Fuqua more was Beggs' role. "I was very uncomfortable about it," Fuqua said. He thought Beggs should have recused himself from the Centaur debate. " . . . I thought he should have. . . . He didn't. He took a very active part in it and finally made the decision to go with it . . . ," Fuqua recalls. Congressman Ronnie Flippo, who chaired the Space Subcommittee at the time, came to

Chairman Fuqua and, according to Fuqua's recollection, asked what could be done about the fact that Beggs was following up on a system he sold to Lovelace while Beggs was at General Dynamics and Lovelace was at NASA. Flippo, according to Fuqua, thought "it looked like he [Beggs] and Lovelace had switched jobs," Fuqua says. "And I said, well, you know I just hope I have enough confidence in them [where] there is nothing wrong there," Fuqua adds.

During the Centaur controversy Beggs was receiving $38,750 a year in deferred compensation from General Dynamics as well as a $1,200-a-month pension. Forms that Beggs filed with the Office of Government Ethics stated he disqualified himself from all decisions regarding General Dynamics until after he sold company stock options that brought him $1,378,034 in September 1981. When a reporter asked Beggs about a possible conflict of interest with General Dynamics over the Centaur, Beggs said he had no intention of removing himself from the debate. He said, "If anything I bend over backwards to be tougher on General Dynamics." [15]

Hollenbeck understood political hardball but he had never quite seen anything like the fight over the upper stage. Kenneth Greenberg, a Hollenbeck aide, said that then Centaur lobbyist Chris Hansen told him that if Hollenbeck did not lay off the issue, the congressman could not count on any more campaign contributions. Hollenbeck remembers Hansen's style. "He got mad when you questioned the sole source. Yeah. Their [General Dynamics'] attitude was, 'We're the big boys. We're the best.' They were the only lobbyists that got irritated when you asked them questions. The only guys who really played hardball and gave the dirty looks and seemed to spread the dough around. It was an arrogance. I realize that spending hundreds of thousands of dollars on congressional campaigns is a cheap way to win billions of dollars from a government contract. But General Dynamics put the arm on anybody who they had an interest with. One of them was [Congresswoman] Claudine Schneider [R-Rhode Island] because of Electric Boat. And who else? Duncan Hunter [the congressman from San Diego] got very personal. I mean I had no ax to grind," Hollenbeck says. In the two-year Centaur fight General Dynamics' Political Action Committee gave $282,369 to members of Congress. Duncan Hunter got $6,500.

But Hollenbeck was incredulous when he found out that his own subcommittee staffer, Jeff Irons, was siding with General Dynamics. Tom Brownell, then an IUS lobbyist, remembers when Irons brought a statement he had written to Hollenbeck's office saying the Republicans on the committee really supported Centaur and Hollenbeck was alone in his opposition. Hollenbeck got angry and told Irons that he worked for the subcommittee, not General Dynamics, and he would write what he was told to write. "Jeff Irons didn't want to make waves. He had to have somebody talking to him because Jeff was a relatively simple person," Hollenbeck recalls.

In September 1982 the heated Centaur debate temporarily ended when the House of Representatives voted on an amendment to give General Dynamics the sole-source contract. Hollenbeck describes what happened. "I don't know the figure but I watched people come onto the floor of the House of Representatives during the upper-stage debate who absolutely did not know what they were talking about. Claudine Schneider actually asked me what the words IUS meant. She asked me what the initials stood for! And then with a prepared statement she spoke vigorously on behalf of General Dynamics' position and against the committee, against the administration, and against NASA. And [Intelligence Committee Chairman] Boland was waving around these dark missions and saying he couldn't talk about the secret things like dark little men on the other side of the moon. He kept saying, 'Trust me. Trust me. Trust me.' I've seen Boland pull that more than once. It's a cheap debater's trick. It just may be a well-intentioned way of winning his point, but it turned out that he won at great expense to NASA and the program," says Hollenbeck. IUS-supporter Tom Brownell watched the debate from the visitors gallery and remembers Boland speaking about the secret "black" program and asking for his colleagues' trust. The next day when Brownell went through his copy of the *Congressional Record* looking for Boland's remarks, the comments were edited so that all references to his request for trust from his colleagues and "black" programs were removed.[16]

The House of Representatives voted three to one in favor of the Centaur. The Sunday after the vote Hollenbeck went to a brunch at Gimbels Department Store in New York. "I spoke to Astronauts Hank Hartsfield and Ken Mattingly who I had met a couple [of] weeks before, after their shuttle flight. We were talking about the vote on the upper stage. They had seen part of it on C-Span and they were bewildered. One of them made the remark, and I'm not sure which one it was, but he said, 'We'd resign from the astronaut corps before we would fly that General Dynamics bomb in the cargo bay of the shuttle,'" Hollenbeck remembers.

On the Senate side of the Capitol, Schmidt was successful in winning the Centaur upper-stage vote for General Dynamics. According to former Senator Howard Cannon, who served as the Democratic leader of the Committee on Commerce, Science, and Transportation, Schmidt was deferred to on technical matters because he was an astronaut and scientist. Once when Schmidt was in New Mexico campaigning, Alabama Senator Howell Heflin attempted to add language to require NASA to at least study an alternative upper stage at some point. The minute Schmidt returned to Washington, he had Heflin's language removed from the legislation. The former Apollo XVII astronaut did a good job for General Dynamics. The windfall to the company was worth more than a billion dollars. But that fall the voters of New Mexico decided not to reelect Schmidt. Cap Hollenbeck was also defeated. But Hollenbeck's subcommittee staffer, Jeff Irons, got his job with General Dynamics.

By 1985, when NASA found itself with massive cost overruns by General Dynamics on the upper stage, Lovelace was running the program. Employees at the plant told DOD investigators, according to newspaper accounts, that work at General Dynamics' Lindbergh Field facility on the stealth cruise missile was charged to NASA's Centaur upper-stage account. NASA sources say millions of dollars in cost over-runs on the Centaur came from the time-card abuse.[17]

Faced with growing deficits for the shuttle and an admin-istration that seemed intent on making NASA into almost a private United Parcel Service for the military, Beggs began secretly to search for a solution to keep NASA in the space business with the space station but take it out of, as he called it, commercial trucking on the shuttle. Paul Dembling said Beggs wanted the shuttle spun off to become self-sufficient. "What Jim Beggs said was, 'This [the shuttle] was a big al-batross around our neck.' If you did not have it, you couldn't get the support of the Congress dollar-wise. He said, 'I don't know how to get rid of it and we shouldn't be keeping it.' . . . That was the dilemma. What do you do with it? . . . How do you get rid of it and not get rid of the support for the space program? Because whenever you had a program that didn't capture the imagination of the Congress and the people, you don't get the money," Dembling explains.[18]

One of the options Beggs seriously considered was pri-vate operation of the shuttle. Beginning with the study he conducted for NASA in 1977, Beggs believed that once the shuttles proved themselves in test flights, the imagination of the business community would be ignited and a commercial operator would be found. Publicly Beggs defended such commercial ventures as a method of getting NASA the funding for the fifth orbiter. Since President Reagan advocated privatization of government activities, Beggs pursued this approach. First Beggs began searching for private companies to run ground operations at the Kennedy Space Center and then to actually operate the shuttle fleet.[19]

And the first to come forward was a familiar face around NASA. Klaus Heiss, who worked with Oskar Morganstern on the questionable Mathmatica Study, came up with the first effort to bring the private sector into shuttle operations. Several years earlier Heiss, a Harvard-educated Austrian national who called himself a "space economist," had been seeking financial backing for his efforts to privatize space. Heiss said that during the 1980 campaign he even briefed Ronald Reagan on his proposals. Despite the fact that Heiss' Mathmatica Study had been widely discredited, he was able to persuade a Princeton, New Jersey, investment banker, William Sword, to form a private company to get involved in shuttle operations. Heiss became president of the Space Transportation Company. Heiss was both admired and shunned by many at NASA for his entrepreneurial efforts. When he first went to NASA in 1981 peddling his ideas, he did not receive a warm welcome. NASA officials like General Counsel Neil Hosinball and General Manager Phil Culbertson listened to him. But no serious negotiations got underway until Heiss recruited high-powered help. Heiss' lack of success at the space agency prompted one of the board members of the Space Transportation Company, Charles Lee, to seek help from his old friend Vice President George Bush.

Lee and Bush went to Yale University together. Bush's press secretary at the time, Peter Teeley, confirmed the two were old friends.[20] Lee wrote to Bush on October 20, 1981:

Dear Mr. Vice President:

For the past two years since the sale of White Weld to Merrill Lynch I have been associated with the international investment banking firm of William Sword and Co., Inc. William Sword and Dr. Klaus Heiss, founder and Chairman of Econ Inc., have spent several years and overseen the expenditure of several million dollars to study the feasibility of privately financing a fifth space shuttle orbiter. Based on their conviction that such financing was feasible, William Sword and Klaus Heiss founded the Space Transportation Co., Inc. Our mutual friend Frank Parker and I have been directors of STC since its incorporation in February 1979. Information on STC's purposes and objectives is enclosed. We would greatly appreciate your consideration of this material and the opportunity to discuss it further with you and/or any of your staff you might suggest. Sally joins me in sending very best wishes to you and Barbara.

Sincerely,
Charles Lee

On the same day another letter arrived in Bush's office, this time from Sword and Heiss asking for a meeting to discuss their proposal. On November 9, 1981, Bush replied to Lee's request. According to Teeley the letter read as follows:

Dear Charlie:

Thank you for your recent letter and the accompanying prospectus of your company's proposal for private industry funding of the fifth and possibly successive space shuttle orbiters. Your proposal is extremely intriguing. As you know, President Reagan is strongly committed to maintaining the United States' leading role in space and also encouraging greater scope and initiative of private industry in many areas. Your proposal is in keeping with these ideas. Unfortunately my schedule is extremely crowded at the moment and I do not believe it will be possible to meet with Dr. Heiss and Mr. Sword for a briefing in the foreseeable future. However as you may be aware the President's Science Adviser, G. Keyworth, and his staff are currently conducting a major space policy review, including options for the space shuttle program. It occurs to me that your proposal fits in perfectly with their work and could make a valuable contribution to the study. I have taken the liberty of passing your proposal along to him and I have asked that his office contact you about it.

Thanks again for thinking of me and very best wishes.

George Bush

In November 1981 Sword and Heiss went to the White House to meet with Frank Van Rensselear and others on the White House staff to discuss the proposal.[21] Shortly after that meeting Heiss and Sword were told to draw up a proposal for NASA. In February 1982 Heiss submitted Space Transportation's proposal to NASA. He said that Space Transportation would buy a fifth orbiter and turn it over to the government in exchange for marketing rights for the entire shuttle fleet. He targeted 1985 as the delivery date for the orbiter. The proposal called for a $150 million down payment on the billion-dollar spaceship. In exchange Space Transportation wanted exclusive marketing rights for the fleet starting in

1983. NASA estimated that profits on the venture could run as high as $2 billion on a $1 billion investment over ten years.

But as NASA listened carefully to Heiss' proposal, the space agency once again was reminded that the fate of the shuttle was not exclusively in their hands. For national security reasons, the Air Force went on record opposing the deal. And to his surprise, Beggs also heard complaints about the proposal from the main shuttle contractor, Rockwell International. Rockwell spokesman Richard Barton raised concerns that were also being expressed in Congress. "The American taxpayer would raise hell if he found out that $10 billion in tax-paid research was about to be turned over to a private company for profit. There are hundreds of problems with this proposal. It is one thing to have someone else routinely launch the shuttle as subcontractor, but when you turn over ownership, that is another matter," Barton said. Ironically Al Rockwell, who no longer had a major holding in the company bearing his name, began exploring a private shuttle operation of his own with the help of former NASA Administrator James Fletcher. William Sword said that as long as his company paid taxes on the profit, the American people should have no objections to private concerns running the fleet.

Heiss and Sword were now courting investors saying they had the Vice President's ear and were actively negotiating with NASA. If Heiss' pitch was not taken seriously at NASA earlier, many took notice when in May 1982, the $60-billion Prudential Insurance Company of North America bought into the Space Transportation Company. Heiss, who had made little headway with NASA or the Congress, was moved aside so that smoother Washington insiders could take over the effort. Because the shuttle production line was threatening to close down, Prudential and Space Transportation pressed hard to finalize a deal.

Beggs, convinced the military would never go for the

Space Transportation Company proposal, contacted Frederick Smith, the head of Federal Express and an old business associate. Beggs was instrumental in getting General Dynamics to loan Smith the funds to get Federal Express off the ground. Smith told Beggs that Sword and Heiss had sold twenty percent of Space Transportation Company to Prudential and were now offering the remainder to Federal Express for $8 million. Exactly what Sword had to sell was not clear since NASA, let alone Congress or the Pentagon, had not agreed to the privatization proposal. But Smith told Beggs that his interest was broader than just the marketing rights for the shuttles. Smith's vice president for advanced projects, Alan McArtor, said, "We want to participate as an operator of the shuttle, not just from a capital investment point of view. We like to operate what we are involved in." But George Keyworth saw Beggs' efforts in the private sector as simply a diversion. "Don't confuse signal with noise. Those [were] noises in the system. The decisions were the space station and ELVs. NASA threw up every conceivable impediment in the way," Keyworth said.[22]

And, independent of Keyworth, there was evidence to indicate Beggs was stalling the White House and not really serious about privatization. Robert Allnut, who handled external relations under Beggs, confirms Keyworth's views. "It is not true to say Beggs was pushing ahead to try and get . . . a private source to buy a fifth [orbiter]. . . . Nobody ever came within a country mile of a deal that . . . I, as a civil servant, would ever sign my name to." Allnut believes Congress would have never gone along. "You couldn't testify with a straight face that it was anything other than a guaranteed loan, that's all it was in those deals."[23] Keyworth said Beggs' methods were hurting his own cause. "I can't tell you of anyone that I can think of in my realm of dealing who had as poor relations with the White House as Jim Beggs," Keyworth said.

Beggs found NASA under attack on another front. Keyworth and other White House officials decided to push the space policy on ELVs harder. The White House decided what Beggs had feared all along—to remove all ELVs from NASA's control. A new commercial space-utilization office was set up at the Department of Transportation. Beggs now faced the prospect of vehicles developed by NASA being used by the Reagan administration to undercut the shuttle. The DOT joined the military in urging NASA to set higher prices for shuttle launches. "That was the argument DOT was making," Beggs said. "They said you ought to set the price very high so that commercial ELVs can come in. The trouble is that argument is very flawed. And it's very seriously flawed because the American ELVs are all twenty-five-year-old technology that nobody is going to buy because they come in at fairly high prices and you have a lot of competitive launch vehicles abroad," said Beggs.[24]

Beggs pushed his argument in the National Security Council. He said that to use Titans and other old ELVs was the equivalent of giving a government subsidy to the contractors to keep the production lines open. Beggs remembered, "That's what I said to this crowd at the NSC. 'Let's put it on the table. What we are talking about here is subsidizing these people. It's not commercial. This is not a government deal. It is a government subsidy. If we're talking about government subsidies, let's talk about the fact that the shuttle system is the latest and best thing that we have got. If you want to subsidize, let's subsidize that.' Oh my God, you know, it was awful. It was sickening, and they would sit around there and say, 'This is a free enterprise system and you just let them take over.' And I said, 'Bullshit, this is not a free enterprise kind of deal. In the first place all the launch facilities are government-owned. The Air Force cannot abrogate the responsibility for the range safety. All the boosters you are talking about were bought and paid for by the government. All the production facilities were set up and bought and paid for by the government. Okay, [if] you give all that investment to them, which I will cheerfully do, you still have got to subsidize them in order to keep making them competitive.' I said, 'That's so dumb it boggles my mind.'"

National Security Council space expert Col. Gilbert Rye said there was a feeling that the Department of Transportation ELV office had "evolved into a lobby group for ELV manufacturers, you know the Martin Mariettas and the General Dynamics and the McDonnell Douglas'. . . . There was a feeling they were just a government-paid lobby group."[25] And with the resurrection of the ELVs, Klaus Heiss, frustrated by the failure of Space Transportation to get its shuttle deal, decided to take advantage of this new angle to profit from space. He joined forces with Martin Marietta and took an option out to sell commercial launches on the Titan 34Ds, the biggest rocket outside of the shuttle.

In order to cover his flanks, Beggs ordered NASA officials to get as much business for the shuttle as possible ranging from communications satellites to private experiment packages. But NASA ran into a major roadblock in these efforts. Arianespace, a private French company with much help from the French government, began marketing the Ariane expendable rocket. The company represents the technical capabilities of eleven European countries. Using the most sophisticated sales tools, Ariane was quickly gobbling up much of the satellite market. They offered cheaper launch prices as a result of a government subsidy for the specific reason of drawing business away from the shuttle. And the Ariane demonstrated how tenuous the economic justifications for the shuttle were. Ariane cut heavily into the shuttle's potential commercial market. For NASA's Chet Lee, who became responsible for selling the shuttle, it was difficult to compete. While Ariane would fly customers to Paris on the Concorde, Lee could only offer less glamorous enticements. "We had an arrangement where we could take our customers to the Air and Space Museum. We could get them tours of the Cape, things like that. . . ."[26]

If Lee did not have enough trouble marketing the shuttle, Beggs created another one. The Air Force wanted the right to bump any flight on national security grounds. Such an open policy would have made it difficult for NASA to book anything commercial on the shuttle because customers paying $50 million for a flight do not want to go standby. Much to the chagrin of some at the Air Force and many at NASA, Beggs negotiated a compromise. In exchange for NASA giving priority to Air Force payloads, NASA would be paid up front for all launches the Air Force thought it was going to make in a given year. Beggs explains the deal. "In return [for the right to bump other shuttle customers] they agreed to pay up front a fixed payment each year to cover the fixed costs of keeping the shuttle flying. As they flew, they would pay the variable costs. They would not only pay the bill but the advantage to that for NASA is pricing. The problem with DOD is they project a certain number of launches. That projection is based upon their assessment of the life of their assets in space. Now being military and conservative people, which you hoped they would be, they are very conservative in estimating life. That means, of course, that the number of launches they tell you they are going to make almost always goes down significantly," explains Beggs.[27]

So Beggs struck a deal with Pete Aldridge, the secretary of the Air Force. "So what I said to Pete was, 'Look, you are forcing us to set aside capacity for, say, six flights a year for your payloads and we are ending up with three. Well, that may not mean anything to you, but it means a lot to us because once we set up our production lines and everything else, that is a significant loss. So we want you to pay the fixed costs of your six flights. You pay that up front early in the year. Then we will just charge you the variable costs which means you can fly your stuff on the cheap.' . . . Variable costs are only about $35 million a flight and that's cheaper than flying on anything else. So he agreed," Beggs said.

Now Aldridge needed a favor from Beggs to keep the uniformed Air Force from openly revolting against the shuttle. Congress slashed funds from the U.S. Air Force's Space Command in Colorado and threatened to cancel the entire $8 billion project. Without the ability to control the launch, Aldridge knew his troops would rebel. Beggs told Aldridge that the Johnson Space Center would take up some of the communications slack so the Air Force would only have to install a minor facility at Colorado Springs. The Johnson Space Center employees were outraged. Led by Center Director Christopher Kraft, the Johnson people were convinced that Beggs had gone too far. Kraft quit under Frosch, and came back to get the shuttle flying under Beggs. This time Kraft, known for his temper, told Beggs the Air Force was turning Johnson into Pentagon, Texas. Secret communications channels, copper flooring, and other devices made Mission Control in Houston "tempest" certified. Morale at Johnson was at an all-time low. Beggs remembers the reaction. "Chris didn't like it at all. But I said to the Johnson boys, 'Look, they are not going to fly but three times a year. That's just not all that much.' That thing was signed in blood by Pete and I. In addition to that, we went into the National Security Council and put in the new pricing which kind of shut out the good old Department of Transportation," Beggs said.

NASA, the administration, and the Pentagon were sending so many confused signals to Congress that the already poor oversight of NASA was becoming a matter of guess-work. Hollenbeck explains the circumstances. "When you're there and everything is swirling around you, you trust that professional staff to make the necessary inquiries and to be inquisitive. Obviously the next question is why aren't they? Well, you have this revolving-door employment policy, an unwritten policy. There's no incentive for them to ask questions because if they ask questions or get too inquisitive the job opportunities are not going to be there on the outside. And the committee to a certain extent falls just short of being a rubber stamp. When NASA flew us down for the first shuttle launch even Fuqua was with us in the visitor viewing stands. We knew less as committee members or as much as anybody from the outside who managed to get seats. We knew nothing more than what was announced on the god-damn loudspeakers. That probably epitomizes the lack of sharing of information and not necessarily of disdain. But NASA only interfaced with you when they needed you. I'll put it that way. They treated you more like VIP guests than as participants in the program or someone who had oversight of the program because that was business as usual. It was a good ole boy business as usual. Fraternization is the word I'm looking for. That's what happened. You have this sort of frat-ernization between the company executives, the lobbyists, the committee, NASA, the astronauts. It's natural. It's a space fraternity really. I was never really part of that. I was looked upon as an outsider because I wasn't in it from the beginning. I was new. I asked questions. I took tough stands. So it was easy to say to the contractors, 'Hey, this guy Hol-lenbeck, he's against your bread and butter.'"[28]

And while Beggs was waging his battles with the White House staff and the Pentagon, the shortcuts taken to build the shuttle on the cheap were coming home to haunt NASA. The cost of each orbiter had gone from $675 million in 1972 to

$1.47 billion by 1983. The external tank, which is not recoverable, was supposed to cost $4.73 million. In fact, the tanks ended up costing $28 million a flight. The payload capacity of the orbiter was supposed to be 65,000 pounds. In reality it never went over 53,000 pounds to low earth orbit. The promised turnaround time between a shuttle landing and a launch was estimated by NASA in 1972 to be 160 hours. Beggs discovered that working full tilt the shuttle took 1,240 hours to refurbish. NASA said that it would cost only $28 million for each shuttle flight and recovery. By 1983 the costs were at $260 million and climbing. And the famous Mathmatica Study's projected price of $100 to $270 per pound of payload orbited by 1983 was in reality more than $5,000 a pound.

By 1983 the fallacy that this remarkable spaceship would be able to pay for itself was known. Beggs knew it and so did his subordinates. It didn't matter. As Fletcher had done under Nixon, Beggs was going to tow the White House line. To get his space station, Beggs would pressure the already overburdened shuttle system to meet the July fourth space policy objective which said: "The first priority of the STS program is to make the system fully operational and cost effective in providing routine access to space."

10

The Politics of Space

IN THE TERRIBLE PLACE THAT NASA BECAME IN THE
years after Apollo, there was someone who tried to stop the
headlong rush to disaster. There was a man who stood up to
Dale Myers and George Low and even James Fletcher and
said you cannot do this. You cannot abandon everything
learned about management in Apollo to build a shuttle on the
cheap. Rocco Petrone was a lone voice. And that is why he
quit NASA in 1975. He did not want to participate in what
he believed to be a combination of self-delusion and lies to sell
the shuttle. He was in charge of manned spaceflight for
NASA, yet this West Point man found himself with less and
less influence over a program he was supposed to be running.
George Low had Fletcher's total confidence. Since Low was
now running Petrone's program, with no apparent objection
from Fletcher, the fear and frustration increased for Petrone.

During 1975, as Petrone spent long nights at Federal Office Building Six studying shuttle design plans and looking at the projected launch rates and costs, he understood where the trade-offs to make it all work would come from. His rule—the rule that von Braun and Gilruth passed on to him—was that when you build machines for man to fly, you put your own life aboard that spacecraft. As he looked at the shuttle design, Petrone understood that this was a vehicle dictated by political and economic considerations. Yes, Low and Fletcher and Myers were right when they called it the most sophisticated spaceship man has ever built. They were right when they said it was the most complicated machine ever built. But they never said that it was also the most dangerous to fly of any manned rocket ever built.

Petrone argued against taking paperwork and management shortcuts. Petrone told his superiors that the one thing NASA learned from Apollo was that accountability led to success. As they found out in the Apollo 204 fire, to remove that accountability could be a fatal error. Yet, to save money, that is exactly the road NASA management selected. Petrone argued that Low and Fletcher were wrong when they said no escape system existed on airplanes and therefore the shuttle did not need one. Because of the success in NASA's track record, Petrone argued that Americans would have great difficulty accepting the loss of astronauts. He said that Americans would not accept astronauts dying. He told them they had to have an escape system. Petrone brought in outside experts to look at the shuttle system. Their findings confirmed his views for the record. Then he left NASA.

For thirty-two years in the Army and at NASA this immense man had been part of space. He looked around his beloved NASA and was disheartened by what he saw. In 1972, when Fletcher put the Johnson Space Center in charge of the other field centers for the shuttle, men like Petrone understood Fletcher and Low were wrecking Webb's carefully crafted management system. But it went nearly un-noticed in Washington. With a stroke of a pen, Fletcher removed from NASA headquarters the control that had kept NASA on top for so long.

The Apollo experience convinced Petrone that promises of shuttle capabilities, cost per launch, and refurbishment time between flights were merely pipe dreams. He did not leak his views to the press. He simply prepared reports for a NASA management that he hoped someday would listen. Petrone left Fletcher, Myers, and Low with their creation and he walked away from NASA where he had hoped to spend the rest of his life. He was one of the veterans who thought the moon was just the beginning. Petrone was trained to play it by the book. He ignored the job offers from defense and NASA contractors. He did not want to get trapped in the revolving door. Instead he went to work for a private foundation. He had little to do with space during his six-year self-imposed exile. For six years, the man who was the natural heir to Webb, Gilruth, and von Braun shut himself out because of his own sense of responsibility and integrity. A few months before *Columbia* was scheduled to fly, Rockwell contacted Petrone and asked him if he would come back and help them fly the shuttle. Petrone made a commitment to return before *Columbia*'s maiden flight. Space was in his blood and he wanted to be there regardless of the success or failure of the shuttle.

What he found when he returned as a contractor was that the NASA he had dedicated his life to had been destroyed. In Washington NASA was dominated by Beggs. Every time he turned around, Beggs was cutting engineers out of the shuttle program. Petrone told Beggs the shuttle was a good vehicle, but it was not perfect. He agreed with others at NASA that Beggs was pushing the shuttle too fast and too hard. NASA veterans knew the engineers were needed to monitor the program. But Beggs would not listen. Petrone and others all too readily recognized the syndrome. Others at NASA, like Lilly and Williamson, say General Abrahamson, who was a super salesman, was powerless in convincing Beggs not to cut manpower.

Petrone and others were amazed at the relationship between Mark and Beggs—the two did not talk to each other a good part of the time. Beggs had mixed emotions about Mark. He respected his deputy's total devotion to the shuttle, if not to the civilian agency. "Hans is an abrasive character. I have always gotten along with him. . . . But many people are not used to Hans, and they have a hard time getting along with him. Hans can be very abrasive. He can be very blunt, very direct. And he can drive you to distraction. Sometimes you have got to say to Hans, 'Alright goddamn it, that's not the way we're going to do it!' I sometimes put it to him, 'Now Hans, you've got a head like a rock, but we ain't going to do it that way.' He's got a German mind," Beggs says.

But the German minds Petrone remembered were the ones of those who helped give NASA that fanatical sense of care during the Apollo years. At the Cape the spirit and dedication Petrone remembered had changed. The abandonment in 1969 of the paper documentation that had been so successful for Apollo was reinstated by 1981. But Petrone and others learned that it wasn't always complied with. Too often, the vastly more complicated shuttle was flying without a complete paper trail to trace responsibility. Problems, such as the creeping into the work areas of uncertified parts and tools that could badly damage the orbiter, were more apparent in the shuttle program. In Petrone's eyes, the discipline that NASA had been so famous for had eroded. As he looked back over the decade-long history of the program, all he could find was one safeguard after another torn away. Many at

NASA say Beggs did not want to hear the bad news. They recall Beggs' big push was for the space station.

To make certain the space station had no competition, Beggs ordered an end in NASA to discussions of a modified shuttle called the Long Duration Orbiter.[1] After a few modifications, such as adding a solar panel to augment the shuttle's fuel cells, the shuttle's operating ability could be extended beyond the current eight days to up to a month in space. Beggs thought this version of the shuttle would hurt his chances for funding for the space station.

To get the space station, Beggs depended on the help of two key people—then Presidential Cabinet Secretary Craig Fuller, whose earlier relationship with Rockwell, according to Beggs, made him a space supporter, and Col. Gilbert Rye, who was assigned to space issues for the National Security Council. Together they provided Beggs time with the president to sell the space station with neither the knowledge nor approval of Domestic Adviser Ed Meese or Science Adviser Keyworth.

In February 1983, Beggs and Mark began to prepare the fiscal year 1985 NASA budget. Their goal was to have the first funding for the space station included in the administration's budget request to Congress. According to Mark's manuscript, in March Mark and Rye decided to arrange a meeting with the president for Beggs. Mark and Beggs established a space station strategy group within NASA. The group included Margaret Finarelli, who would represent NASA in an intergovernmental working group established by SIG-Space. She was selected not only because she came from NASA's International Affairs Office, but also because she had a comprehensive intelligence background. She could argue the intelligence benefits of the space station with the CIA and Department of Defense, both of which were absolutely against the project.

The most Beggs hoped for from SIG-Space was that other government agencies would not kill the space station until he had a chance to make his case directly to the president. On April 7, 1983, Beggs was ushered into the Oval Office. Beggs began to lay out his ideas for the space station. The president asked him about a mission to Mars. Beggs says he told the president: "'You know a mission to Mars would be terribly exciting but,' I said, 'it's something that would probably take us ten to fifteen years to accomplish and a great deal of money. So let's do the space station first and then we can go anywhere we want to.'" Beggs says Reagan had trouble with the concepts of space. "He was almost technically ignorant. Not quite, but almost. He grasps a few of the broader concepts, but when you start talking to him in any kind of detail about the broader aspects of the program, his eyes glaze over. You lose him very fast. I found out," Beggs remembers.[2]

Beggs sold the space station to President Reagan on national security grounds as an edge on the Soviets. If the United States program had one shortcoming, Beggs told the president, it was lack of continuous experience of man in space. The Soviets had stuck with their aging technology but flew astronauts to orbital workshops for missions lasting months while the U.S. astronauts remained grounded waiting for the shuttle. And Beggs was not asking the president for a courageous commitment. After all, the bulk of the money would not be needed until after Reagan left office. Money was an issue that Reagan did not want to deal with. "He didn't like to talk about money at all. What he would say when you got to the point of talking about how much it would cost, he would either turn to Meese or in most cases to Fuller, and say, 'Well let's work this out with David [Stockman].' And he'd stop. That's what we ultimately did. Stockman would say, 'How much is this going to cost?' And I said, 'Well let's pick the $8 billion number.' That $8 billion is $12 billion in real terms, that is if we could get the Europeans and Japanese to come along for another $3 or $4 billion."

By the end of the meeting the president was favorably disposed to the space station. Beggs and Mark attribute the success of the space station campaign in large part to Gil Rye. Originally Rye "was sent in [by the DOD] as a spy. And it turned out he was converted and turned out he was decent," Mrs. Beggs says.[3] But Beggs did not have the close, personal relationship with then Cabinet Secretary Craig Fuller one might expect. "He was one of the few people who positively pitched the program to the president. Keyworth never did. Keyworth was all in favor of the military space program. Craig was all in favor of a civilian space program and he as far as I know . . . was very positive with the president. But he was not in my court. That was just his position. I know for a fact he was out after my scalp because he told several people who reported to me," Beggs recalls. Beggs thinks Fuller wanted to be the NASA administrator.

Beggs and Mark also credit the support of the Europeans and the Japanese for the space station in helping them make their case to the president. "But we did get a lot of interest from the folks over at ESA [the European Space Agency], and the Japanese expressed interest. The Japanese, in fact, I think in one of the various exchanges with the president, the Japanese expressed interest that if the United States was going to go forward with the space station, they would be interested in joining. And that was helpful. I think the President was impressed," says Beggs.

For Keyworth the loss to Beggs on the space station was a bitter defeat. He thought little of Beggs' helpers. He describes Craig Fuller as " . . . a complete airhead . . . caught up in the space world." Keyworth thought that Hans Mark, using his Air Force connections, got Rye, who he describes as "Hans Mark's shill," installed on the National Security Council (NSC). As Rye successfully made a case for Beggs' and Mark's space station before the NSC, Keyworth became more and more embittered. Rye was selected to head up a task force to examine the space station and prepare options for the president. Rye says, "We had all the concerned agencies on it. . . . Then we had a cabinet meeting that everyone attended and expressed their views. Keyworth's view, by the way, was that we ought to set as an objective [of] going back to the moon, which almost met with uproarious laughter from those at the table."

Keyworth remembers events differently. "In fact, the president walked into that last NSC meeting with a wonderful twinkle in his eye and [in] one of Ronald Reagan's 'I am excited about this moods,' and he walked in before almost anyone else and he said, 'Jay before we talk I have an idea.' Now unfortunately he fingered me by giving me a big wink and so on. He said that the space station is interesting but how about a manned mission to Mars. Craig Fuller jumped up and said, 'Mr. President, I believe that due process has been violated. We have been holding consensus building mechanisms to present you with options and Jay Keyworth has gone around that.' And the president sort of chuckled. The president is not a bureaucrat to say the least and Jim Beggs came and said, 'Well Mr. President, of course the space station will be exactly that. It will be a step on our way to the moon [or to Mars],'" Keyworth remembers.[4] Keyworth believes Beggs lied to the president when he told him that. Keyworth says that the space station design does not allow it to be used as a staging platform for future lunar or Mars missions. But Keyworth saves his greatest anger for Rye. In Keyworth's opinion, "Gil Rye is a thug, an absolute thug. I have said that Jim Beggs wasn't smart enough. Hans Mark wasn't self-consistent. But Gil Rye was a thug."

Keyworth thinks Rye took advantage of senior administration officials who relied upon him for facts. Keyworth said that normally no one would dare do such a thing because of what Keyworth calls the "sheer awesomeness of the presidency." "You know, it is a rare individual who can be base around the president. You know, you just have a feeling—here is the last resort. This man is really vulnerable. And you can screw anybody but don't screw him. . . . Gil Rye put documents in front of the president for his signature the president didn't read. Now that is absolutely verboten. I never saw that done by anyone else," Keyworth says. Rye, now a senior official at the Communications Satellite Corporation, denies Keyworth's charges. He says that even if he wanted to do such a thing, which Rye says he didn't, he did not have the access to the president to do it.

In the spring of 1983 Beggs was well on his way to winning the space station battle and was holding his own with the Pentagon. He thought Keyworth and other White House opponents simply could not get to him. But Beggs soon learned that by going around Meese, he made an enemy. And in the world of the Reagan White House, that could be a fatal mistake. Interest was building for the first flight of an American woman in space, Dr. Sally Ride. Beggs' wife, Mary, says that Ride's parents live in the Santa Monica, California, Assembly district of Tom Hayden, the former radical and now very liberal Democrat married to actress Jane Fonda. Hayden, according to Jim Beggs, called NASA's Los Angeles office and asked for an invitation to the launch for himself and his famous wife. According to Beggs, Hayden had a fascination with the shuttle and had shown up for many of the landings at Edwards Air Force Base. Following the practice since Apollo for local public officials such as Hayden, NASA immediately sent Hayden and Fonda an invitation for the June 18, 1983, lift-off of STS-7.

In addition to Fonda, NASA invited a planeload of other

professional women to the launch. Most of them were Reagan administration political appointees. Beggs remembers the day well. "So Fonda and Hayden show up for the Sally Ride launch down at Kennedy. And of course, as you would expect, the press swarmed around Fonda like bees do around honey. She got a lot of press. And it was favorable press." According to Mrs. Beggs who was there, NASA public relations man Brian Duff was talking to a *Washington Post* reporter and began pointing out women at the event, including Ms. Fonda, who could be role models for children. PBS newsman Jim Lehrer said to Mrs. Beggs how terrific it was that Jane Fonda was there "because it showed that a broad spectrum was being included in this program."

The next day the Style Section of the *Post* included favorable coverage of Fonda's visit to the launch. And Beggs heard about it quickly. "Well, the White House was furious. Deaver called me the next day and said, 'What the hell was Jane Fonda doing there?' I said, 'Well, I didn't invite her.' I said, 'Goddamn it Mike, we don't have any restrictions on launches. It's open to the public.' He said, 'Yeah, but she got all that press.' I said, 'We didn't give her all the press.' Then he said, 'Well Nancy Reagan is mad and I am mad and everybody is mad,'" Beggs remembers Deaver saying. Reagan officials wanted a sacrificial lamb from NASA to calm the White House outrage. And in this case the target was Brian Duff. Deaver demanded Beggs fire Duff immediately. Beggs, furious over the pettiness of Deaver, managed to get Duff placed in a similar public relations job at the National Air and Space Museum. Mrs. Beggs said she was "amazed at the pettiness over this." "Well, we didn't treat this that seriously and it didn't occur to me until after I left the agency and was thinking about it. Mary and I were invited to the White House several times before the Fonda incident and never afterwards," Beggs recalls.

To Beggs, the Fonda incident was a minor irritant. To Meese, Keyworth, and other White House staffers who understood the ultraconservative petty politics in the White House, it was the chink in Beggs' armor they had been waiting for. Keyworth says that the Fonda incident allowed him to push the effort to try to get rid of Beggs. "I'd been working on it for years. Listen. First of all you've got to realize we were talking in the White House. I don't mean me alone. The senior people at the White House were talking about a replacement for Beggs years before," Keyworth says. According to Keyworth, beginning in 1982, Frank Borman's name was being tossed around to replace Beggs. Keyworth says the delays in getting rid of Beggs went right to the top. "Ronald Reagan's only weakness, and you can say it is because he is too nice, but it's not that. It is because Ronald Reagan is so aloof. It's why he is such a great leader. It is also one of the reasons people don't understand him. He's so warm and human and unbelievably considerate. And when he sheds a tear at a person suffering, it is real as can be. . . . But he is very, very aloof. And he does not, let's say, occupy his mind. He probably didn't even know who Jim Beggs was [when he was first appointed], to put it bluntly," Keyworth explains.

While the president supported the space station privately, a meeting he had with Secretary of Defense Casper Weinberger brought up the issue again. Reagan heard further opposition to the project from CIA Director Casey, Adm. James Watkins, Chief of Naval Operations, as well as Meese and Baker. According to Mark, these meetings caused Beggs and Mark to doubt that the president's support for the space station would stick. Both Casey and Weinberger preferred spending the funds for their own pet projects. Beggs' attempts to sell them the space station for defense and intelligence purposes were ignored.

On December 5, 1983, OMB informed Beggs that $150

million was included in the FY 1985 budget for the space station. For Mark and Beggs their long battle was over. In his memoirs Hans Mark wrote, "Beggs would be remembered along with Jim Webb and Jim Fletcher as one of the NASA administrators who had succeeded in persuading a president to do something brand new." In fact, the difference between Webb and the others was that Webb did not need to convince his president. It was Kennedy, not Webb, who was bent on convincing the country to do something brand new. Mark says he was upset when, at a dinner party attended by authors, ex-astronauts, and others interested in space, he only got a lukewarm reaction to the approval of the space station. Most people at the dinner party felt the space station just wasn't enough.

Rocco Petrone, becoming more and more frustrated over trying to deal with Beggs, must have winced when he heard the news that once again NASA was going to manage a major program from field centers and not from headquarters. Again Johnson was named the "lead center." A few weeks later President Reagan gave his State of the Union Address announcing the space station as if it were the Apollo lunar landing. The differences were enormous. The planned early funding for the space station was less than a fourth of what was spent on Project Mercury a quarter century earlier. In reality, there was no space station victory, and no massive commitment, something Beggs now acknowledges. Reagan would be out of office by the time major appropriations were required to pay for the station, "so it wouldn't make any difference to him. It wasn't an issue that we'd face then," Beggs said. And Beggs expected cost overruns on the space station to equal the thirty percent overruns of the Space Shuttle.

The Jane Fonda incident was not Beggs' only brush with Michael Deaver. After Beggs sent over a note to the White House suggesting a private citizen be allowed to fly on the shuttle, preferably a schoolteacher, the White House embraced the suggestion as its own. After a rigorous selection process was completed, a buoyant young mother and teacher named Christa McAuliffe was selected. A few days after Mrs. McAuliffe was chosen, she gave an interview saying that she was an admirer of President Kennedy and the Kennedy family. It did not take long for the White House to respond. "And that made the White House upset," Beggs said. "Deaver told me to tell her not to talk. I told the folks down at the astronaut office to say, 'Look Christa, we can't tell you not to talk to the press; obviously you will be besieged by the press, but recognize the fact that you are in a very sensitive position politically and try not to be partisan because this is a nonpartisan agency and we have over the years tried to be strictly nonpartisan in our approach.' And she observed that very carefully in subsequent discussions," Beggs remembers.

Deaver also did not hesitate to call Beggs after he left the White House to set up his own lobbying firm. One of his clients was the Coca-Cola Company. Much was being made out of the fact that Coca-Cola had built a special can for zero gravity and was going to fly the first can of the soft drink on the Space Shuttle.

To complicate matters, Beggs said that Pepsi insisted on being on the same flight as Coca-Cola. "And I said, 'Jesus, why do you want to do that?' 'Well we have to be on the same flight and you can't deny us that because there is room on the flight.' They had already been to Johnson, and Johnson said, 'Yeah, we can book you on that.' So I capitulated and that's when I got the call from Deaver. He wanted me to throw the competition off the flight. I said, 'No.' . . . He was kind of nasty about it. He bothered me on the phone several times. Of course a lot of people bothered me about silly things. Of all the things that were done on the shuttle, the one that caused the most aggravation was the goddamn cola war. And, you know, part of that was a tempest in a teapot. We had run into that because everybody was coming in saying we want to fly this or that. Alright, goddamn it, if they want to pay their way, we'll fly. But no publicity in space. We won't put their names on the side of the shuttle. . . . And Deaver said, 'Why did you do that?' And I said, 'Well they found out that we had space available.' And I said, 'You know I am a poor dumb government official. I can't discriminate between colas.' . . . Well he was awfully upset and he was mad. . . . And I said, 'Mike I can't do anything . . . but I will look again to make sure that we made no special arrangements for them.' "5

To reach an accommodation, Beggs agreed to let the astronauts try Coke first, since they had booked the flight before Pepsi. When the astronauts tasted the soft drinks they found, according to Beggs, "it tasted terrible. Warm and terrible. And it was a bloody failure." Beggs said it was not necessary for Deaver to threaten him to keep Pepsi off the shuttle. Beggs said, "You know they all imply. Whether they threaten you or not, the implication is there . . . he's got ties to the president and so on. He still had his White House pass."

But Deaver was Beggs' smallest worry compared to what was happening in the White House. What Beggs had accomplished with his space station victory was to anger the far right, which had adopted a militarized vision of space as the future. Beggs, who in any previous administration would have been considered a conservative, had now earned the enmity of organizations like the Heritage Foundation as well as the White House staff. Beggs had gone around Edwin Meese in making his successful run for the space station. He had made enemies out of an unforgiving group. All he needed to do was supply the opportunity and motive for his downfall, and almost on cue he did both.

By late 1984, Hans Mark, a mercurial man, saw little future at NASA. He had gotten approval for his space station and his Centaur upper stage and the shuttle was flying. He worked hard to meet the goals he had set for himself. A man of strong convictions, Mark was proud of his accomplishments. Beggs had stuck by Mark, in the view of some at NASA, to the detriment of the civilian space program. Mark's relations with the White House were not going well. His hope of having a major role in Star Wars diminished as General Abrahamson's ascended. After all, to members of the Reagan administration, Mark was still a Democrat. "I am a Democrat. I call the shots as I see them. The point is that . . . I voted for Reagan twice. You know, here I was a member of the Carter administration [and] I voted for Reagan because I thought Carter was incompetent. I don't believe that party affiliation means that much in this country. . . . And those turkeys don't understand that," Mark says.[6]

The University of Texas, cashing in on the end of the resurgence in oil prices, was spending big money for talent. Mark landed the job of chancellor at the Austin, Texas, school. According to Mary Beggs, Mark did not want to leave Washington. Jim Beggs says Mark left because he was afraid that people in the Reagan White House would either fire him or take other action that would destroy his career. "He thought the White House did not like him. Hated him. They were going to assassinate him sooner or later. . . . That's what he told me."[7]

Mark's resignation left Beggs without a deputy at a critical time. The flight schedule for the shuttle was being vastly increased. The Centaur project was in technical and financial trouble. Already the cost overruns were numbering in the tens of millions. The General Dynamics' victory in winning the fight to be sole-source contractor for Centaur was haunting NASA and draining funding for fixes that were badly needed on the four shuttles. And the TDRSS program was not faring any better. After numerous technical difficulties delayed the satellite, it was now time for NASA to begin paying up. "So NASA started in '84. November of '84 was our first payment. No, we made a payment in August, I think, too. And we pay every year now and it is $227 million a year and will run out through '93 and then there is a partial payment in '94. . . . A considerable amount of the cost is interest. In fact, a billion [dollars] is interest in the program," the head of the TDRSS program, Bob Aller, explains.[8]

Beggs wanted to fill Mark's position as quickly as possible. But Beggs' haste played right into the hands of his increasing list of enemies at the White House. Keyworth said he only wanted one thing out of a new NASA official when Hans Mark left. "We had no communication with that organization. We wanted communication. So sure, I wanted somebody I trusted in there. So did Don Regan. So did everybody. We wanted somebody who was as straight as an arrow. In that sense it was a reaction. We wanted someone who was loyal to the president," Keyworth explains.[9]

For all his experience in the corporate and political world, Jim Beggs was not prepared for the Reagan White House. He did not understand that appearance meant more than substance. That outward adherence to doctrinaire conservative philosophy meant more than the quality of the work. That success was measured more in terms of who you defeated rather than what you achieved. He made a classic mistake in trying to replace Mark. Instead of sending over to the White House a list of those he wanted considered for the job, Beggs simply told Personnel Director John Herrington that he needed a deputy. It was the kind of fatal political error that James Webb made a career out of avoiding. But Beggs, a no-nonsense personality, did not allow much thought for political machinations. An old-line Republican, Beggs considered people like Science Adviser George Keyworth and others in the administration "right wing nuts" for whom he had little patience. He was convinced that they had no real influence with the president. Beggs says he had always looked upon Keyworth as a minor player in White House intrigue. That was a mistake. The Jane Fonda affair and other incidents gave Keyworth the ammunition he needed to convince his White House colleagues that Beggs could not be trusted and that they needed someone loyal to Reagan at NASA.

It was against this backdrop that Beggs asked the White House for a successor to Mark. Beggs never thought Herrington would send him someone without NASA experience. The number-two job at the agency had in the early days been held by giants like the late Hugh Dryden. As the agency expanded, large-scale management experience became more important than NASA experience. Beggs particularly wanted someone with plenty of management experience because the shuttle was flying nearly once a month and NASA was short on both manpower and money to keep the program going. Beggs said he told Herrington, "I had to get a guy who can hit the ground running because if I were to fall down in an airplane [crash], we needed somebody [who could take over immediately] because what we do is so dangerous and it is risky. Lives could be lost. We have got to have people who are competent and who know what they are doing."[10]

Beggs finally got a list of perspective deputies back from Herrington and on it "were some very good names," Beggs says. "John Young was on it. Jack Townsend of Fairchild was on it. Cliff Duncan of NASA in the Apollo days was on it. And Bill Graham. And I reviewed the list and called back and said, 'Some of these guys are completely acceptable to me and I would be happy to take anyone of them and I will interview them all if you would like, but this guy Graham has no qualification. I have nothing against Bill Graham, but I have read his resumé and he is not qualified for this job.'" Graham, who came from the world of military consulting and nuclear warfare, was Keyworth's personal choice. Keyworth had coached him and sold him to the White House. It was Keyworth's chance to get even.

Beggs said he told Herrington that the largest group Graham had managed was twelve analysts at the Rand Corporation. With 20,000 highly decentralized employees at NASA, Beggs argued that Graham just wasn't up to the task. But Beggs had deeper concerns. Beggs had dismissed as nonsense talk that NASA was being militarized by the joint participation of the Air Force in the shuttle program. He already had suffered an open revolt in Houston by Chris Kraft and other pioneers in manned flight. As Beggs went over Graham's resumé, one thing stuck out. Graham was, like Keyworth, a nuclear weapons expert. For the first time the reality of what Beggs' colleagues at NASA had been saying hit home. This appointment was coming from the White House, not the Pentagon.

Beggs shared Graham's resumé with his General Manager Phil Culbertson. Culbertson, known within the agency as politically sensitive, took the resumé and distributed it to some former old-line NASA officials. A meeting was held. The advice they gave Culbertson was that this political appointment could be a death-blow to the civil space program.[11] Beggs, far less emotional than the retirees, was largely concerned about Graham's qualifications, but agreed with the others at NASA that Graham was also politically intolerable.

Beggs said he told Herrington that Graham was simply not acceptable. "Herrington told me, 'We understand, we understand,' but they said it was a political problem for us and 'Would you please interview˝ him. It would do us ever so much good if you just interview him.'" So Beggs interviewed all the candidates including Graham and called Herrington and told him that all but Graham were acceptable. "I made it clear Graham was not," Beggs says. That was in late February 1985. That spring Donald Regan and James Baker switched jobs. Herrington was leaving the personnel job at the White House to head the Department of Energy. Beggs recalls the conversation. "His assistant called me and said, 'We would still like you to consider Graham for your deputy.' I said, 'No way.' I said, 'Look, I have told you before and I am telling you again, there is no way I will take that guy, okay.' And bang goes the phone."

In late March, just before Herrington left the White House, he took care of the matter. When Beggs called to check on the status of the deputy's job, he was told that Herrington had left, but his successor, Robert Tuttle, would find out the status. According to Beggs, "It turns out that the son of a bitch Herrington went to Meese and they walked Graham's nomination into the president and got him to sign it without ever telling me. He calls me back and says, 'Oh my God, before they left here, they walked Graham's nomination through to the president and it's signed and I can't walk it back. I don't have any power.' I said, 'Okay, who does have that power?' He says, 'You are going to have to see Don Regan,'" Beggs remembers angrily.[12]

Beggs went over to see Regan and explained his concerns about Graham. Regan assured Beggs that Graham was not his choice for the job. Regan told Beggs he would see what he could do. Then Beggs heard from Regan. "So I get a call from him about two weeks later and he says, 'I can't do anything. This guy has strong support from the West Coast.' He told me, 'It's done. It's a fait accompli. The president signed it and he wouldn't unsign it. This guy has support on the West Coast from friends of the president. People like Henry Salvatore.'" The oil-rich Salvatore was one of Ronald Reagan's earliest supporters for governor of California.

Beggs trusted Regan. "I told Regan, 'We do risky things and it is hazardous to fly in space.' When Regan called me back I said, 'I would like to see the president.' He said, 'That is your privilege, but if you see him, I am warning you that you are going to lose this one.' This one had strong political support that could not be walked back. Well, I trusted Regan. I shouldn't have. I got had. So I said I wouldn't go see the president but I am not going to take him [Graham]. It turns out that the president didn't know a damn thing about it. He [Regan] says, 'You have got to take him.' I said, 'No way I am gonna take him.' I said, 'I am gonna play dog in the manger on this one,'" Beggs remembers.

Beggs refused to approve the appointment for the entire summer of 1985. With no strong number-two man to rely on, the backlog of major decisions was growing. NASA General Manager Phil Culbertson attempted to fill the vacuum left by Mark, but he got little cooperation from the centers. To many at NASA, Culbertson was one of the space agency's lesser lights. And many in the centers viewed Beggs as a Republican hack who was giving away the store to the Air Force on all shuttle decisions. One of the changes Beggs made when he came to NASA was to end Frosch's practice of allowing all eleven center directors to report directly to the administrator. Under Beggs, they reported to Mark and later Culbertson. In effect, by promoting people who were not held in high esteem by NASA's "marching army," and by not allowing his executives in the field to deal directly with him, Beggs isolated himself from the scientific credibility and technical expertise of the agency.

As his attentions were consumed with his political battle with Donald Regan, Beggs was inundated with other problems. The promises Mark talked Beggs into making to the Air Force to keep them flying on the shuttle came at a high price to NASA. In addition to supplying the Centaur upper stage for future, secret Air Force missions, NASA began building a new, spun-filament lightweight solid booster system for the shuttle. Officially, NASA said that the spun-filament boosters, which were much lighter than the steel solids, could be used on both military and civilian flights. But the mobile launchers at Kennedy could not launch the new solids without extensive modifications. And unlike their steel counterparts, the new boosters were for all practical purposes throwaways. The reusable steel boosters saved NASA an estimated $26 million each time a shuttle flew.

The spun-filament boosters were being built to help the shuttle carry heavier payloads from the new Vandenberg launch facilities. The shuttle could not carry the weight that NASA originally promised the Air Force. The fifteen-by-sixty-foot cargo bay could only carry 53,000 pounds, not the promised 65,000, into orbit from the Kennedy Space Center. NASA engineers knew that without the help of the earth's rotation which the Kennedy launch site provided, 30,000 pounds would be the limit for the West Coast launches at Vandenberg. This loss of payload capability understandably caused great consternation among Air Force officials. They had the job of orbiting a 35,000-pound Keyhole 12 surveillance satellite from Vandenberg for the Central Intelligence Agency and that was the weight NASA originally promised. The Air Force claimed that NASA misled them.

The Marshall Space Flight Center's solution was the lightweight boosters and a proposal to certify the three main shuttle engines far beyond their original design limits. Marshall said that if the engines were flown at 109 percent of their rated power instead of 104 percent, combined with the spun-filament boosters, 35,000 pounds from Vandenberg was possible. Some of the engineers argued that the worst that could happen is the main engines would have to be replaced after this kind of flight. Others protested that the engines' turbopumps could fail and the entire shuttle could be lost. The new lightweight solids Beggs ordered for Air Force launches and the increased certification for the engines would reduce safety margins and increase the cost of shuttle operations. But Beggs says he did it to keep the Air Force on board the shuttle and since "so few" flights would require such power, his decisions would not have a serious impact on the shuttle program. But costs on the project were escalating, and other shuttle work was being set aside, including the O-ring problem that kept showing up on flights.

One project set aside was a redesign of the seals attaching the steel solid booster segments. A troublesome burn-through had been noted on flight after flight. In March 1984, Hans Mark ordered a review of the solid rocket motor joints. Mark said, "The O-ring seal problem did gain my attention again just before I left NASA. On the tenth flight we noticed some charring of the O-rings in the lower field joint. This phenomenon had been observed once before on the second flight, but when it did not reappear we thought it was a one-time event. When we saw it again on the tenth flight, the question of what should be done was discussed at the Flight Readiness Review for the eleventh flight. After the completion of the Flight Readiness Review, I issued an 'Action Item' asking for a complete review of all the solid rocket motor seals and joints. . . . Unfortunately this review was never held. I made the decision of leaving NASA about two weeks after signing out the 'Action Item' so the matter was apparently dropped."[13]

Mark continues, "Both the people at the Marshall Space Flight Center and Thiokal apparently decided that they would develop a plan to fix the O-ring seal problem rather than review the problem with higher-level NASA management. It is for this reason, of course, that nothing was done for fifteen months." Mark says he discussed the O-rings and the burn-through with Beggs. Beggs denies it. Mark says, "I find that hard to believe, but things do slip the memory. You know, I certainly knew about them." Mark says remarks he has seen from upper-level NASA officials denying they were aware of the O-ring problems "seem very strange to me. Those were not the kind of things we would keep secret," Mark explains. [14]

After Mark left in mid-1984, all communications between Marshall and Beggs were funneled through Phil Culbertson. Culbertson had much of the pressure of the entire shuttle program dropped on his shoulders after General Abrahamson left the shuttle program to head the new Strategic Defense Initiative (SDI, also known as Star Wars). And the pressures Culbertson felt were clearly instigated by Beggs, Congress, and the White House. Culbertson states, "It was a matter of money. Sure . . . it was encouraged. Everybody was sort of caught up with the spirit of yes, we must become operational. And we felt, and I think it is a rational thought, that if we became operational, whatever the term really means, the more responsive we could be to the true customers. The more we could keep things on schedule. . . . We were needing to be competitive. . . . It was clear the greater the launch rate, the more economical the system would be to operate. And the more effectively we drew missions to the shuttle, the less it was gonna cost NASA for shuttle missions." [15]

Compounding Culbertson's problems in filling the void left by Mark was Beggs himself. "Beggs is not a very approachable guy. He is not easy to go in and sit down and say, 'Jim, I have got a problem and I think you're the cause. And I would like to talk it over.' You didn't do that with Jim Beggs, even after you worked closely with him. Some people you can, some people you can't. . . . On the other hand, Beggs was not too inclined to call people in and sit down and say, 'Look, I've got a lot of respect for you as center director but there are some things down there that you're causing me problems on. . . . Let's talk about them and see what's wrong.

. . . If we can come to an accommodation, we'll go on. Maybe we can't come to an accommodation and then, I'm the boss.' . . . Jim wouldn't do that. . . . He would tend to gradually freeze somebody out. You know he didn't do it in a vindictive sense at all. It was his nature," Culbertson recalls.

Culbertson said that because the center directors found Beggs less approachable than past administrators, they were reluctant to bring their problems to him. One center that did not bring problems to him was Marshall. Culbertson says this was because of a long tradition of independence from Washington in solving problems, not passing them on. But several current and former officials at Marshall said that in their opinion neither Culbertson nor Beggs wanted to hear anything that would disrupt the flight schedule of the shuttles. And they say the O-ring problem would have stopped the shuttle program in its tracks had it shown up in the NASA of von Braun.

In August 1985, Robert Tuttle, from White House Personnel, called Beggs and said Regan was demanding that a decision be made on Graham. Beggs remained adamant. "He [Tuttle] says, 'We've got to do something about this.' I said, 'What have we got to do?' I said, 'I don't have to do a goddamn thing about it and I am not going to take him and you can't send his nomination if I won't agree.'" Then Tuttle asked Beggs to talk to Graham one more time to explain why he could not accept him as his deputy. Tuttle hoped that the conversation would resolve the situation.

So Beggs called Graham and invited him in for a talk. "I said, 'Look Bill, I have nothing against you personally, I don't even know you. I have nothing against your background or anything else.' Although I had been warned by this time that the guy was a right-wing kook, a nut, I said, 'I don't know anything about your background, but you are not qualified.' I said, 'I need somebody in this job who is qualified.' I said, 'If I thought you were qualified, I would take you in a minute because you are a nice guy and comb your hair right.'" Beggs said that based on Graham's credentials he could place him in another job at NASA but Beggs did not think that Graham was qualified to be the second in command. Beggs recalls what transpired. "He [Graham] said, 'Let me think about it.' He thought about it for a week. He called me back and said, 'No, the only job I'll take is deputy.'" Graham denies Beggs ever offered him an alternative position at NASA.

Beggs called Tuttle and told him of his conversation with Graham. "He [Tuttle] said, 'This is really bad and let me think about it.' So a week or so later he called me up and said, 'You have just got to take this guy and do us a favor.' I don't know what happened. It was a weak moment or something. So I said, 'Alright, I'll take him.' Well I said, 'You guys owe me a whole bunch.' They said, 'By God, we'll take care of you. This is the last one, nothing else. And we'll give you anything.'"

Later Beggs says he realized how serious a mistake he made by agreeing to accept Graham as his deputy. But his job was to protect the civilian space program. By giving the White House this one appointment, he believed they would be more receptive to NASA's needs. But Beggs says the first thing Graham did was to try to install [in Beggs' opinion] "some of his right-wing cronies as his deputies." Beggs describes what occurred. "The first thing he told me was he [Graham] would like to bring in two men as special assistants. One is Charlie Kupperman and the other is Jonathan Thompson. And I said, 'Bring me their resumés.' So he sent me their resumés and I read them and I called him back and I said, 'No way.' And I said, 'Neither one of these guys is going to come into NASA.' And he said, 'Why not? I need them.' He said he particularly needed Charlie. He did because Kupperman programmed him like a computer. I said, 'No.

Kupperman has no background in space and he has no background in technology.'" Beggs told Graham that he could pick any aide in NASA he wanted or he could go over to the Department of Defense and select an aide on loan to NASA. "Oh, he was in a terrible tizzy. Well, now I know why. Because Kupperman is his brains. And this guy Jonathan Thompson apparently got promised to do something for him. . . . He had apparently been chased out of the White House," Beggs recalls.

In the fall of 1985, Beggs' days were filled with budget discussions on the space station and increasing problems with the Centaur upper stage for the shuttle. Every awful prediction about safety problems for the Centaur was coming true. "If there was ever a time I needed a qualified deputy it was then. Little did I know what I was in for." Beggs was alone at home on the first Saturday in September 1985, when the phone rang. The caller "said he was with the FBI and asked me if I was going to be in my office on Monday. I said, 'Yeah.' He said he had a letter to deliver to me," Beggs remembers. On Monday two FBI agents walked into the NASA administrator's office and said they were told to deliver the letter to Beggs. "Well, it turns out that these two guys had been up to their ears in this investigation from the beginning. But anyway, they knew what it was all about and that was the first inkling I had. I opened the letter in their presence and I read it. It said you are the subject of a grand jury investigation, not a target, a subject, investigating the DIVAD [Divisional Air Defense weapon] prototype contract and it gave the number. And the investigation covers offenses covered by the following group of laws and followed by a lot of legal mumbo jumbo. And I mumbled something like I didn't know what the hell that is and they said that is white-collar crime. And I said, 'Fine.' And they left."

Shocked, Beggs picked up the phone and called the General Dynamics' general counsel and asked him what was going on. "'Oh,' he said, 'that case.' And [he] said that this had been going on for years. And I said, 'Why the hell didn't you tell me?' And he said, 'Because we didn't take it seriously. We didn't think it was serious,'" Beggs says the lawyer told him. Jim Beggs was now facing the possibility of a felony charge concerning a government contract he had very little to do with and he could barely recall. Hardly the type to believe in conspiracies, Beggs became convinced that the struggle over Graham and the criminal investigation had to be linked. As he sat in his office, all he could think of was why now? Why so many years after the fact and after he agreed to take Graham as his deputy did this thing start? Beggs realized that the probe not only threatened his career, but it also was happening at a time when someone totally unqualified, installed at NASA under White House orders, was next in the leadership line. Now if he had to step down, someone favorably disposed to the Pentagon and the administration's more extreme elements would be in a position to make the civilian program impotent.

Beggs' legal troubles originated during the 1973 Yom Kippur War. The invasion on Yom Kippur was described as a sickening surprise by the late Israeli Prime Minister Golda Meir. But she was certain that the amazing Israeli Air Force would be able to rout the invading Egyptian tank force as it had in 1967. Israeli Air Force commanders ordered one hundred planes in the air for the attack. The battlefield commanders believed this would be enough aircraft to end the advance. The lead aircraft flew at less than one hundred feet over the Sinai. The pilot went in for his run on the tanks. The other planes followed at high speed. With any luck they would all make it back to their base within half an hour. Israel, after all, is a small country. But something was amiss. The lead plane was cut to ribbons by high-speed cannon fire that was amazingly accurate. As other planes made their low-level runs, the Israeli Air Force was being destroyed over the Sinai. The great counteroffensive to the Arab invasion was ending in shambles.

The damage to the Israeli Air Force from that afternoon encounter was kept secret. But CIA sources say that out of 350 planes, the Israelis lost forty. Never in the short history of that country had they suffered such aerial destruction. With aid from the United States, the Israelis fought back and won. But the weapon that did so much damage to the world's greatest air force caught the U.S. Army's attention. Atop the Egyptian armor was a new Soviet-supplied radar-directed, high-speed cannon. The United States had nothing like it. The Army wanted one, except faster and more sophisticated. A design competition to build the prototype was held. The two best bidders would combine the best of each design and build a prototype, one of which the Army would select for production. General Dynamics and Ford won the rights to build the prototypes. The Army decided it would let the prototypes battle each other rather than combine the best of both. By General Dynamics standards, the funding for the prototype was not much for a company used to being paid billions to build nuclear submarines and fleets of aircraft.

General Dynamics successfully built their prototype within government specifications at their Pomona, California, facilities. But the competing Ford prototype ran into some problems. Its 40-mm gun was having trouble hitting its targets. Just four months before the field competition for the contracts, the Army published a new lethality model for what exactly would constitute hitting a target. Beggs explains what happened. The "lethality model is the computer model by which you judge the effectiveness of the system. And, unfortunately, my division people did not [fully] judge the importance of what they [the Army] had done. What they did was reassess the kill capability of the system. What they did was give a higher score to a proximity quotient. And why did they do that? Because the 40-mm gun [the Ford gun] had trouble hitting the targets," Beggs recalls.

Ford was given the DIVAD contract and it was worth billions. To Beggs it was puzzling. The General Dynamics machine hit twice as many targets as the Ford prototype. In the field competition, the Ford prototype could not keep up with the M-60 tanks it was supposed to protect. One clear violation of the rules of the competition occurred when the Ford machines' automatic loading system failed. Instead of shutting down, the Ford prototype continued on. Beggs was disappointed in the results of the DIVAD competition but left General Dynamics shortly after the contract loss to Ford to assume his new job at NASA in June 1981.

Almost immediately after Beggs left General Dynamics, the DOD transferred their regular auditor at General Dynamics' Pomona, California, facility and installed a new one. The new auditor claimed that General Dynamics had cheated the government on its DIVAD prototype contract. Los Angeles Assistant U.S. Attorney Gary Black visited the Pomona facility and began an investigation into how General Dynamics spent its $39 million government contract for its losing system. After investigating General Dynamics over the summer of 1982, Black concluded there was no basis for prosecuting either the company or any employees. Beggs says he was never notified of any investigation involving DIVAD, including the one Black closed. But by the fall of 1985 Black had been transferred to the civil division of the Justice Department in Washington and a new lawyer had taken over the case in Los Angeles.

When Beggs' legal troubles began, General Dynamics was in its second year of scandal involving overbilling to the government for unjustified expenses. The DIVAD investigation was one of the smaller embarrassments, and General Dynamics failed to notify Beggs of the investigation. When Beggs did reach a lawyer at General Dynamics, he reassured Beggs and said that the Justice Department had no case. Beggs told the General Dynamics lawyer that Randy Bellows, the prosecutor who replaced Black, apparently did plan to proceed. With that, the lawyer told Beggs that as a director and officer of General Dynamics, he was entitled to legal coverage and recommended the NASA chief hire a lawyer.

By the time Beggs discovered he was using the same St. Louis law firm the dozen or so other defendants were using, the bizarre nature of the investigation was becoming clear. According to Beggs, Ford, who won the Pentagon contract, spent $2 billion building a failed system and was not under scrutiny. Shortly before Beggs knew he was under investigation, it became apparent that the Army assisted Ford in covering up test results which showed Ford's version of the DIVAD should never have been put into production. In late September, the lawyer representing Beggs as well as the dozen other General Dynamics defendants went to Los Angeles to find out just how serious prosecutor Bellows was. Afterwards the lawyer met with Beggs. Beggs remembers the conversation. "He told me I just had a meeting the likes of which I have never had before. And he said, 'Well, I walked into his [Bellows'] office and sat down and he said, 'I could offer immunity for any of your clients if they will give testimony against Beggs.' And, gee whiz, that surprises me a little bit. 'Have you got anything to offer Beggs?' He says, 'I might be ready to let Beggs cop a plea if he will offer evidence and testimony against Lewis [David Lewis, chairman of General Dynamics].' He said, 'What do you think of that?' I [Beggs] said, 'Well what I think of it is you can go back and tell the son of a bitch,' and that is what I look at him as, 'that I don't have any evidence to offer against Lewis and even if I did I wouldn't take up his offer of immunity. Tell him to go to hell,'" Beggs remembers telling his lawyer.

By October it was clear that Beggs was the one the prosecutors were after. But even then Beggs had trouble taking the case too seriously. He learned that the U.S. attorney orchestrating the case was Robert Bonner who became famous as the man who had John Delorean on videotape making cocaine deals with the FBI and who failed to convict him. In Beggs' opinion: "It was obvious to me this guy was an idiot. Towards the end of October they sent me another letter this time saying you are now a target." By now Beggs was seriously concerned and hired his own attorney, Vincent Fuller, of Williams and Connelly, one of the more powerful Washington law firms. Beggs also asked his daughter, a New York lawyer, to work on his case.

It had now been more than four years since the case was opened and no one from the DOD or the Department of Justice had ever questioned Beggs about the specifics of the case. The statute of limitations was about run out. "In the third week in November, just before Thanksgiving, the Justice Department had discussions with the attorneys and came back to all of the employees who had been targeted and they said, 'We think you have raised some interesting points on this whole thing. If all the defendants, including the company, would waive their rights under the statute of limitations, we would consider continuing our discussions to see if this can be worked out.' Well, they called everybody including the company and we all agreed. We said, 'What the hell, what have we got to lose,'" Beggs remembers.

For the first time Beggs felt like the holidays might not be so bleak. On the day before Thanksgiving, Beggs got a call from the Washington office of General Dynamics. According to Beggs, "They dropped the letter off at GD's attorney's office in town. It said that they had changed their minds and they were going to proceed with an indictment on Monday and they did. The Monday after Thanksgiving. So I was indicted. So I called Don Regan and said, 'I am indicted.' I said, 'This is a cockamamy case, and I don't understand it.' And I said, 'Obviously, I have got to take a leave of absence while this ends. But . . . I would like that courtesy.' Well, he had a meeting with his staff. And they came back and said, 'No, we want you to resign.' And I said, 'I ain't gonna resign unless the president asks me to resign.' I said that Ed Meese went through that horrible thing and they took care of him. So my lawyer went over and talked to Len Garment [at the White House]. And he [my lawyer] said, 'This is totally inequitable. You have done this for others, why don't you do this for Jim Beggs.' And Len agreed. And Len apparently went to Regan and said, 'We can't do this.' So they agreed to let me take a leave."

The timing of the indictment could not have been worse. He was turning over NASA to a complete novice with a political agenda. Beggs' entire tenure at NASA had been a balancing act. He appeased the military and kept the manned program going. Keeping the manned program going meant keeping the space science programs going. And he had gotten Ronald Reagan to commit to a space station by the early 1990s.

Beggs was in shock. He believed that Graham was part of a setup to get him out of NASA. "I think Graham knew I was going to get indicted when he first came over to talk to me and refused to give up the job. Now how did he know it? Well Lois Herrington, John Herrington's wife, is an assistant attorney general and Becky Norton Dunlap, who was Herrington's deputy at the White House, is now in Ed Meese's office. Becky and Lois are still very well plugged into the Brownies in the White House. I think they told Graham,

'You get over there . . . then Beggs is going to be indicted and he'll be gone.' The thing they didn't count on is that the president would give me a leave. They thought that he would immediately accede to the administration position and that he [Graham] would be off and running NASA," says Beggs. Graham stepped into the job of acting administrator eight days after he came to NASA. Keyworth had won round two.

11

Death of a Dream

When Beggs had first learned of his indictment, his initial reaction was to call a NASA headquarters staff meeting and announce his intention to stay in office during the legal proceedings. He even called a press conference for the next day to tell the public that he would not leave. But Don Regan would have none of it. He told White House aide Leonard Garment that Beggs would not have to resign until his guilt or innocence was determined, but he would have to take a leave of absence from NASA.

Dr. William Graham had been at NASA less than two weeks prior to Beggs' indictment. Beggs said Graham came into his office and said, "'I'd appreciate it very much if you'd introduce me at your farewell speech and give me a chance to say something.' I said, 'Fine.' I said, 'I'd really hoped that we could work together on this thing . . . because you are going to have difficulties. This is not an easy agency to run and you are going to be working in a tough year where you try to launch fourteen or fifteen times. . . . It's going to require some hands-on managing.' So, I gave my farewell speech and I called him up and said, 'I want you all to meet Bill Graham. He's going to be acting administrator and I have full confidence he'll do a good job and here's Bill.' So he raced forward and from that day until this, he never said a word to me except to thank me when I came in and told him what he ought to do after the accident. That was all. I mean he didn't ring my bell. He didn't write me any memos asking for advice. He never came into my office again," Beggs remembers.[1] That same day Graham, a tall and austere-looking man, told a reporter, "I'm in full charge and I intend to run this agency as though I am."

Although NASA was about to launch three important shuttle missions and begin its most ambitious launch year yet, the administrator and the acting administrator were not talking to each other. Only Beggs had the information to instruct Graham on how to operate the agency, and the shuttle program's problems were mounting. Graham said he believed that no matter what the two men's differences, people's lives were on the line. Graham says, "It seemed to me that if I were in a job and a deputy had come in, even if he hadn't been my choice, I would at that point have taken some interest in trying to . . . assure myself that he was obtaining the information he needed. That he was coming up to speed on the appropriate issues. . . . But with Beggs, the output was exactly zero. It seemed to me his agenda . . . might be that he was going to prove the president wrong [in demanding my appointment to the deputy's job] and him right by providing me with zero information here."[2]

Instead of leaving NASA, Beggs remained in an office down the hall from his old office. The White House told Graham that Beggs would stay on to provide "continuity and consultation" to his replacement. In fact, Beggs said nothing to Graham. Graham said he asked his assistance on a matter and found Beggs "aggressive and hostile." In the late fall of 1985, the atmosphere at NASA headquarters was divisive, and morale was reaching its lowest ebb in the entire history of the space agency. Beggs was still meeting with Culbertson on a regular basis. For Graham it presented a serious management problem. Graham found that NASA employees seemed to be intimidated by Beggs' presence. As acting administrator, Graham believed that he was being undermined because Beggs kept telling NASA executives that he would soon be back in charge. Graham says that Beggs was putting career NASA employees in a position of choosing between the two men, that Beggs was, in effect, "leaning" on the NASA staff. "It put the staff in a tough position because they'd just say, 'Well, if I do something that Beggs finds objectionable and he comes back, he'll be in a position where he can make my life very difficult,'" Graham remembers.[3] General Manager Phil Culbertson, who played a "jack of all trades" role for Beggs after Hans Mark left, remained loyal to Beggs. This allegiance compounded Graham's problems. Graham contends that Culbertson was not passing on critical information to him.

Before Beggs' leave of absence, Graham had busied himself with his first Flight Readiness Review for the twenty-third shuttle flight. The November 26, 1985, mission was assigned the task of orbiting three communication satellites. The cargo bay of *Atlantis*, the fourth shuttle in the fleet, also featured a large structure that would help determine the best way to construct the space station in orbit. But Graham, an engineer by training, did not like what he saw at the meeting. "I was sitting in this Flight Readiness Review briefing for 61-Charlie . . . for two and a half hours, and one view graph comes up and says 4,000 hertz resonance have occurred in these three engines," Graham remembers. For Graham it was a red light. He was convinced someone inserted the graph into the briefing to send him a message. Graham explains his reaction. "It was like the dog that didn't bark. The view graph didn't have to be in there because those engines were not going to be used on this mission. . . . So immediately after the meeting I got a couple of those guys aside and asked them what is this 4,000 hertz resonance. Very high frequency vibration. . . . Well the next question was, what was the amplitude of it? And they said, 'Well, it was somewhere between 30 and 90 Gs on the engine.' I said, 'My God, those engines can't stand that kind of vibration.' They said, 'No, if we leave that on very long, it will start causing cracks to form and things to potentially fail in the engines,'" Graham recalls.[4]

Graham ordered the engineers to find out what was causing the excessive vibration. They told him they were already "working on it." The answer made Graham nervous. "Well, that is an answer you have to be careful with because if you have a car and it's got a history of the axle breaking or something, if you call the factory and they say, 'yeah, we know about that and we're working on it,' that doesn't make it any safer for you to go down to the beltway the next day." But Beggs recalls that "In December they had all those troubles and I think it scared him because we did have a whole succession of things and it was obvious he didn't understand what was going on down there. . . . My friends down at Kennedy called me and asked me to tell them about this guy." Beggs charges that Graham concerned himself with secrecy. ". . . Whenever he made phone calls, he went back to his motel to a private line. He never made calls on the federal system."[5] Beggs says that Graham also had a new private line put in the administrator's office.

When Graham went to the Cape, he said he found launch crews that were grossly overworked by Beggs' increased launch schedule. And he knew it was going to get worse. "It is a little bit like calling American Airlines and saying, 'Okay, last year you ran an airline of size x. Next year we want you to run an airline of size 2x.' Airlines don't change operations that fast. And changing NASA's operations that fast was extremely ambitious," Graham points out. The next shuttle flight was scheduled for December with a congressman as a passenger. Graham was becoming so concerned about Beggs' launch schedule that he postponed that flight until early 1986 to give the launch crews some time off during the holidays.[6]

Colleagues say Rocco Petrone was worried about the work crews too, but for a different reason. Petrone shed no tears for Beggs' departure. Petrone was now trying to deal with what he considered the worst of Beggs' decisions. In order to reduce the costs for shuttle operations, Beggs contracted with Lockheed, which had nothing to do with building the shuttle, to process the vehicles for launch. That meant that for the first time, Rockwell, Martin Marietta, and other major contractors were not servicing the vehicles they understood so well. In some cases damage was done to the shuttle system by workers who were unfamiliar with it. Rockwell had built it. They understood it and they understood it was far from perfect. They understood that the shuttle was not an airliner.

Petrone learned from his engineers that Lockheed Corporation, who won the launch operations contract, was using unauthorized tools and small parts around the four orbiters. Although Lockheed was responsible for the launches, Petrone understood all too well that if a major system failure took place, it would be Rockwell that would take the heat. Now Petrone faced the added problem of having a shortage of engineers to monitor the still young system to see if some major flaw had not been detected. Petrone had been in manned flight since the beginning and what he was seeing seemed foolhardy.

Due to a chronic shortage of spare parts, the shuttles were being cannibalized from flight to flight. Because of the extraordinary budget pressures Beggs put on the system to try to make it economical, shuttle parts were being taken from one orbiter for use in another to keep the system going on schedule. The chairman of NASA's Oversight Committee in the House of Representatives was worried. Congressman Don Fuqua (D-Florida) wondered, "How do you get the development contractor out of it? There is no way Lockheed knows more about that bird than Rockwell or that they know more about the external tank than Martin or that SRB than Thiokol. Now you had to get the price down and I was supporting that and urging Jim [Beggs] to do that. But I did have a concern about what might happen."[7]

What Fuqua did not know was that the SRB seals had failed *ten out of twenty-three flights* by the end of 1985. To prevent an interruption in the flight schedule, waivers were signed that allowed the flights to continue despite the safety threats. Hans Mark's memo had been ignored for more than a year. In fact, NASA was flying the shuttle on backup systems and that procedure was a violation of a mission rule that had been in effect since Alan Shepard flew a quarter century earlier.

Graham also inherited the first planned launch using the Centaur upper stage set for May 1986. While he had not yet looked at the cost overruns, Graham was well aware that NASA needed to launch within a thirteen-month window or the mission would have to be postponed another thirteen months. And the scheduled date of May 1986 was cutting it close. But NASA soon discovered that many of the Centaur components were substandard. These problems put further pressures on the tightening launch schedule. There were less than seven months before the first scheduled flight of the most dangerous payload man had ever carried into space—a combination of the Centaur stage and the nuclear-powered Galileo probe. And Graham found NASA "behind the power curve on parts, the components, and somewhat behind the power curve on full checkout. . . . It [the Centaur] hadn't yet been integrated into the shuttle, much less put in the launch complex," Graham notes.

From Beggs' point of view, Graham's management behavior reflected his background and inexperience. "I had an office there and they [the White House] leaked to the press that I was coming into the office and there was an article in the *Post* [*The Washington Post*] saying Beggs is still using his office. Well, I was. And it also said he was still using his car, which was not true. And using government franked envelopes and so forth, which wasn't true. But I did go about twice a week to pick up my mail and answer phone calls which were numerous. All the NASA people wanted to tell me what he [Graham] did today. The first thing he did was issue a lot of directives. He acted like a typical analyst. He sat in his office with the door closed and he wrote directives. The first directive he wrote described how you were supposed to wear your NASA badge. The second directive he wrote was a standards of conduct memo on what was permissible and what was not permissible for NASA employees. Of course that raised the hackles of everybody because NASA has got a bunch of free spirits," Beggs explains.

But what distressed Beggs the most was Graham's actions to undo the launch agreement that NASA had negotiated with the Department of Defense over the past three years. That agreement called for the Air Force to pay yearly all costs for its projected shuttle flights up front in exchange for a price break on the variable launch costs. Beggs describes what happened. "That thing was signed in blood by Pete [Aldridge] and I. . . . So what Graham was doing was letting Pete off the hook on his agreement by allowing him to get a larger number of Titan backups and saying, 'Okay, you don't have to pay this up front payment.' And he told the folks in the Manned Space Office, we're not going to take anymore commercial customers. . . . He was going to unwind everything," Beggs contends.[8]

Beggs was angry because he believed these actions were the precursor to a move by the White House to turn the manned spaceflight program over to the Air Force. "I went to my friends on the Hill, people like Jake Garn and Jack Danforth, and told them they've got to tell the White House he [Graham] cannot be confirmed as administrator. By that time they had made an independent assessment and decided he was [a] loose cannon and didn't want him either. They both called [Don] Regan and said, 'No way, now get a proper administrator in there.' Regan said, 'Well we can't appoint a proper administrator while Beggs is there.' So they called me and said, 'If they appoint a proper administrator will you resign?' And I said, 'Sure. I'll quit just as soon as they appoint somebody proper.'" Beggs then entered into a long negotiation with the White House over who the new administrator would be. He said he was adamant. He wanted James Fletcher or somebody with that level of experience. Beggs said he refused to resign until that arrangement was completed.

The idea of flying private citizens on the Space Shuttle did not appeal to many at the Johnson Space Center, especially the astronauts. But Beggs was convinced that it was just the kind of publicity the program needed. He wanted to show that the shuttle made spaceflight an ordinary activity. He wanted to prove that the shuttle was "operational." Beggs agreed to allow Senator Jake Garn, the chairman of the NASA Senate Appropriations Subcommittee, to be the first politician to fly in space. But former Congressman Don Fuqua opposed the idea and made his feelings known to Beggs. "He [Beggs] said, 'Jake Garn is really putting the heat on me about flying in space.' And I said, 'Well, Jim let me make one thing clear to you. I'm not asking. I would love to fly. I think it would be one of the most thrilling experiences a person could ever witness. . . . But I don't think I or any other politician has got any damn business up there.' First of all you don't have the time to adequately train to do the job and contribute to the flight," Fuqua argues.[9]

Fuqua wrote Beggs a letter protesting the Garn flight. He was even more incensed when his own subcommittee chairman, Congressman Bill Nelson, requested to fly. "He [Nelson] said, 'I know how you feel about this.' And he said, 'This is the most important thing in my life.' And I said, 'Bill, I am not going to go out and wave my arms to try and stop it,'" Fuqua remembers. Because both Nelson and Garn insisted on flying, Fuqua said a former Air Force engineer named Gregory Jarvis, who designed satellites for Hughes Aircraft Company, was bumped from both those flights. He finally was reassigned to fly aboard *Challenger* on Mission 51-L.

Graham's first flight experience as acting administrator was the January launch of *Columbia* with Congressman Bill Nelson aboard. On January 6, 1986, the countdown was being turned over to the automatic sequencer at T minus 31 seconds. The computers aboard *Columbia* detected a temperature drop in the main engines below launch safety limits and terminated the countdown. NASA quickly diagnosed the problem. The launch crew had inadvertently drained 18,000 pounds of liquid oxygen from the main tank. If they had overridden the temperature indicator warning light, *Columbia* would not have had enough fuel to make it into orbit.

It was a sobering experience for Graham. NASA told the

press a "mechanical failure" postponed the flight. Although Graham had delayed the flight by a month to ease the pressures on the launch crew, the flight processing demands had many workers putting in forty straight twelve-hour days. There was another dangerous incident on the Nelson flight. A member of the launch team broke off a temperature probe in the prevalve of the orbiter. The broken probe went through the plumbing and endangered one of the shuttle's main engines. Had the fueling incident not stopped the launch, the shuttle would have taken off with the probe in the engine valve. When actuators shut the valve, it must be done very precisely or enormous quantities of oxygen flow into the engine forcing the flow of hydrogen to be out of balance. If that happened, the engine would consume itself in flight and destroy the crew and the vehicle.

On January 15 the Flight Readiness Review was held for *Challenger* mission 51-L. The mission had two primary objectives. From NASA's standpoint the deployment of their second Tracking and Data Relay Satellite was vital. NASA was, after all, paying nearly $270 million a year in payments on the system. The sooner the space agency had a full complement of satellites in orbit, the sooner its far-flung, ground-based tracking network could be closed. The second objective was to deploy a small Spartan satellite that was going to examine Halley's Comet and then be recovered. But that experiment paled compared to the Halley's Comet encounters the Soviets and Europeans had launched. For the public, the highlight of the flight was Christa McAuliffe. She had been training for the flight since July. Unlike some of the other "passengers" the astronauts had to contend with, including one who had to be restrained on an earlier spaceflight, Ms. McAuliffe was considered a professional who trained very hard for the flight. Judith Resnick, Gregory Jarvis, Colonel Ellison Onizuka, and Ronald McNair were the mission specialists. Piloting *Chal-*

lenger was U.S. Navy Captain Michael Smith, a rookie astronaut. Francis Richard Scobee was the mission commander on his second flight.

In December as the big solids were stacked for 51-L, none of the seven crew members was aware of field joint problems in the Solid Rocket Boosters (SRBs) or the esoteric problems of shipping and assembling the boosters. They also would have no way of knowing that a 1977 Consumer Product Safety Commission ruling banning asbestos in certain paint products would have a tragic effect on the flight. NASA had used an "off the shelf" putty manufactured by the Fuller O'Brien Paint Company in San Francisco to help seal the field joints of the SRBs through the first ten missions. Fuller O'Brien, fearful of legal action because of the asbestos ban, stopped manufacturing the asbestos-based putty. When a low-level budget analyst named Richard Cook warned in a July 23, 1985, memo about O-ring problems that needed attention, he said of the burn-through: "Engineers have not yet determined the cause of the problem. Candidates include the use of a new type of putty (the putty formerly used was removed from the market by NASA because it contained asbestos)." NASA began buying a different putty from a New Jersey company. The SRB experts at Marshall noted the new putty did not seem to seal the joints as well as the old putty, but they continued to use it anyway.

The mission was to last six days and *Challenger* was assigned a circular, 153-nautical-mile orbit. The original launch date was set for January 22, 1986. But work slippage on the flight carrying Congressman Nelson caused the launch to be postponed to January 26, Superbowl Sunday. For NASA a launch on the same day as the championship football game was a public relations bonanza. Although all of the television networks, except Cable News Network, had quit covering the launches live, news stories on the lift-off were certain to catch some of the public's attention.

Beggs, Kennedy Space Center Director Dick Smith, and others remember that Graham was very concerned about the guest list for the 51-L launch. Beggs said he received a phone call a few days before the scheduled launch of 51-L from the Public Affairs Office. "They said, 'What's with this guy Graham?' And I said, 'I don't know. What's he doing now?' And they said, 'Well, he is reviewing in detail the whole guest list.' And I said, 'What's he doing?' Well, he [the Public Affairs Officer] says, 'He's [Graham's] scratching names out he says he is going to get in trouble with the Hill.'" The public affairs people told Beggs that Graham was taking Democrats and any others he perceived to have liberal leanings off the list.

The day before the scheduled Sunday launch of Mission 51-L, Congressman Fuqua visited the crew quarters and then went flying with an astronaut. "You could see the weather. You could see all the way to Orlando. It was beautiful. . . . You could see Daytona Beach. Gorgeous weather. I had been to Jacksonville that morning and it had been raining there, but John Young (the Chief Astronaut) told me he had flown all the way to Pensacola and the weather was coming but it was probably going to be Monday before it got there." At dinner in a nearby restaurant Fuqua was called and told the mission was scrubbed because of weather. Fuqua awakened at his Patrick Air Force Base VIP quarters to a beautiful Superbowl Sunday morning. The scrubbed launch caused Vice President George Bush to cancel a last-minute visit for the lift-off. "I saw Graham back in Washington on Sunday," Fuqua recalls, "and I said, 'Who the hell called that shot off?' And he said, 'I did.' And he said, 'All the weather people swore in blood it was going to be bad.'" But the Air Force predictions of terrible weather on Sunday were wrong.

The launch was recycled twenty-four hours to Monday, January 27. Fuqua was sitting in his Rayburn Building office watching preparations for the flight on closed-circuit NASA television with former X-15 test pilot and committee staffer Scott Crossfield. Crossfield was briefing Fuqua on the newly proposed Transatmospheric vehicle. During the briefing Fuqua would glance up and look at how the countdown was progressing. Fuqua said, "That's when they went up and [found that] someone had wrung a bolt off in the door latch." Rocco Petrone, watching the same picture on closed-circuit television in the firing room at the Cape, would not discover for a week that an illegal tool had been used on *Challenger* that morning. Fuqua was furious. "Instead of signing for it and saying, you know, there is a door latch broken, nobody ever admitted it, ever signed for it. You are supposed to sign all the way up to supervisor that it's clean. Well secondly, the normal procedure when we are getting ready to launch is that the launch crew takes an emergency kit, kind of like a doctor's kit, which has got all kinds of tools you might need . . . last minute tools for closeout. They didn't have that. They had to go get a tool so they could fix that bolt. Scobee insisted that they fix it. They got the tool, an electric drill, and the battery was dead. So they had to send somebody over to the industrial area—a twenty-minute drive—to get the tool and come back up and fix it. So you lose almost an hour just picking up the drill. Everybody is sitting there waiting and I am taking my anger out on Scott and Scott had nothing to do with it," Fuqua recalls. Crossfield told Fuqua that everything seemed to be sloppy the last couple of shuttle flights. The angry Fuqua sent word to shuttle program boss Mike Weeks "that if the general public saw all that, NASA would be the laughingstock of the country and they'd better get their act together." By the time the repairs were made, the crosswinds familiar to the Cape began blowing across the shuttle runway.

An abort landing would be difficult in the high winds. The launch was scrubbed at 12:36 P.M.

Within half an hour a teleconference was held, involving Thiokol personnel and NASA officials at Marshall who discussed the effect of extremely cold temperatures on the Solid Rocket Boosters if *Challenger* were launched in twenty-four hours. Meetings went on all afternoon and through the night. Morton Thiokol Project Manager Allan J. MacDonald voiced his concerns about low temperatures affecting the O-rings to his superiors in Utah. At 8:45 Monday evening in a teleconference, Thiokol engineers urged NASA not to launch unless the temperatures of the O-rings were at least fifty-three degrees Fahrenheit. At 11:15 Monday night Kennedy Space Center officials told Allan MacDonald not to concern himself with either the high seas affecting the booster recovery area or the cold affecting the O-rings. Arnold D. Aldrich, manager of the shuttle system in Houston, was not informed of the O-ring concerns and Culbertson did not pass the information on to Graham. Throughout the night the weather got colder and the seas got rougher. The ocean reached Sea State Six, too rough a sea for successful recovery of the SRBs after launch. The loss of the booster casings could cost NASA $26 million for the flight of 51-L.

At Rockwell headquarters in Downy, California, a complete control center displayed launch data similar to the control room at the Cape. At 4:30 A.M. (PST) Petrone, who had returned to Los Angeles, walked into the center and looked at the NASA closed-circuit television of Launch Complex 39B and saw the ice formations, some of them several feet long. He expected the count to be stopped. The highest ranking official of NASA at the launch of 51-L was Phil Culbertson.

Although it was only Graham's second launch as acting administrator, he decided to leave the Cape and return to Washington that Sunday. Many at NASA found this strange since traditionally either the administrator or his deputy was on hand for every shuttle flight. One reason Graham wanted to go back to Washington was Beggs had been causing him political problems on Capitol Hill. It had become obvious that Beggs was not only dealing directly with NASA officials like Culbertson on agency issues, he was also talking regularly to several senators, including Jake Garn.[10] Beggs conceded that he was doing everything he could to sidetrack Graham's campaign to be named permanent administrator. Graham returned to Washington to do a little political fence mending. He had an appointment that Tuesday morning with the Republican leader of NASA's Oversight Subcommittee, Congressman Manuel Lujan. Although the time of the meeting conflicted with the launch of *Challenger*, Graham arrived punctually at Lujan's office.

At 3:10 A.M. the launch crew began pumping in liquid hydrogen and liquid oxygen into the separate tanks inside the giant external tank of *Challenger*. The twenty-seven-degree temperature felt cold to the ice teams on the pad as the ten-mile-an-hour wind blew against the shuttle. The fuel in the external tank, at less than 400 degrees below zero, contributed to the cold, and the launchpad was a bitingly uncomfortable place to be that morning. The field joints, the O-rings, and the putty sealing them now reached a temperature of twenty-nine degrees. The O-rings were already shrinking and hardening from the cold at each of the field joints on the two fifteen-story-tall SRBs. The shrunken O-rings were so cold that the surrounding putty had congealed to a cold greasy substance. The ice team does not report surface temperatures routinely. So the twenty-five degrees on the left booster and the eight-degree temperature on the right booster were never reported to the launch team in the firing room.

On the clear and cold morning of January 28, Beggs left his large comfortable home in the affluent Westmoreland Circle section of Washington for NASA headquarters. He walked through the double doors leading to the seventh-floor executive suite. He walked past the portraits of those administrators who had given NASA such a flawless history in manned flight. He greeted the receptionist and secretarial staff. He turned on the closed-circuit NASA television set and saw ice all over the launch tower. Beggs says he was shocked that the countdown was still going forward. He said it was not so much ice damage to the tiles that concerned him; all that would do was lengthen the turnaround time for the next flight. What worried him was "internal ice." "With condensation you get internal ice around the piping of those main engines and you change the frequency of vibration. . . . When you get a frequency of vibration you get a cascading effect and you can shake yourself to pieces." Beggs then learned that the sea state was marginal at best for recovery of the $26-million solid boosters. "So I wouldn't have launched. . . . It was a bad decision. I was in my office that morning and I told two people—who shall be unknown—'You ought to go call those people and tell them to think hard about launching.' I said, 'I can't tell them, but you can call them and tell them.'"[11]

Phil Culbertson, who had gone to Beggs for advice several times, was on his own for the launch of 51-L. He was the senior NASA person on the scene and the one individual who could say no to launching under such extreme conditions. Culbertson had been worried about the space transportation system after the earlier problems in January with Bill Nelson's flight. He was concerned that in an operations mode, NASA was "more reliant on individual initiative than on a very elaborate chain of communications where any kind of problem is brought to the top."[12] In fact, few problems had risen to the top of NASA in the last six months. Culbertson remained in a small glass enclosure above the main floor of the firing room watching the countdown. A few minutes before lift-off Culbertson left his station and took an elevator to the top of the fifty-story-tall Vehicle Assembly Building for a good view of the launch from Pad 39B.

Graham arrived at the office at 7:15 A.M. Tuesday morning. He says he turned on the monitor in his office to watch NASA's closed-circuit television to check on the progress of the launch. He remembers having a conversation with an official at the space center, probably Center Director Dick Smith. They discussed problems with getting the SRB recovery ships in position for the launch. "I think it is more like they weren't in position but they were getting in position," Graham recalls. Graham remembered seeing the ice on NASA television. He made the "presumption that the people who were working there knew what they were doing. It didn't worry me in [that sense] because they had ice there before."

Beggs did not see Graham the morning of the launch. Graham left before the launch for his meeting on Capitol Hill with Congressman Lujan. For the first time in shuttle history, an administrator or a deputy administrator was not sitting in the control center in Houston or at the Cape. Before he left, Graham failed to remind Phil Culbertson to keep an open phone line between headquarters and the Cape. Graham feared that if there were a launch emergency "everybody picks up the phone at once . . . and there are only so many lines and you just sit there without even a dial tone. . . . "

A NASA driver took Graham and his assistant Jack Murphy to the Longworth Building for the 11:00 A.M. appointment. Lujan "was delayed slightly from other business," according to Graham. Graham and Murphy talked with a congressional aide while they waited. In the adjoining building, Congressman Fuqua was in his office watching launch preparations on NASA television. With him was House Science Committee Staff Director Dr. Harold Hansen. Fuqua and Hansen watched the seven-member crew climb into the shuttle and the white-room crew close out the hatch. Flight controllers broke into mocking applause since the closeout crew had so much trouble with the hatch the day before. Because of ice and frozen ground support equipment, including a problem in the fire protection system, the launch was delayed two hours.

At Pad 39B the flight crew was ensconced in *Challenger*. On the middeck Onizuka sat next to the shuttle hatch in a little entryway into the ship. Sitting in front of him were McAuliffe and Jarvis. The entire crew were lying on their backs strapped in their seats. The three crew members on the middeck had no assignments for lift-off. They simply waited. Upstairs on the flight deck, Pilot Smith sat on the right-hand front seat. Behind him was Ronald McNair. Scobee sat in the commander's seat on the left side. Behind and to the right of his seat, Resnick was strapped in. On the flight deck Smith and Scobee were busy going down the long checkout list and communicating with Kennedy launch control. A few minutes before the lift-off, Graham remembers turning up the television set in Lujan's office. Fuqua did the same in his office. At NASA headquarters, Beggs watched NASA television. Aboard *Challenger* the final minutes to lift-off were filled with banter and technical references. Three miles away the crew's families shivered in the cold on the bleachers at the visitors site. The wind blew across the roof of the VAB as Culbertson arrived on top of the enormous structure to watch the launch. At T minus 30 seconds, Scobee told those sitting on the middeck "thirty seconds down there." At 16:37:53.444, 6.566 seconds prior to the Solid Rocket Booster (SRB) ignition, *Challenger*'s general purpose computer issued the first of three commands to fire the main engines. Scobee said, "There they go, guys." After checking all of *Challenger*'s systems, the same general purpose computer decreed *Challenger* fit for flight, and at zero, lit the solids. In the time between zero and one second, at precisely T plus .650 seconds, the fate of *Challenger* and her crew was sealed. The O-rings and new putty did not react well to the cold. The enormous pressure from the gases inside the SRB caused the boosters to expand. As the SRBs expanded, the booster segments rotated against each other. Although the falling ice, the distance, and the steam obscured it, a puff of ominous black smoke streamed out of the lower field joint of the right booster as *Challenger* broke its mooring bolts and lifted off.

At the end of the first second, Smith told the crew, "Here we go." At T plus 7 seconds the big stack began to roll over on its back. The flame was still pouring out of the SRBs and main engines. Every second the pressure against the lower joint increased and the tiny opening that was emitting the smoke became the catalyst for instant destruction. At twelve seconds the surging heat in the booster melted the O-ring and putty and created a temporary seal. At T plus 19 seconds Smith commented on the stiff winds buffeting *Challenger*. At T plus 28 seconds *Challenger* was traveling half the speed of sound and reached 10,000 feet. Now the power of the rockets was telling. At T plus 40 seconds *Challenger* tore through the sound barrier at 19,000 feet.

At T plus 43 seconds *Challenger* throttled down its main engines to sixty percent of their thrust. The solids, which cannot be throttled down, continued to provide eighty percent of the enormous power it takes to climb into earth orbit. As *Challenger* entered Max Q, the period when the shuttle faces its greatest dynamic pressure, the ride shook the stack and the vibration broke the temporary seal. The O-ring failed.

At T plus 57 seconds, Scobee announced that the main engines were being throttled up. At T plus 60 seconds the main engines reached 104 percent. As the crew felt the unbelievable rush of power, they had no idea what was happening to the right Solid Rocket Booster propelling them. Mike Smith yelled, "Feel that mother go."

Heat at 5,800 degrees began to emerge from the joint in a plume of flame. It traveled around the entire lower-right SRB failed joint. The thrust from the plume caused the struts connecting the right solid to the external tank to break loose. The swiveling booster at T plus 72.1 seconds smashed into the stubby right wing of *Challenger* and a fraction of a second later swiveled back to smash through the thin aluminum skin of the external tank. That blow breached the walls of the hydrogen and oxygen tanks. The thin skin of the giant external tank became the target of the wayward plume of flame.

Fuqua looked at the television screen and watched the explosion. "And first I thought it was staging because the solids came off and then I looked at my clock and I said, 'Holy shit! That's not two minutes.' Something has happened because they burn [for two minutes] and it's been a little over a minute, seventy-three seconds." A block away in Lujan's office Graham watched *Challenger* climb, his wristwatch programmed to the length of time it would take for the solid booster to burn. Graham looked at his watch and could not believe what he saw. All he could think of was, "No way the solids can go like that because they are basically locked in a ball joint until the thrust drops off to something like ten percent. . . . So that can't happen. But you say it just did happen. That's not right, which it wasn't. I turned to Lujan and I said, 'Something's very wrong here. . . .'"

Nine miles above the Atlantic, the nightmare NASA had feared for twenty-five years was playing itself out in a horrifyingly long ordeal for the crew. Mike Smith could now see the nightmare outside his window on the right side of *Challenger*. Seventy-three seconds after the launch, he said, "Uh, Oh!" What looked from earth like a disintegrating orbiter caught in a fireball was not. The explosion was, in fact, less than fifteen percent of the energy *Challenger* was capable of releasing had everything possible gone wrong. The aerodynamic stress of the solids breaking away caused *Challenger* to come apart. But this shuttle, which had been reused more than any other, behaved as it was supposed to until the awful end. After the external tank blew, the last of the telemetry told ground controlers, just as it was supposed to, that a main engine shut down due to lack of fuel.

The force of the explosion separated the pressure vessel, or the crew cabin, from the aluminum and tile structure that was once the orbiter. The crew cabin careened to 65,000 feet. The force of the blast probably did not seriously injure any of the crew members. Evidence indicates that Dick Scobee's emergency egress air pack was never turned on. But Michael Smith's air pack was probably turned on by either Resnick or McNair. That action meant that for as long as it took for a crew member to activate Smith's air pack, at least two of the seven *Challenger* astronauts were aware that they were hurtling to their deaths. The recovered gauges showed that much of the air in the emergency egress packs had been used. A crew member was breathing for several minutes. Once the crew cabin separated from the orbiter, only cabin and emergency breathing air was available. The cabin dropped 65,000 feet in two minutes and forty-five seconds. *Challenger*'s cabin and crew slammed into eighty feet of water at 207 miles an hour. No one survived.

Phil Culbertson could only look at the empty and smoldering launch complex and watch the twisted clouds in the sky that had been *Challenger*. "I ran back downstairs, went back in the firing room and met with Jesse Moore and Dick Smith and told Dick we needed a room in which we could gather people together and develop a course of action. I didn't say it quite that rationally but it was something like that." It would be an hour before Graham spoke to Culbertson. In the meantime, Beggs instructed Culbertson over the phone. Immediately after the accident, Beggs looked around the office for Graham and asked, "Where the hell is he?" Beggs says, "He should have been down there, particularly in view of the troubles we've had. But he was on the Hill. I said to his gals out in the office, 'As soon as he gets back, let me know because we need to do some things and do them quickly.' So he came in about half an hour later and I said, 'Bill, two things. One you should get on an airplane and get your ass down to Kennedy immediately. . . .'" Beggs also suggested Graham form an internal investigation board immediately because he feared data from the launch could get "cold" and be lost.

Beggs recalls that "Culbertson and Milt Silveira, the Chief Engineer, urged him [Graham] to appoint me to the accident review, but he wouldn't do it. . . . Apparently he was told by the White House not to do that."

Graham remembers Beggs handing him a list of names for an investigating committee. "And I said, 'Thank you, very much.' Those were literally the first words he [Beggs] had spoken to me since he had been indicted." Graham spent the afternoon at the White House where he met with President Reagan, who was, according to Graham, genuinely affected by the explosion.

Graham now realizes that for him the bottleneck in communications at NASA was Phil Culbertson. Graham says, "I tried to give him the benefit of the doubt in the process. Afterwards, unfortunately, there were a couple of instances where it became very clear he wasn't communicating important information. . . . One was . . . the problem with the O-rings. He'd been deeply involved in the shuttle system before he went to the space station. . . . He worked for Yardley and then in the front office in shuttle activities. So he was intimately familiar with the system and . . . he was the senior guy down at the launch, in fact, and was involved in looking at the accident down there soon after that."

According to Culbertson, Graham's account of the events surrounding the *Challenger* accident was not true. Culbertson said he had indications the O-ring was the cause of the loss of 51-L within two hours of the tragedy and so informed Graham. "I didn't want to talk to him too long because he was in a hurry to get to the White House. . . . I called him a second time to let him know that we had an indication it was an SRB. . . . Yeah, from one of the camera [positions] there was evidence. I told him it was either an SRB or a rupture in the main tank, because we had, with one of the early camera shots, seen flame at the aft end of the external tank. And I said that the press has those films and so you must be aware as you go to the White House that it could show up in the press at any time," Culbertson recalls.

Yet Graham maintains, "They told me ten days later. And as the general manager, one of his [Culbertson's] jobs was to act as the communications channel from the line programs, in particular the Office of Space Flight and so on, to me. And here I was put in the position of talking to the media, talking to the president, testifying. . . . It was, I think, ten days after the accident that he finally came to me and said, 'Say, there's going to be an article in the *New York Times* tomorrow and it mentions O-rings and I thought maybe you ought to know about the O-ring problem.' And that's when I first found out about the O-ring, the leak there, the erosion and some of the concerns about the design."

Graham said he called Culbertson in and said "this was a major breach of his obligation . . . and this couldn't occur again." Graham continues, "And it was unconscionable in my view this was done." Graham, profoundly shaken by the loss of the shuttle and fearful his own staff was not telling him the truth, decided to decertify the shuttle fleet so it could not fly.

Graham thought his troubles with Culbertson were over, but he was wrong. "He was never terribly communicative but he was adequate. Not what I would call high by industry standards. . . . We were . . . in very important and somewhat difficult negotiations with [an] intergovernment, interagency group on a replacement orbiter and commercialization and all the related matters. . . . I was trying to establish some NASA credibility in that process. I turned on the evening news one night. I was here [at NASA] to about 7:00 P.M. and saw Dan Rather say that NASA had just signed a contract to launch three more satellites," Graham recalls.

Graham called Chet Lee, who ran commercial services for NASA. "I said, 'Chet did you sign that?' He said, 'Yes.' I said, 'Well, on what authority?' And he said, 'Culbertson.' I checked it and Culbertson had agreed to it. And so I called Phil and I said, 'Did you do that?' He said, 'Yes.' I said, 'You know your specific instructions are that policy matters are to be referred to me and you're to provide communication on all activities going on.' . . . And he said, 'Well, it's the right thing to do.' And this was his justification." Graham tried to fire Culbertson as general manager but discovered civil service rules prevented that. And Graham said, "Culbertson must have immediately turned to the Hill because I started receiving calls from senior members of Congress. How could I remove such a loyal and valuable member of the staff."

Appearances Graham made on weekend television after the tragedy did not endear him to either NASA or the White House. In one case Graham told his audience that it was possible for the orbiter to successfully break away from the exploding rocket stack while the solids were firing. Rocco Petrone understands perhaps better than anyone else how wrong Graham was. He knew instantly that the crew was lost. There was no way for them to get off of the solids. There was no escape system.

On May 6, 1986, James C. Fletcher was confirmed by

the Senate to return to NASA as administrator. The choice of Fletcher was no coincidence. He had been selected by two presidents for loyalty. The irony of selecting a man who was selling Star Wars for Ronald Reagan was not lost on people at the civilian space agency. Fletcher is the same man who failed to build a consensus for a civil space effort under Richard Nixon. He is the same man who made the decision to build the shuttle on the cheap, using solid rockets. Some old NASA hands say it is poetic justice that Fletcher is having to live with what he largely created. He isn't the only one. Dale Myers, who ran the program under Fletcher's first stint at NASA, has been brought back again. The cast of characters who assisted Fletcher in bringing us the broken promises of the shuttle is being reassembled in Washington.

Although Fletcher talks of replacement orbiters and even a bigger shuttle fleet, his commercial customers have been taken away from him by the White House. "I am worried more about cancelling current contracts. I think that would be a devastating thing. NASA would lose its credibility if you cancel all of those commercial contracts," Fletcher said in July 1986. And that's precisely what the White House did less than a month later.

And the military, wanting off the shuttle for a decade, is getting a new Titan booster, an ELV that will launch as much weight and as big a payload as the shuttle. The NASA that had lifted our spirits and our pride is gone. The spirit and perhaps the last vestiges of that old NASA was spread over 93,000 square miles of ocean last January twenty-eighth. The Department of Defense, in fact the United States Air Force, has offered to provide a pair of old empty Minuteman silos at the Canaveral Air Force Station to bury the remnants of *Challenger*. A plaque should be put up that reads:

THE NATIONAL AERONAUTICS AND SPACE
ADMINISTRATION 1958–1986.

Notes on Sources and Interviews

CHAPTER 1

1. The meeting took place on May 12, 1986.
2. The interview with Col. John Fabian took place on July 11, 1986.
3. See Dwight David Eisenhower's *Waging Peace* (pages 205–226), published by Doubleday, 1965.
4. Interview with Dr. George Keyworth on July 11, 1986.
5. See *Waging Peace* by Dwight David Eisenhower (page 211).
6. Interview with William Lilly on May 20, 1986.
7. Interview with David Williamson on June 3, 1986.
8. Much is to be learned about the early Soviet program from Walter McDougall's benchmark history *The Heavens and the Earth*, published by Basic Books in 1985. See chapter 1.
9. Interview with Dr. T. Keith Glennan on July 9, 1986.
10. The papers of Richard Hirsch, the late aerospace assistant to the National Aeronautics and Space Council.
11. Interview with Paul Dembling on May 8, 1986.
12. See chapter 2 of *The National Aeronautics and Space Administration* (Praeger 1973) by Richard Hirsch and Joseph John Trento.
13. Interview with Dr. T. Keith Glennan on July 9, 1986.
14. Interview with David Williamson on June 3, 1986.
15. Interview with Dr. T. Keith Glennan July 9, 1986

16. See Dwight David Eisenhower's *Waging Peace* (page 558).
17. Interview with Dr. T. Keith Glennan on July 9, 1986.
18. Interview with Willis Shapley on April 30, 1986.
19. Interview with David Williamson on April 15, 1986.
20. See *This New Ocean—A History of Project Mercury* (National Aeronautics and Space Administration, 1966) for a detailed account of the program.
21. Interview with Dr. Robert Gilruth on April 26, 1986.
22. Interview with Dr. T. Keith Glennan on July 9, 1986.

CHAPTER 2

1. Interview with Dr. T. Keith Glennan on July 9, 1986.
2. Interview with Dr. Robert Gilruth on April 26, 1986.
3. See *This New Ocean—A History of Project Mercury*, published by NASA in 1966. The authors, Loyd S. Swenson, Jr., James M. Grimwood, and Charles Alexander, paint a complete technical picture of that pioneering effort.
4. Interviews with Charles Mathews on April 16 and 23, 1986.
5. Interview with Dr. T. Keith Glennan on July 9, 1986.
6. Interview with David Williamson on April 15, 1986.
7. Interview with Dr. T. Keith Glennan on July 9, 1986.
8. From Dr. Jerome Wiesner's report on space to the President-elect.
9. Interview with Dr. T. Keith Glennan on July 9, 1986.
10. Interview with Willis Shapley on April 30, 1986.
11. Interview with James E. Webb on September 4, 1986.
12. Interview with David Williamson on April 15, 1986.
13. From the papers of Richard Hirsch, former aerospace assistant to the National Space Council.
14. Interview with John Disher on April 8, 1986.
15. Interview with Dr. Robert Seamans on July 26, 1986.
16. Interview with David Williamson on April 15, 1986.
17. Interview with Dr. Robert Gilruth on April 26, 1986.
18. Interview with James E. Webb on September 4, 1986.
19. Interview with James E. Webb on September 4, 1986.
20. Interview with David Williamson on April 15, 1986.

CHAPTER 3

1. Interview with Paul Dembling on May 8, 1986.
2. Interview with Dr. Robert Seamans on July 22, 1986.
3. Interview with Dr. Robert Gilruth on April 26, 1986.
4. Interviews with Charles Mathews on April 16 and 23, 1986.
5. Interview with James E. Webb on September 4, 1986.
6. For an excellent history of the overlooked Gemini Project see *On the Shoulders of Titans—A History of Project Gemini* published by NASA in 1977 and written by Barton C. Hacker and James M. Grimwood.
7. Interview with James E. Webb on September 4, 1986, and also see *Chariots for Apollo—A History of Manned Lunar Spacecraft*, published by NASA in 1979 and written by Courtney G. Brooks, James M. Grimwood, and Loyd S. Swenson, Jr.
8. For an excellent history of the early Soviet program see *The Heavens and the Earth*, published in 1985 by Basic Books and written by Walter A. McDougall.
9. According to David Williamson, the late Charles Shelton of the Library of Congress became the primary fountain of "leaked" U.S. intelligence information about the Soviet program.
10. Interview with James E. Webb on September 4, 1986.
11. Interview with Willis Shapley on April 30, 1986.
12. A job given to Dr. Robert Seamans according to Webb.
13. Interview with Dr. Robert Seamans on July 22, 1986.
14. Interview with Capt. Charles Mathews on April 16 and 23, 1986.
15. Interview with James E. Webb on September 4, 1986.
16. Interview with Paul Dembling on May 8, 1986.
17. Interview with James E. Webb on September 4, 1986.
18. That NASA official asks not to be identified.

CHAPTER 4

1. Interview with Dr. Robert Gilruth on April 26, 1986.
2. Interviews with James E. Webb by the staff of the National Air and Space Museum.
3. Interview with Dr. Thomas Paine on July 18, 1986.
4. Interview with James E. Webb on September 4, 1986.

5. Interview with Richard Smith on June 26, 1986.
6. Interview with Dr. Thomas Paine on July 18, 1986.
7. Interview with James E. Webb on September 4, 1986.
8. Interview with Dr. Thomas Paine on July 18, 1986.
9. Interview with Dr. Robert Gilruth on April 26, 1986.
10. Interview with LeRoy Day on May 9, 1986.
11. Interview with Dr. Thomas Paine on July 18, 1986.
12. Interview with Dr. Robert Seamans on July 22, 1986.
13. Gilruth confirmed this.
14. Interview with James E. Webb on September 4, 1986.

CHAPTER 5

1. Interview with LeRoy Day on May 9, 1986.
2. Interview with William Lilly on May 20 and July 3, 1986.
3. Interview with Richard Callaghan on April 24, 1986.
4. Interview with Paul Dembling on May 8, 1986.
5. Interview with Dr. John Naugle on May 14, 1986.
6. Interview with Dr. Thomas Paine on July 18, 1986.
7. Interview with Dr. Robert Seamans on July 22, 1986.
8. Letter from Robert Seamans to Vice President Spiro T. Agnew, dated August 4, 1969.
9. Interview with LeRoy Day on May 8, 1986.
10. Interview with Dr. Thomas Paine on July 18, 1986.
11. Interview with Willis Shapley on April 30, 1986.
12. Interview with Charles Donlan on May 7, 1986.
13. Interview with Dr. James Fletcher on August 7, 1986.
14. Interviews with William Lilly on May 20, 1986, and with Willis Shapley on April 30, 1986.
15. Interview with Dr. Thomas Paine on July 18, 1986.
16. Interview with Dr. James Fletcher on August 7, 1986.
17. Interview with Willis Shapley on April 30, 1986.
18. Interview with William Lilly on July 3, 1986.
19. Interview with William Lilly on July 3, 1986.
20. Interview with Dr. James Fletcher on August 7, 1986.
21. To be published by Duke University Press in 1987.
22. Interview with Dr. Robert Seamans on July 22, 1986.

23. Interviews with William Lilly on May 20, 1986, and Willis Shapley on April 30, 1986.
24. Interviews with William Lilly on May 20, 1986, and Willis Shapley on April 30, 1986.
25. Interview with William Lilly on May 20, 1986.
26. Interview with Dr. James Fletcher on August 7, 1986.
27. Interview with Dr. Robert Gilruth on April 26, 1986.
28. Interview with Dr. John Naugle on May 14, 1986.
29. Interview with Dr. James Fletcher on August 7, 1986.
30. Interview with Dr. John Naugle on May 14, 1986.

CHAPTER 6

1. Interview with David Williamson on April 14, 1986.
2. Interview with David Williamson on June 3, 1986.
3. Interview with Ambassador Edward M. Korry in November 1976.
4. Interview with William Lilly on July 3, 1986.
5. Interview with Dr. James Fletcher on August 7, 1986.
6. Ending in 1986 with the total cost for the facility at over $4 billion and the Air Force putting off activation of the site until the 1990s.
7. Interview with Willis Shapley on April 30, 1986.
8. Interview with Dr. James Fletcher on August 7, 1986.
9. Interview with William Lilly on July 3, 1986.
10. Interview with Dr. Thomas Paine on July 18, 1986.
11. Interview with Robert Aller on April 25, 1986.
12. Interview with Gen. Jacob Smart on May 6, 1986.
13. Interview with David Williamson on June 3, 1986.
14. Interview with William Lilly on July 3, 1986.
15. Interview with William Lilly on July 3, 1986.
16. Interview with John Yardley on August 6, 1986.
17. Interview with Willis Shapley on April 30, 1986.
18. Interview with Paul Dembling on May 8, 1986.
19. Interview with Dr. James Fletcher on August 7, 1986.
20. Interview with Dr. Robert Gilruth on April 26, 1986.
21. Interview with James Webb on September 4, 1986.
22. Interview with Dr. Robert Frosch on July 1, 1986.
23. Interview with Charles Donlan on May 7, 1986.
24. Interview with William Lilly on July 3, 1986.

CHAPTER 7

1. Interview with Robert Frosch on July 1, 1986.
2. Interview with Willis Shapley on April 30, 1986.
3. Interview with Dr. Hans Mark on July 16, 1986.
4. Interview with Willis Shapley on April 30, 1986.
5. Interview with William Lilly on May 20, 1986.
6. The Air Force and CIA began to pressure NASA to activate an emergency polar orbit launch plan out of the Kennedy Space Center a few days after the loss of *Challenger*.
7. From Dr. Hans Mark's manuscript entitled *The Space Station—A Personal Journey*.
8. Interview with Dr. Robert Seamans on July 22, 1986.
9. Interview with Dr. Hans Mark on July 16, 1986.
10. Interview with William Lilly on July 3, 1986.
11. Interview with William Lilly on July 3, 1986.
12. Interview with Dr. Robert Frosch on July 1, 1986.
13. Interview with Dr. John Naugle on May 14, 1986.
14. Interview with Willis Shapley on April 30, 1986.
15. See "Report of the Seasat Failure Review Board," released by NASA on December 21, 1978.
16. Interview with David Williamson on June 3, 1986.
17. Press refused to be interviewed for this book.
18. See a series of articles in the *Wilmington News Journal* between October 1978 and 1981 by Joseph J. Trento and Richard Sandza detailing this security disaster.
19. Interview with Dr. Robert Frosch on July 1, 1986.
20. Interview with David Williamson on June 3, 1986.
21. Interview with Robert Aller on April 25, 1986.
22. Interview with Dr. Robert Frosch on July 1, 1986.
23. Interview with Dr. Hans Mark on July 16, 1986.
24. Interview with Dr. Robert Frosch on July 1, 1986.
25. A series of documents were generated by this lobbying effort culminating in a document from Lewis justifying the non-competitive procurement for the Centaur upper stage that was circulated within NASA in early 1981.
26. Interview with Dr. Robert Frosch on July 1, 1986.
27. Interview with William Lilly on July 3, 1986.

28. From *The Space Station—A Personal Journey*, written by Dr. Hans Mark.
29. This center was created by James E. Webb to give NASA and the country an edge in electronics. But Thomas Paine closed the center because of declining NASA budgets.

CHAPTER 8

1. Lovelace did not respond to repeated telephone calls requesting an interview.
2. The letters from Lovelace to O'Neill and other congressional officials about the Centaur can be found in the NASA history office file on Centaur.
3. Interview with Dr. Robert Frosch on July 1, 1986.
4. Interview with William Lilly on July 3, 1986.
5. Interview with William Lilly on May 20, 1986.
6. Interview with Mrs. Beggs on June 4, 1986.
7. Interview with William Lilly on May 20, 1986.
8. The record shows that Beggs lobbied both Dr. Robert Frosch as well as Al Lovelace.
9. Interview with William Lilly on July 3, 1986.
10. Interview with Mrs. Beggs on June 4, 1986.
11. Interview with William Lilly on July 3, 1986.
12. Interview with William Lilly on July 3, 1986.
13. Interview with Dr. George Keyworth on July 11, 1986.
14. The facility in California cost nearly $4 billion as of this writing and is still not suitable for launches.
15. Interview with John Yardley on August 6, 1986.
16. As described in his manuscript *The Space Station—A Personal Journey*.
17. Interview with Dr. George Keyworth on July 11, 1986.
18. This was changed to 1992 after the *Challenger* blew up.
19. Interview with James Beggs on August 7, 1986.
20. Interview with James Beggs on June 18, 1986.
21. Interview with Dr. George Keyworth on July 11, 1986.
22. Interview with James Beggs on August 7, 1986.
23. Interview with Robert Allnut on May 16, 1986.

CHAPTER 9

1. See the *Chicago Tribune*, page 1, December 19, 1982, "U.S. probes Rockwell use of space funds."
2. Interview with Paul Dembling on May 8, 1986.
3. Interview with Dr. George Keyworth on July 11, 1986.
4. Interview with James Beggs on August 7, 1986.
5. Interview with Dr. George Keyworth on July 11, 1986.
6. Interview with William Lilly on July 3, 1986.
7. Interview with former Congressman Harold "Cap" Hollenbeck on July 27, 1986.
8. Interview with Dr. George Keyworth on July 11, 1986.
9. Interview with former Congressman Harold Hollenbeck on July 28, 1986.
10. Interview with former General Dynamics lobbyist Chris Hansen on July 18, 1986.
11. See White House press release titled "National Space Policy," released on July 4, 1982.
12. Interview with Dr. George Keyworth on July 11, 1986.
13. August 4, 1982, before the House Science and Technology Committee.
14. Interview with Congressman Don Fuqua on July 17, 1986.
15. The author was the reporter, then working for the *Wilmington News Journal*.
16. Interview with Tom Brownell on August 27, 1986.
17. See the *New York Times*, page D-1, February 5, 1986, "Workers Accuse Dynamics."
18. Interview with Paul Dembling on May 8, 1986.
19. This grew into the so-called "Shuttle Processing Contract" that marked the first time someone other than a booster contractor was responsible for the launch preparation of a space vehicle.
20. The correspondence between Bush and Space Transportation Company was released to the author by Teeley when Teeley was Bush's press secretary.
21. According to Heiss.
22. Interview with Dr. George Keyworth on July 11, 1986.
23. Interview with Robert Allnut on May 16, 1986.

24. Interview with James Beggs on June 18, 1986.
25. Interview with Col. Gil Rye on July 16, 1986.
26. Interview with Chester Lee on April 29, 1986.
27. Interview with James Beggs on June 18, 1986.
28. Interview with former Congressman Hollenbeck on July 27, 1986.

CHAPTER 10
1. Interview with Dr. William Graham on August 28, 1986.
2. Interview with James Beggs on June 18, 1986.
3. In an interview on August 7, 1986.
4. Interview with Dr. George Keyworth on July 11, 1986.
5. Interview with James Beggs on August 7, 1986.
6. Interview with Dr. Hans Mark on July 16, 1986.
7. Interview with James Beggs on August 7, 1986.
8. Interview with Robert Aller on April 25, 1986.
9. Interview with Dr. George Keyworth on July 11, 1986.
10. Interview with James Beggs on June 18, 1986.
11. Interview with William Lilly on July 3, 1986.
12. Interview with James Beggs on August 7, 1986.
13. From a letter from Hans Mark to the author, dated July 18, 1986.
14. Mark's memo on the O-ring problem is dated May 30, 1984, and was sent to Lawrence Mulloy.
15. Interview with Philip Culbertson on July 11, 1986.

CHAPTER 11
1. Interview with James Beggs on June 18, 1986.
2. Interview with Dr. William Graham on August 28, 1986.
3. Interview with Dr. William Graham on August 28, 1986.
4. Interview with Dr. William Graham on August 7, 1986.
5. Interview with James Beggs on June 18, 1986.
6. Interview with Dr. William Graham on August 28, 1986.
7. Interview with Congressman Don Fuqua on July 17, 1986.
8. Interview with James Beggs on August 7, 1986.
9. Interview with Congressman Don Fuqua on July 17, 1986.
10. Beggs confirms this.
11. Interview with James Beggs on June 18, 1986.
12. Interview with Philip Culbertson on July 11, 1986.

Index